New York City

Big City Food Biographies Series

Series Editor
Ken Albala, University of the Pacific, kalbala@pacific.edu

Food helps define the cultural identity of cities in much the same way as the distinctive architecture and famous personalities. Great cities have one-of-a-kind food cultures, offering the essence of the multitudes who have immigrated there and shaped foodways through time. The **Big City Food Biographies** series focuses on those metropolises celebrated as culinary destinations, with their iconic dishes, ethnic neighborhoods, markets, restaurants, and chefs. Guidebooks to cities abound, but these are real biographies that will satisfy readers' desire to know the full food culture of a city. Each narrative volume, devoted to a different city, explains the history, the natural resources, and the people that make that city's food culture unique. Each biography also looks at the markets, historic restaurants, signature dishes, and great cookbooks that are part of the city's gastronomic makeup.

Books in the Series
New Orleans: A Food Biography, by Elizabeth M. Williams
San Francisco: A Food Biography, by Erica J. Peters

New York City

A *Food Biography*

Andrew F. Smith

ROWMAN & LITTLEFIELD
Lanham • Boulder • New York • Toronto • Plymouth, UK

The publisher has done its best to ensure that the instructions and/or recipes in the book are correct. However, users, especially parents and teachers working with young people, should apply judgment and experience when preparing recipes. The publisher accepts no responsibility for the outcome of any recipe included in this volume.

Published by Rowman & Littlefield
4501 Forbes Boulevard, Suite 200, Lanham, Maryland 20706
www.rowman.com

10 Thornbury Road, Plymouth PL6 7PP, United Kingdom

British Library Cataloguing in Publication Information Available

Library of Congress Cataloging-in-Publication Data
Smith, Andrew F., 1946–
  New York City : a food biography / Andrew F. Smith.
    pages cm — (Big city food biographies series)
  Includes bibliographical references and index.
  ISBN 978-1-4422-2712-5 (cloth : alk. paper) — ISBN 978-1-4422-2713-2 (electronic : alk. paper) 1. Food—New York (State) —New York—History. 2. Food habits—New York (State) —New York—History. 3. Food industry and trade—New York (State) —New York—History. 4. Cooking, International—History. 5. New York (N.Y.) —History.
I. Title.
  TX360.U63N498 2014
  641.59747—dc23   2013032098

♾™ The paper used in this publication meets the minimum requirements of American National Standard for Information Sciences—Permanence of Paper for Printed Library Materials, ANSI/NISO Z39.48-1992.

Printed in the United States of America

~

Contents

~

Big City Food Biographies, Series Foreword

Cities are rather like living organisms. There are nerve centers, circulatory systems, structures that hold them together, and of course conduits through which food enters and waste leaves the city. Each city also has its own unique personality, based mostly on the people who live there but also on the physical layout, the habits of interaction, and the places where people meet to eat and drink. More than any other factor, it seems that food is used to define the identity of so many cities. Simply say any of the following words and a particular place immediately leaps to mind: bagel, cheesesteak, muffuletta, "chowda," and cioppino. Natives, of course, have many more associations— their favorite restaurants and markets, bakeries and donut shops, pizza parlors, and hot dog stands. Even the restaurants seem to have their own unique vibe wherever you go. Some cities boast great steakhouses or barbecue pits; others, their ethnic enclaves and more elusive specialties like Frito pie in Santa Fe, Cincinnati chili, and the Chicago deep dish pizza. Tourists might find snippets of information about such hidden gems in guidebooks; the inveterate flaneur naturally seeks them out personally. For the rest of us, this is practically unchartered territory.

These urban food biographies are meant to be not guidebooks but rather real biographies, explaining the urban infrastructure, the natural resources that make each city unique, and most importantly the history, people, and neighborhoods. Each volume is meant to introduce you to the city or reacquaint you with an old friend in ways you may never have considered. Each biography also looks at the historic restaurants, signature dishes, and great cookbooks that reflect each city's unique gastronomic makeup.

These food biographies also come at a crucial juncture in our culinary history as a people. Not only do chain restaurants and fast food threaten the existence of our gastronomic heritage, but also we are increasingly mobile as a people, losing our deep connections to place and the cooking that happens in cities over the generations with a rooted population. Moreover, signature dishes associated with individual cities become popularized and bastardized and are often in danger of becoming caricatures of themselves. Ersatz versions of so many classics, catering to the lowest common denominator of taste, are now available throughout the country. Our gastronomic sensibilities are in danger of becoming entirely homogenized. The intent here is not, however, to simply stop the clock or make museum pieces of regional cuisines. Cooking must and will evolve, but understanding the history of each city's food will help us make better choices, will make us more discerning customers, and perhaps will make us more respectful of the wonderful variety that exists across our great nation.

Ken Albala
University of the Pacific

~

Chronology

1626   New Amsterdam is founded as a fur-acquiring operation by the Dutch West India Company. Old World plants and animals are introduced into what will become New York.

1664   English warships capture New Amsterdam and change the city's name to New York. English immigration.

1762   Samuel Fraunces opens a tavern, first named the Queens Arms, later named for its owner. Today, the building is the oldest surviving structure in New York City.

1763   The Seven Years' War ends; the British acquire Canada and all of North America east of the Appalachian Mountains to the Mississippi River. American merchants thrive during the war, supplying the British army and navy with food and other necessities.

1764   To help pay for the war, the British parliament begins to pass bills taxing products imported into North America to help cover the costs of British troops that are stationed in Canada. New Yorkers form Sons of Liberty in New York and launch resistance to the British laws, particularly to the Sugar Act and a series of other revenue measures imposed by parliament.

1773   British parliament lowers the tax on tea; the British East Indies Company rushes ships with tea to America assuming that colonials will buy the lower-costing tea. The ships containing tea are turned back; tea is thrown into New York Harbor, just as it had been previously in Boston.

1775   The War for American Independence begins; British forces occupy New York City the following year and continue to do so for more than seven years. Surrounding farmers refuse to send food into the city, and the British garrison and the loyalists living in the city depend on shipments of food from Ireland to survive.

1783   Peace treaty is signed granting independence to the United States; British forces leave New York. General George Washington celebrates by dining at Fraunces Tavern in lower Manhattan.

1784   The sailing ship *Empress of China* sailed out of New York Harbor headed for China and returns with a load of tea; it is the first American vessel to trade with China.

1789   George Washington is inaugurated first president of the United States in New York City; he hires Samuel Fraunces, proprietor of a city tavern, to cater his food during his tenure in New York.

1807   William Havemeyer opens a sugar refinery in New York; the company he founded will become one of the most important sugar companies in nineteenth-century America.

1812   War of 1812 with Britain begins; international trade is greatly reduced until its end in 1815.

1819   Canning of salmon, lobster, and oysters begins in New York City.

1825   Erie Canal is completed; grains and agricultural goods from upstate New York and the Midwest flow into New York. The city increases financial, commercial, and manufacturing operations, especially for flour and sugar refining.

1827   The Delmonico brothers, immigrants from the Italian region of Switzerland, open a café in New York; it will blossom into one of the city's most famous upper-class restaurants, which survives until 1923.

1830s Large numbers of German immigrants begin arriving in New York— they will continue to arrive until World War I. They establish larger beer breweries, delicatessens, grocery stores, street vendors—one of whom will be credited with inventing the American hot dog—and restaurants, which serve hamburger steak.

1832   Vegetarian and health reformer Sylvester Graham lectures in New York, arguing for temperance and vegetarianism; supporters open Graham Boardinghouse in New York, which followed his advice about food and beverages.

1840s Irish immigrants begin flooding into New York; they open saloons and grocery stores, and work in boardinghouses. The "swill milk war" begins with newspapers and magazines publishing exposés about the city's milk, beer, and distilling industries.

1860s   Italian immigrants begin to flood into the city, creating Little Italy. The Great Atlantic & Pacific Tea Company (soon shortened to A&P grocery store) chain opens in New York.

1861   The Civil War begins; New Yorkers join regiments to fight for the Union; the war ends four years later. New York restaurants thrive during the war.

1863   Riots in New York against the draft require U.S. military to help control parts of the city.

1864   Union League Club launches effort to give Union soldiers and sailors a turkey dinner on Thanksgiving.

1867   Charles Feltman, a pushcart vendor on Coney Island, New York, is credited with selling sausages on white rolls. These are considered the first hot dogs.

1869   The transcontinental railroad completed; New Yorkers can travel by train to San Francisco, and food can be shipped across the continent. The grocery store chain that will eventually become A&P establishes stores outside of Manhattan and will eventually become the largest chain in America.

1870s   Chinese immigrants begin to move into the city, eventually creating Chinatown.

1880s   Bagels are sold by street vendors.

1890   Jacob Riis publishes the exposé *How the Other Half Lives: Studies among the Tenements of New York*, reporting that more than half a million people living in the tenements were either begging for food or subsisting on charity.

1894   Charles Ranhofer, the former chef at Delmonico's, publishes *The Epicurean*, with the recipes that made the restaurant famous.

1898   Five boroughs—Manhattan, Brooklyn, Staten Island, Queens, and the Bronx—merge to form Greater New York.

1902   New York's first Automat opens. They survive until 1991.

1903   America's first pizzeria opens in New York's Little Italy.

1916   Nathan Handwerker, a Polish immigrant, opens a hot dog stand at Coney Island, New York; it's soon known as "Nathan's Famous."

1917   United States enters the war; Congress passes restriction on making beer and spirits as a way to help conserve grain for use by the military and to send to allies. New York distilleries and breweries decrease or halt production of beer and spirits. "Wheatless, Meatless, and Porkless" days are declared by the mayor to support the war effort.

1919   Eighteenth Amendment to U.S. Constitution is approved, outlaw-
        ing the manufacture, sale, importation, and transportation of alco-
        holic beverages in America; the following year, Prohibition begins.
        Saloons, bars, breweries, distilleries, and many restaurants close in
        New York; speakeasies open, and bootleggers flourish.
1930   Michael J. Cullen opens one of the nation's first supermarkets—
        King Kullen—in Jamaica, New York.
1933   Prohibition ends; bars and a few breweries reopen.
1939   New York's World Fair opens in Flushing Meadow, Queens. It has
        more than eighty restaurants that introduce New York fairgoers to a
        wide variety of foreign foods. Two restaurants emerge from the fair
        and will influence the city's future restaurants for decades.
1941   The United States enters World War II. *Gourmet* magazine
        launched, and Henri Soulé opens Le Pavillon restaurant in New
        York's plush Upper East Side. Both will reintroduce haute cuisine
        into New York.
1942   Rationing goes into effect and will not completely end until 1947;
        New Yorkers plant Victory Gardens to help the war effort.
1945   World War II ends. Veterans return with an experience of and taste
        for European and Asian food cultures.
1957   Craig Claiborne is hired as a food columnist by *New York Times*;
        his cookbook, *The New York Times Cook Book* (1961), sold more
        than three million copies; it familiarized New Yorkers with regional
        American, European, and some Asian recipes.
1959   Four Seasons restaurant created by restaurant impresario Joe Baum
        opens.
1965   Immigration Act makes it possible for immigrants from all over the
        world to bring their food cultures to America; New York restau-
        rant kitchens benefit from the influx of culinary professionals from
        around the world.
1968   Gael Greene is hired as the restaurant critic and later food colum-
        nist for *New York Magazine*.
1973   Michael and Ariane Batterberry publish *On the Town in New York:
        From 1776 to the Present*, New York's first food history.
1975   Mimi Sheraton is hired as the *New York Times* restaurant critic and
        transforms the genre of newspapers reviewing restaurants. She de-
        scribes her techniques in her memoir, *Eating My Words: An Appetite
        for Life* (2004).

1976   Windows on the World, designed by the team led by restaurant impresario Joe Baum, opens in the World Trade Center. New York's first Greenmarket opens; today, fifty-four Greenmarkets are open in all boroughs of the city.

1990   Molly O'Neill is hired as a reporter for the *New York Times* and later becomes a weekly food columnist for the paper's Sunday magazine. She publishes three cookbooks in the 1990s, including *New York Cookbook* (1992).

1993   Food Network is launched in New York; its programs—as well as those of other networks—popularize food preparation and other culinary matters.

1994   *Saveur*, a food magazine, is started in New York.

1997   Amanda Hesser becomes a food reporter for the *New York Times*, and later the food editor for the newspaper's Sunday magazine. Her cookbook, *The Essential New York Times Cook Book*, was published in 2010.

2001   The World Trade Center is destroyed; New Yorkers pull together to move beyond the tragedy. Construction begins on a new World Trade Center, which is completed in 2013.

2009   William Grimes publishes *Appetite City: A Culinary History of New York*, the city's second book-length culinary history.

2010   *Gourmet* magazine closes, ending an era of upscale food publishing. Lidia Bastianich, her son Joe Bastianich, and Mario Batali extend the reach of their interpretations of Italian cuisine with Eataly, a fifty-thousand-square-foot emporium that is devoted to Italian food and culinary traditions.

CHAPTER ONE

~

The Material Resources

Land, Water, and Air

Twenty thousand years ago there wasn't much to see—or eat—where the culinary capital that is New York City now rises. There was no Manhattan Island, Hudson River, or Long Island Sound, and no forests, fish, animals, or ocean; the Atlantic, at that time, was 130 miles to the east. There was nothing but a wintry wasteland of snow and chunks of ice, for this was the southeastern boundary of the Laurentide ice sheet. When the ice sheet retreated, it created the physical characteristics of the future city—its islands and hills, and its rivers and shoreline. Tundra and grasslands expanded into the void left by the glacier, and big game—woolly mammoths, mastodons, bison, bears, sloths, giant beavers, caribou, and saber-toothed tigers—roamed into the area. Small bands of Paleo-Indians followed them. Little is known about these hunters other than they were highly mobile and their principal weapon was a small spear propelled by a spear thrower. The small spear points, made from antler or stone, easily penetrated the hide of their prey but also slipped out easily, permitting their reuse. The big game disappeared—likely due to the expert hunting skills of the Paleo-Indians and climatic fluctuations.

The climate and geographical features stabilized about eight thousand years ago. Forests grew, and dozens of different habitats provided homes for a complex array of trees, plants, animals, fish, shellfish, and birds. The most comprehensive early account of the natural features of the New York area was recorded by Adriaen van der Donck, a Dutch lawyer and colonist who arrived in New Amsterdam in 1641. He was later given an estate north of Manhattan that would later become a city named after him, Yonkers. Van der Donck carefully studied the natural flora and fauna of the colony and published his observations in *A Description of the New Netherlands* (1655). The winters were colder in New Netherland than in Holland at the time, he reported. This was likely true, as the Little Ice Age that had arrived a few hundred years before greatly lowered temperatures in eastern North America. It would continue to affect the climate until the early nineteenth century. He also reported that the summers were warmer and the soil was perfect for farming, especially on Long Island and Staten Island.

The food plants native to the area, Van der Donck recounted, included "several kinds of plums, Wild or small cherries, juniper, small kinds of apples, many hazel-nuts, black currants, gooseberries, blue India figs, and strawberries in abundance all over the country, some of which ripen at half May, and we have them until July; blueberries, raspberries, black-caps, &c., with artichokes, ground-acorns, ground beans, wild onions, and leeks like ours, with several other kinds of roots and fruits, known to the Indians." There were also ample fowl, particularly wild turkeys, which were easy to hunt year round, and migratory birds, such as "geese, ducks, widgeons, teal, brant and many more," which were available much of the year.

The Hudson estuary, much of which was below sea level, was a tidal oasis for fish, shellfish, and sea mammals. Anadromous fish (those that spawn in freshwater rivers and annually migrate to and from the ocean)—shad, herring, sturgeon, striped bass, salmon, sea trout, and others—frequented the Hudson River and migrated annually through the bay to the ocean. In the surrounding bay and waters, there was plenty of herring, mackerel, halibut, scoll, sheepshead, "carp, snook, forrels, pike, trout, suckers, thickheads, flounders, eels, palings, brickens and lampreys," noted Van der Donck. They became a major food source for the area, as did turtles, crabs, lobster, mussels, scallops, eels, and clams. Some lobsters, claimed Van der Donck, were "five to six feet in length; others again are from a foot to a foot and a half long, which are the best for the table." The most common shellfish were the oysters; according to later estimates, the New York Bay and Long Island Sound had the most prolific oyster beds in the world. The bay was also frequented by marine mammals—seals, porpoises, and the occasional whale—which were occasionally stranded on beaches. Just offshore in the Atlantic was yet another abundance of oceanic fish and seafood. All in all, the New York City area was a natural culinary wonderland.

The Lenape

About 6,500 years ago, the Munsee—a loose collection of groups of Delaware Indians who settled the area from eastern Connecticut to central New

Jersey and eastern Pennsylvania—arrived in the New York area. They spoke dialects of Algonquian, as did hundreds of other indigenous groups living in eastern North America. In New York, the Munsee called themselves Lenape, or "real people." Archaeologists have identified about eighty Lenape habitation sites in the five boroughs of New York, but few remains have been located. How many Lenape lived in the area when the Europeans arrived in the early seventeenth century is unknown. Estimates vary from a low of 3,800 to a high of 15,000. Based on the number of archaeological sites, Staten Island likely had the largest Indian population.

The Lenape operated in small autonomous bands that varied in size from a few dozen to hundreds of members. Each band maintained fishing and hunting "rights" within the particular territory where they lived. Their villages were typically situated on hills near freshwater sources; larger villages were surrounded by palisades. Their wigwams—small round structures— and longhouses—larger multifamily buildings—were constructed of grass, wood, and bark. The hearth was located in the center of their abodes, and a hole in the roof permitted the smoke to escape. The Lenape's only domesticated animal was the American dog used for hunting and, occasionally, as a pack animal. It disappeared shortly after Europeans introduced Old World dogs into the area.

Native peoples enjoyed a rich and diverse diet. With spears, stone axes, and traps, men hunted birds and animals. They acquired bows and arrows about 2,800 years ago, and this greatly enhanced their hunting efficiency. They also collected eggs from wild birds and gathered a wide variety of readily available plant foods: grapes, gooseberries, raspberries, strawberries, fruit, chestnuts, hickory nuts, acorns, roots, barks, and leaves. They caught shad, herring, eels, alewife, turtles, and other sea animals with spears or bag-shaped nets. They gathered shellfish, particularly clams, oysters, lobsters, and mussels. From white or purple seashells found at Long Island Sound, the Lenape made wampum, small beads pierced with a central hole so that they could be strung together. Wampum was used for ritual and ornamental purposes. The Lenape strung them together to make belts and ornaments. When the Dutch arrived, wampum became a medium of exchange, and eventually it was recognized as legal tender throughout the Dutch colony of New Netherland.

The Lenape developed a network of trails throughout the area that gave them easy access to wooded areas for hunting and coastal areas for fishing and gathering shellfish. They made pitch-sealed bark buckets and fired clay pots. The pot walls tapered to a thin rim, making them lighter and easier to move from place to place, if relatively fragile. Still, if a pot broke in transit, it was easy enough to make a new one, which they found preferable to carrying heavier, sturdier vessels. The pots and buckets were used for cooking by filling them with water and dropping in heated stones, which quickly brought the water to a boil.

Lenape bands did not settle into towns, at least as Europeans understood the term. They were seminomadic; they moved occasionally depending on soil productivity and game availability. They employed the slash-and-burn method of agriculture, creating fields by felling big trees and burning small trees and underbrush. In these open areas, they planted corn, beans, and squash, which had been domesticated in Mesoamerica but had been disseminated into the New York area about a thousand years ago.

In the fall, when the harvest was done, the Lenape burned their fields, as well as nearby woods and meadows. In the spring, they burned off any vegetation that had grown on the fields before they planted their crops. Burning the woods cleared the area of entangling underbrush and improved the productivity of the land. The fires did not usually harm large trees, which only lost their outer bark and lower branches, thus ensuring a supply of nuts or fruits. The clearings also created a habitat for animals, which could then be hunted more easily. (This practice was so useful that Dutch colonists would later do the same thing.) They remained in a specific place for several years, until the productivity of the land diminished; then they moved to another location and started over.

Lenape women prepared fields for planting by making small molehills about two and a half feet apart. In April, they planted five or six grains of corn in each hill. When the plants were two or three feet high, the women sowed beans under them, and the bean vines climbed the cornstalks like trellises. Occasionally, squash seeds were planted between the mounds and grew along the ground: they help to keep the soil moist between showers. The beans, corn, and squash were harvested in the fall; some of the produce was eaten fresh, and some was dried for use during the winter and spring. Dried food was stored in clay pots, pitch-sealed bark buckets, woven baskets, or bags made of rushes or wild hemp. These were buried in pits dug into the house floors or stashed beneath sleeping platforms. For sustaining winter meals, they boiled fresh meat with dried corn or beans until soft enough to eat. They also boiled beans with corn to make a type of succotash.

The Lenape may have also planted Jerusalem artichokes (*Helianthus tuberosus*) and sunflowers (*Helianthus annuus*), which grew wild in the area. The sunflower had been domesticated by North American Indians about five thousand years ago. The seeds were dried, shelled, and eaten; they were combined with corn and beans to make succotash. The sunflower plant was closely related to the Jerusalem artichoke, a somewhat knobby, thin-skinned underground tuber that was usually boiled or roasted. The dried tubers and dried sunflower seeds were also ground into flour. These were the only two plants that were domesticated in eastern North America and widely disseminated in pre-Columbian times.

During the summer months, women weeded the fields and piled more dirt on the mounds. In August, they removed barren cornstalks and sucked out the sweet sap, which was one of the few natural sweeteners available to them. In the fall, the adult men and some women left the village to hunt and fish, leaving other women, the elderly, and children in charge of the fields to keep deer and other animals from gobbling up the fields. The hunters were absent for months at a time. They ate as much as they could, becoming fat, which helped them survive the long winter and spring. They also dried meat and fish and brought them back to the settlement.

In the spring, men fished with dragnets that they had knitted from wild hemp fibers. They mainly caught shad and white salmon, which, according to an early European account, was "of very good flavor . . . it has white scales; the heads are so full of fat that in some there are two or three spoonfuls, so that there is good eating for one who is fond of picking heads." In the summer, the men hunted "deer, fawns, hares, and foxes and all such" with bows and arrows reported another European. They commonly boiled their meat and fish, and also dried both for later consumption. When needed, the leathery dried fish or meat was pounded into powder and boiled with ground cornmeal. This was a common dish in late winter and early spring, when other provisions had been exhausted. If the supply of dried food gave out, the Lenape went out hunting again or headed for the bay or sound, where shellfish were usually abundant.

Dried corn was the Lenape's most important staple, particularly during the winter and spring when other food sources were at a premium. To render it edible, they boiled it and then pulverized it with a stone on a block or with a wooden mortar, usually a hollowed-out tree stump. With the coarser cornmeal, the Lenape made porridge, which they called *sappaen*; this was a mainstay of their winter diet. They sifted out the fine flour, mixed it with lukewarm water, and kneaded it into dough. This was molded into round, flat cakes, which were heated in the hot ashes of a fire. When the Europeans arrived, some were unimpressed with the Indian cornbread, which did not taste or look like the wheat bread they expected. As one later explained, "They gave us a small piece when we entered, and although the grains were not ripe, and it was half baked and coarse grains, we nevertheless had to eat it." Despite bad reviews, early European colonists adopted it as a staple of their diets.

The Lenape also made cakes and porridge out of acorns. As most acorns contain a toxin (tannic acid), this was a complicated process. The nuts either were subjected to long soaking or were repeatedly boiled and rinsed. When waterlogged, the shells were cracked open and the nutmeats removed. The acorns were pulverized with a mortar and pestle and the resulting mush soaked additional times to leach out the tannin. Then it was dried in the sun and finally pounded into a powder. They used acorn flour as they did cornmeal, to make porridge or cakes.

The Indians had no set schedule for meals; each family ate when they were hungry. They shared all of their meals with anyone who wanted to eat, with no expectation of compensation, reported early European settlers. The exceptions were ceremonial dinners, where each family in a community contributed delicacies. When the Lenape entertained, their special foods were beavers' tails, bass heads, or very fat meat stewed with parched cornmeal and bruised shelled chestnuts, reported a Dutch colonist. When the Lenape traveled and had no expectation of finding or hunting for food along the way, they carried small bags of parched cornmeal, which took up little space. When water was added to the meal, the parched corn expanded and provided a filling meal. According to the Dutch, the Lenape could subsist on a quarter of a pound of this mixture per day for several days, if necessary.

The Lenape did not eat excessively, even on their feast days. The quality and quantity of food were the same for all; higher status did not entitle one to more or better food or the special culinary luxuries that Europeans expected. No food was wasted.

Their main beverage was water, but when grapes were in season, the Lenape occasionally crushed them and drank the juice. They also drank the water in which their food was cooked. They consumed no alcoholic beverages until the arrival of the Europeans. Once exposed to alcohol, some drank to excess, becoming malicious, "insolent and troublesome," reported Dutch observers. Once Indians became accustomed to alcohol, however, Van der Donck reported, they bore "it as well as our own people do." Most refused to drink alcohol, and they called those Indians who drank to excess fools. The Dutch government forbade the sale of alcoholic beverages to Indians as did other colonial governments. Despite the laws, Europeans regularly traded or gave alcohol to them, and alcoholism contributed to their dissolution of families and their communities.

When the Dutch West India Company made the decision to establish a settlement on Manhattan, Peter Minuit, the director of the colony of New Netherland, bought the island in April 1626 for about sixty guilders worth of goods (estimated today to be worth about four thousand dollars) from some Lenape, who, according to the Dutch, were empowered to speak for all Lenape on Manhattan. The Lenape had agreed, claimed the Dutch, to move north of the island to what is today the Bronx. How many Lenape lived on Manhattan at the time is variously estimated to have been as few as 300 or as many as 1,200, and they lived in several different communities. Later, the Dutch made similar accommodations with other groups on Long Island and Staten Island. Europeans identified these groups with the places where they lived, such as the Jamaica (beaver place), Canarsies (grassy place), and the Rockaways (sandy place).

Some Lenape never left the area, and others returned to the places where they had once lived. It was estimated in 1628 that three hundred Lenape still inhabited Manhattan. Relations between them and the colonists deteriorated. A Dutch observer complained that the Indians were "a bad race of savages, who have always been very obstinate and unfriendly towards our countrymen." The friction was abetted by conflicting systems of agriculture. Dutch introduced Old World animals that roamed freely, eating Lenape crops, and the Dutch destroyed their hunting grounds. Conflicts erupted over stolen pigs, cattle, and even peaches. These escalated into wars that ended with the Lenape's defeat.

War, the disappearance of game, the growth of alcoholism, and the introduction of viral diseases by the Dutch all contributed to the destruction of the Lenape. They disappeared from Manhattan by the end of the seventeenth century, but small groups survived in Brooklyn, Staten Island, and the Bronx until the nineteenth century.

European colonists altered the area's natural environment, fashioning it into a traditional European landscape. They chopped down forests to make way for buildings, roads, and farms, which quickly dominated Manhattan and the other boroughs. Hills were leveled; valleys were filled in; and ponds, swamps, springs, and streams were covered over. Wharves, built to enable ships to sail right up to the island and easily load and unload, destroyed sandy beaches and wildlife habitats. Rocks, debris, garbage, trash, and construction materials were dumped into the surrounding waterways, which expanded the size of Manhattan, Long Island, and other islands in the harbor. The Hudson River, the East River, and the harbor became polluted; the aquatic and avian diversity that once thrived and fed the city's inhabitants disappeared.

These natural losses were noted and mourned by the mid-nineteenth century. New Yorkers preserved some natural habitats by creating parks, and the results are some of the nation's most beautiful urban parks, sanctuaries, and botanic gardens, such as Central Park in Manhattan, Prospect Park and the Brooklyn Botanic Garden in Brooklyn, Van Cortlandt Park and the New York Botanic Garden in the Bronx, and the Jamaica Bay Wildlife Sanctuary in Queens. Only during the last forty years have New Yorkers become particularly concerned with water and soil pollution. Good progress has been made: wetlands have been preserved; water pollution has declined; and some native fish, shellfish, and birds have returned. Oyster beds have been planted in the harbor to help filter the pollution out of the water and improve biodiversity. These were important steps, but they have not re-created the area's abundant natural environment that existed before the arrival of large numbers of Europeans in the seventeenth century.

CHAPTER TWO

~

From Colonization to the Present

Henry Hudson, an English explorer, was engaged by the Dutch East India Company to find a northern route to the Pacific coast of Asia. If a northern passage could be found, it would shorten the distance and time to reach the wealth of India and China. Hudson sailed northward along the eastern coast of North America when, in September 1609, he sighted a large bay. Hudson sailed his ship, de *Halve Maen* (the *Half Moon*), through those narrows and into the bay, and he traveled up the estuary called the Great River of Mountains. He turned back near where the city of Albany is today. Along the river he traded with native peoples, acquiring corn, oysters, and fruit. One sailor proclaimed, "They haue great store of Maiz or *Indian* Wheate, whereof they make good Bread." A Dutch officer on board reported that the Indians possessed "an abundance of provisions, skins, and furs, of martens and foxes, and many other commodities, as birds and fruit, even white and red grapes, and they traded amicably with the people." The sailors themselves netted "ten great Mullets" and a ray so large that four men had difficulty wrestling it onboard the ship.

Back in Holland, the Dutch were impressed with the furs that Hudson brought back from his voyage. Other Dutch ships soon arrived in the bay and further explored the river, which they named the North River. (It wouldn't be called the Hudson River until 1909, when New Yorkers celebrated the three hundredth anniversary of Hudson's voyage.) The Dutch commenced a fur-trading enterprise with the Indians, which proved so lucrative that in 1614, the Dutch established a small outpost at Fort Orange,

9

today Albany. Early Dutch traders found an abundance of game, migratory fowl, fresh and saltwater fish, shellfish, turtles, and even buffalo. They were solely focused on acquiring furs (beavers, otters, minks, and other animals). From local Indian tribes they acquired maize and other foodstuffs. They neglected to establish the gardens, farms, and orchards necessary to sustain their growing community.

A growing food shortage was not the worst problem they faced, however: the English claimed all of eastern North America and had complained to the Dutch about their fur-trading activities along the Hudson River. The English were serious about their claim: in 1620, English colonists, many of whom ironically lived in Holland, were granted authority to establish a community at the mouth of the Hudson River. For reasons that remain unclear, these English colonists, later called Pilgrims, settled at Plimoth Plantation, in Massachusetts. Had this group settled in New York, the Dutch trading center upriver would have been cut off and New York's culinary history would have been very different.

The Dutch created the West India Company in 1621, and the fur-trading venture in North America became one of its responsibilities. In 1625, the company ordered the director general of its North American trading operations to concentrate colonists in a single settlement. The southern tip of Manhattan Island was selected, and construction was begun on a small fort to protect the colony. More colonists arrived from Europe, bringing cattle, dogs, sheep, hogs, horses, and agricultural implements. By November 1626, 270 colonists were living in New Amsterdam, as the settlement was called. They established farms, planted crops, and raised animals, but their main activity was fur trading, and food shortages emerged. In 1628, the Reverend Jonas Michaëlius, the first minister of the Dutch Reformed Church in the settlement, reported that the colonists failed to "obtain proper sustenance for want of bread and other necessaries." Butter and milk, he wrote, "cannot here be obtained" except at "very high price." He urged the West India Company to send more farmers and dairymen. This complaint worked. Dairy farmers were recruited to settle in New Amsterdam, and milk, butter, and cheese became staples, as they were in Holland.

Colonists planted wheat, but the early varieties did not fare well. Having learned from the Lenape how to plant corn, the Dutch ground the kernels and made cakes by mixing cornmeal with water and baking the dough in hot ashes—just as the local Indians had taught them. Dutch colonists also ate the Indian corn dishes *samp* (a type of hominy) and *suppawn* (a thick cornmeal porridge), but they mixed these with butter, a European ingredient unknown to the Lenape. Colonists planted other Old World grains, such as barley, and a wide variety of fruits (apples, berries, cherries, and grapes), nuts (almonds and hazelnuts), and vegetables (onions, peas, and turnips).

Unlike Boston, New Amsterdam never developed a large deep-sea fishing fleet; Boston was closer to the Grand Banks, where cod, the premier fish of the day, thrived, so that city had a geographical advantage. But there was a more important reason. The streams, rivers, lakes, bays, Long Island Sound, and the nearby Atlantic offered such abundance and diversity of fish, shellfish, and seafood that fishing hundreds of miles offshore was simply unnecessary. According to Adriaen van der Donck, "All the waters of the New-Netherlands are rich with fishes." In early June, sturgeon were extremely plentiful in the rivers, but they were not preferred and were not eaten at all when large. In fact, he reported that no one took the trouble to catch them for profit, and among those who caught sturgeon for sport, the "roes from which the costly *caviaer* was made" were discarded. This resource would later be recognized as a valuable commodity, and in the nineteenth century New York City became the world's largest caviar exporter until the sturgeon disappeared due to overfishing and pollution.

Oysters were so abundant in the bays and harbors around Manhattan and Long Island that they were considered a cheap everyday food rather than a luxury, but Van der Donck complained that they didn't have any valuable pearls in them. Oysters from the bay and East River were highly praised. Two visitors in 1669 exclaimed that the oysters "are large and full, some of them not less than a foot long, and they grow sometimes ten, twelve and sixteen together, and are then like a piece of rock. Others are young and small. In consequence of the great quantities of them, everybody keeps the shells for the purpose of burning them into lime."

It took time for Old World wheat varieties to acclimatize to the New World, but by the 1640s wheat grew abundantly in the Hudson Valley and on Long Island; it was shipped to New Amsterdam, where flour was milled and made into wheat bread and bakeries were in operation. After annexation by the English, New York became the world's largest milling center. Grain, flour, bread, and biscuits became major export items, and New York, along with New Jersey and Pennsylvania, would later be called the "bread colonies." Ships leaving New York Harbor stocked up on bread, hardtack, and flour before venturing out to sea. By the 1760s, 75 percent of New York's exports were agricultural products in the form of flour or biscuits. During the following decades, the city became the world's largest merchant-milling center.

Few natural sweeteners were available in the New Netherland colony. American Indians did draw sap from several trees, the most productive of which was the sugar maple, but sugar from the maple was not manufactured extensively until the following century. Honey would have been another possibility, but American bees produced little of it. About 1638 the Dutch introduced the Old World bee (*Apis mellifica*) into New Netherland, and this honey-producing strain quickly established itself throughout colonial America. The Indians called the bees "white men's flies."

The rapid expansion of sugarcane planting in the Dutch (and other) colonies in the Caribbean and South America gave New Amsterdamers easy access to refined sugar, although it was expensive and only the wealthy could afford to buy a lot of it. Sugar was occasionally granulated but more often came in clumps or in seven- to ten-pound "loaves," which were large, solid, white cones. Shears, mini-axes and hammers were used to snip off pieces of the sugar cone, which would then be placed in water to dissolve. A much cheaper sweetener was molasses, a by-product of sugar refining. Molasses was the sweetener used by the poor, but it would later find its way into a wide variety of foods, including cookies, cakes, and porridge, and was also used to flavor stewed vegetables and meats.

Rather than expend time and effort raising and growing all of their own food, New Amsterdamers acquired game from the Indians; imported spices, coffee, tea, and wine from Europe; and bought beef, pork, wheat, butter, lamb, fish, butter, malt, salt, fruit, and cider apples from Long Island, New England, and Virginia. As the profitability of fur trapping dwindled, the West India Company faced financial ruin. The Dutch never emigrated in large numbers to New Amsterdam. Officials permitted immigrants and refugees with diverse national, religious, ethnic, and linguistic backgrounds—including peoples from Germany, Italy, Spain, and England—to settle in New Amsterdam.

The colony had another problem: it was geographically between two rapidly expanding English colonies, New England to the north and Virginia to the south. In an attempt to provoke a war with the Netherlands, the English sent four warships into New Amsterdam's harbor, and the Dutch colony surrendered without firing a shot in 1664. The Second Anglo-Dutch War broke out several months later, and the Dutch occupied English sugar plantations in what is today Surinam, a country in northern South America that few New Yorkers have ever heard of. In the seventeenth century, sugar was extremely valuable, so when the Dutch came out on top during the war, they kept the lucrative sugar plantations, and the English were stuck with the floundering fur-trading colony, which they renamed New York, in honor of James Stuart, Duke of York, the future King James II.

At the time, the city had a population of about 1,500, and only about half were of Dutch/Walloon heritage. Despite this small population, decisions made and actions taken during the Dutch period greatly affected the city's culinary future. These included the introduction of a wide range of Old World plants and animals along with the establishment of dairying and baking. These set the city and its environs on the path to becoming an agricultural powerhouse that survived for two centuries. Just as significant was the willingness of the Dutch to allow many different nationalities and religious groups to settle in the region, a tradition that continued when the colony was turned over to the English. Each new wave of immigrants enriched the city with their own foodways, a precedent that would create an incredible culinary mosaic that is enjoyed by New Yorkers to this day. Yet another significant contribution of the Dutch was their view that New Amsterdam was an economic operation; trade and commerce have continued to shape the city and the food produced and consumed in it.

Colonial New York

Under English administration, New York left its origins as a small, unprofitable fur-trapping colony behind and became a major Atlantic trading center. The Hudson River was navigable father than any other river on the eastern seaboard. The Hudson valley was a rich agricultural area, especially for growing wheat, which was shipped down to New York City; the city became an important milling center and a "bread basket" for other colonies and for stocking ships. Other commodities, such as livestock, timber, and apples, were also shipped down the Hudson to New York, where they were converted into salable products such as flour, bread, wooden casks, and hard cider. These were shipped to other American colonies but mostly to the West Indies, where sugarcane was the dominant cash crop. Molasses, sent back from the islands, came to be the most widely used sweetener in America. More important, molasses could be converted into rum, which quickly became New York's spirit of choice.

The West Indies also shipped raw sugar to New York; these partly refined cane sugar syrups were sweeter and more expensive than molasses, but they could be refined into pure sugar. When the first New York sugar refinery was established is a matter of debate. Historian Mary L. Booth claimed that the city's first sugar refinery opened in 1689 on Liberty Street. Sugar historian Noel Deerr deemed this too early, placing the date in 1725, when the New York legislature granted a monopoly to Robert Hooper to create a refinery. Others soon followed. By 1728 another refinery, run by Samuel Bayard, was operating on Wall Street; it sold refined loaf sugar, powder sugars, and candy. In 1754, the Livingston family constructed a six-story refinery on Crown

Street, and John van Cortlandt established one on Liberty Street. William Rhinelander opened the Rhinelander Sugar House at the corner of Rose and Duane Streets in 1763, and later the family acquired another refinery. Refineries were the largest buildings in the city at the time, and sugar refining was one of the city's most important industries.

Revolutionary New York

During the Seven Years' War (1756–1763), Great Britain defeated the French army in North America, and as a result of the treaty, it acquired Canada along with a vast territory west of the Allegheny Mountains that extended to the Mississippi River. The war had been costly, and many members of the British parliament concluded that the American colonists, who had gained much from the war, should pay a portion of the debt and the cost of upkeep of the British troops stationed in the newly acquired territories.

The British colonies had indeed reaped tremendous benefits from the war. Merchants had made profits supplying the British army and navy with food and equipment, and more important, the greatest and only real military threat to the colonies—the French in Canada—had been removed. In 1764, the British parliament passed the Sugar Act, which levied a tax on American imports of five products, the most important of which was molasses. A British tax on molasses imported from the French, Spanish, and Dutch colonies in the Caribbean had already been on the books for thirty years, but colonists had simply subverted the law through smuggling and bribing customs officials. The Sugar Act actually *lowered* the existing import duties from six pence to three pence, but it also had stiff enforcement provisions, which, if carried out, would harm the American sugar-refining and whiskey-distilling industries. Many colonists also viewed the tax as a restriction of their liberties.

The Sugar Act was vigorously opposed by New Yorkers. Some opponents engaged in public demonstrations against it in front of the Merchants' Coffee House, a central location in the city. Others protestors were more destructive. An angry mob trashed Vauxhall, a tavern and pleasure garden (a small private park), after its owner, a former British army officer, came out in favor of the act. Still other opponents created the Sons of Liberty, a semi-secret organization that met at taverns and would soon organize resistance to other acts passed by the British parliament and the royal governor's appointed by the Crown.

It was no surprise that New York taverns played such an important role in revolutionary activity that led to the American Revolution. Taverns were more than just places to drink, eat, and occasionally stay the night: In colonial America, taverns functioned as community centers. Their owners were generally well informed about current happenings, and they shared what they knew. Meetings of groups such as militiamen were frequently convened at taverns and public houses. Men congregated at taverns, passing on information and discussing current events. Many taverns provided newspapers and magazines for customers to peruse.

The protests worked. The British parliament rescinded the Sugar Act but continued to pass a series of acts intended to reaffirm its right to levy a tax on the colonies. These acts generated even bigger protests, culminating in the outbreak of the Revolutionary War in Massachusetts in 1775.

A few months after the British evacuated Boston in March of 1776, British forces landed on Staten Island and, a few weeks later, on Long Island. Within a matter of days they had captured New York City and more than three thousand American soldiers. Supporters of the Revolution fled the city, loyalists returned, and the city was occupied for the next seven years—longer than any other American city. Thousands of British troops and German mercenaries were garrisoned in the city. In addition, thousands of loyalists and escaping slaves from the surrounding areas and colonies flocked to New York. The city's population swelled from seventeen to thirty-four thousand during the war.

Several thousand American soldiers captured by the British ended up imprisoned in abandoned churches and sugar refineries. The unlucky ones ended up in the holds of decommissioned British ships anchored off the coast of Brooklyn. These facilities were overcrowded, and thousands died from the lack of food and clean water, as well as from typhus and other diseases, for which no medical assistance was provided.

Throughout out the Revolutionary War, British and American military forces engaged in guerilla warfare in the hinterland around New York. Cattle rustling and crop burnings were common. Farmers on Long Island and New Jersey eventually supported the War for Independence and refused to sell their products to the British occupiers of New York City. The British army had to import commodities by ship, and the cost of food in British-occupied New York jumped 800 percent during the war. When food shipments failed to arrive, the British considered abandoning the city. Only the timely arrival of a victualing fleet from Ireland prevented mass starvation.

Peace negotiations began in April 1782; in mid-August 1783, the British governor of New York informed General George Washington that his forces were withdrawing from the city. During the next three months, twenty-nine thousand British military personnel, loyalists, and freed slaves left the city, while those who had fled in 1776 trickled back to reclaim what was left of their property. New York was in a shambles. Fires had swept through the city in 1776 and 1778, and an explosion on an ammunition ship in the East River had damaged the docks and other port facilities. When the war ended, more than one-third of the city's buildings had been destroyed, replaced by shanties that housed penniless loyalists and military personnel.

One tavern that survived was owned by Samuel Fraunces, who was born in the West Indies. Like most tavern owners, Fraunces offered a set dinner as well as alcoholic beverages. He prepared meals in the English style, and his desserts were particularly popular. Fraunces left New York City when the British took over. He later returned and resumed running his tavern. Fraunces aided American prisoners of war during the British occupation, for which a grateful Continental Congress awarded him two hundred pounds in 1782. Many British soldiers drank and ate in his tavern, and he reportedly passed on information gleaned from his guests to Washington's army, which was encamped outside the city.

The Treaty of Paris was signed on September 3, 1783, ending the Revolutionary War, and the British military authorities officially turned over New York City on November 25, 1783. Called "Evacuation Day," New Yorkers would celebrate it with revelry and alcoholic beverages for the next sixty years. George Washington and the Continental Army marched down Broadway to cheering crowds. That night, a public dinner was held for Washington at Fraunces Tavern, and there, nine days later, Washington gave his farewell address to the officers of the Continental Army.

Revitalizing a City

The city slowly reinvented itself, an undertaking it would repeat many times in the centuries that followed. As New York reestablished its trade and financial center, the city took a commercial lead over its rivals, Boston and Philadelphia—a margin that continued to increase during the following years. After the U.S. Constitution was approved in 1788, New York became the nation's temporary capital. When George Washington was inaugurated president at Federal Hall in 1789, he selected Samuel Fraunces as his head steward. While in New York, Washington hosted dinners and receptions lavish enough to shock some members of his cabinet and Congress. An observer described one such dinner in August 1789: "First was the soup; fish roasted and boiled; meats, gammon, fowls, etc." It was followed by dessert: "apple pies, pudding, etc.; then iced creams, jellies, etc.; then water-melons, muskmelons, apples, peaches, and nuts."

The city's population almost doubled—from thirty-three thousand in 1790 to sixty thousand by the end of the decade—and swelled even more during the early nineteenth century. This created a large concentration of potential customers that made commercial production of bakery products, refined sugar, and canned goods financially viable.

Bakeries

Bakeries had been in operation in the city since early colonial days, but during the early nineteenth century city dwellers opted to pay for the ease and convenience of buying bakers' bread, and the housewife's chore of baking bread shifted to the task of buying it. Bakers sold their goods retail or wholesaled their products to grocery stores, restaurants, and street vendors. Commercial bakeries were subject to market forces: local laws controlled the price and characteristics of bakers' bread, making it difficult for bakers to make a profit. Bakers responded by reducing costs: they adulterated their products with powdered chalk or plaster to make the bread whiter and heavier, or at least so claimed Sylvester Graham, a Presbyterian minister, temperance advocate, and outspoken advocate for vegetarianism. Graham frequently spoke to large crowds in New York and elsewhere, inveighing against bakers and their pallid, impoverished bread, as well as butchers. He believed that women should bake bread at home, eschewing refined white flour and using coarse, unbolted (whole grain) wheat flour instead. His views caught on in New York City, and beginning in 1833, Graham boardinghouses, which institutionalized his views, sprang up in the city to enable his adherents to follow Graham's health food regimen.

Graham's views toward professional bakers were not, however, shared by most New Yorkers, who increasingly bought commercially baked loaves. The city's baking industry was regularly renewed by an influx of professional bakers from abroad. By the early nineteenth century, Scots-Irish bakers dominated the industry. When German and Irish immigrants began to arrive in the 1830s, many went into baking. By 1855, however, Germans, many of whom were Jewish, dominated the city's commercial bakeries. As other immigrant groups entered the city, they, too, opened bakeries that offered goods particularly associated with those groups. Both the quality and diversity of bread and other baked goods improved throughout the nineteenth century. By the early twentieth century, few New Yorkers made bread at home.

Large commercial bakeries and hundreds of small artisanal bakeries—many owned by immigrants—sustained city dwellers in the late nineteenth century. In 1889, six bakeries united to create the New York Biscuit

Bird's eye view of Manhattan. Courtesy of the Library of Congress. Reproduction Number: LC-DIG-pga-03183

Company. Other bakeries joined the organization, and in 1898 the company was renamed the National Biscuit Company, which in 1971 officially shortened its name to "Nabisco." It operated a manufacturing facility in New York until after World War II.

Nabisco created many of America's favorite cookies and crackers, including Uneeda Biscuits, Triscuits, Barnum's Animal Crackers, Oreos, Nilla Wafers, and Ritz Crackers. It has grown into a huge corporation by acquiring other companies, including those that produced Shredded Wheat, Planters Nuts, and LifeSavers. Its most iconic New York brand was Mallomars—cookies with a round biscuit base (similar to a Graham cracker), topped with a dome of marshmallow and coated with dark chocolate. The former Nabisco plant in Manhattan, at Ninth Avenue and Fifteenth Street, is now home to a very successful and upscale "mini-mall" of food purveyors called Chelsea Market. The Food Network's headquarters and studios, and several high-end restaurants, are in the same building.

Sugar Refining

New York's sugar-refining industry quickly revived after the Revolutionary War. A German immigrant, William Havemeyer, arrived in New York in

1799. He had been superintendent of a sugar refinery in London. In New York, he ran Edmund Seaman & Company's sugar house on Pine Street and then opened his own refinery in Manhattan in 1807. His son, William F. Havemeyer, joined the family business, later going into partnership with a cousin, Frederick C. Havemeyer.

New York was an ideal location for the sugar-refining industry. Its port facilities were the best on the East Coast, and it was easy to transport raw sugar into the city from the Caribbean. The city had a large population that wanted the sweetener, and the city's transportation grid meant that the refined product could be easily transported to other regions of the country. By 1830, the city had eleven sugar-refining companies. Thirty years later, this had increased to twenty-six, which were collectively valued at thirty-five million dollars (today somewhere between one and five billion dollars). New York City dominated sugar refining in America, and this dominance increased over the years. Eventually, as manufacturing methods improved and production rose dramatically, sugar prices took a steep drop in the nineteenth century. Several companies went out of business, but the surviving firms expanded their dominance of the industry. In 1864, the Havemeyers constructed the largest and most technologically advanced sugar refineries in the world in Williamsburg.

By 1872, New York processed 59 percent of the sugar imported into America; fifteen years later, this had risen to 68 percent. As a result of mass production, the price of sugar continued to decline. In 1887, the Havemeyers and seven other sugar industry leaders formed the Sugar Trust. Its intent was to lower production in order to raise prices and profits for all the companies. The trust was taken to court, and in 1891 it was allowed to reorganize. It acquired additional companies, and the resulting conglomerate was named the American Sugar Refining Company. Inefficient plants were closed while others were combined, and American Sugar Refining unofficially, but effectively, fixed the price of refined sugar. In 1900, the company created a subsidiary, Domino Sugar, to market the sugar that the parent company refined. By 1907, the American Sugar Refining Company controlled 97 percent of all production of refined sugar in America. Although this percentage declined after 1921, when the company lost a major antitrust case, it continued to dominate American sugar refining throughout the twentieth century. New York's refineries were slowly closed as more efficient—and less costly—factories were built elsewhere. The large Domino sugar refinery in Williamsburg, the last sugar refinery in New York, closed in 2004. The property is being redeveloped; preservationists hope that at least one building, emblazoned with "Domino Sugar" in big yellow letters resembling a box of sugar, will be landmarked.

Sugar was used in many ways, but one of the most important was confectionery, and industries making candy emerged in New York City. Tootsie Rolls, a perennial American favorite, were created by Leo Hirschfield, an immigrant from Austria. In 1896, he began turning out small, log-shaped, chewy chocolate caramels in his candy store. In 1905, he named the candy after his daughter, Clara, whose nickname was "Tootsie," and began manufacturing them. Tootsie Rolls were the first penny candy to be individually wrapped. Hirschfield named his business the Sweets Company of America, and in 1917 he began advertising nationally. In 1931, the company introduced the Tootsie Pop, which was a hard candy lollipop with a Tootsie Roll center. During World War II, Tootsie Rolls were placed in soldier's ration kits, mainly because they could survive extremes of temperature and humidity. After the war, the company targeted its advertising on youth by sponsoring popular children's television shows. The company was renamed Tootsie Roll Industries, Inc., and today it is headquartered in Chicago.

Samuel Born, a Russian Jew who immigrated to New York in 1910, invented the "Born Sucker Machine," which automatically inserted sticks into lollipops, thereby revolutionizing the lollipop trade. In 1917, he opened a retail candy store in Brooklyn. In 1923, Born started his own manufacturing company: Just Born. In 1932, the company relocated to Bethlehem, Pennsylvania. Its most famous product is Peeps, marshmallow chicks in bright Easter colors.

Yet another candy company was launched by Edward Noble, owner of the Mint Products Company of New York. In 1913, he acquired the rights to manufacture LifeSavers, ring-shaped mint candies that had been invented the previous year in Ohio. Noble packaged stacks of the candies in foil and sold them for a nickel a roll. They were distributed to bars, where displays were installed next to cash registers. The idea was that mint candy served as a "lifesaver" for drinkers, disguising the smell of alcohol on their breath. In 1915, the United Cigar Store chain placed the displays in their many stores, and Noble also marketed LifeSavers to drugstores, grocery stores, and other retailers. LifeSavers became one of the most successful hard candy lines in America. The company was eventually sold to Wrigley Company, best known for their chewing gum.

Many food and beverage corporations were headquartered in New York, and many operated factories, but beginning in the mid-twentieth century most manufacturing operations left the city. During the early twenty-first century, the New York City Economic Development Corporation encouraged food startups, particularly in Brooklyn and Queens. Today, dozens of small companies have been launched, including Kombucha Brooklyn (tea-based beverages), Empire Mayonnaise, McClure's Pickles, Brooklyn Soda Works, Steve's Ice Cream, Madécasse (chocolate bars), People's Pops (ice pops), Cuties Pies, King County Jerky Co., ten breweries, and one distillery.

Fresh, Pickled, Canned, and Bottled

From colonial times, raw oysters were sold on the streets and later in oyster houses, saloons, cellars, and restaurants. Oysters were also pickled, packed in small casks, and sent to other colonies and the Caribbean. In 1748, Swedish-Finnish botanist Peter Kalm described the elaborate process in which New Yorkers pickled them. The oysters were first shelled, boiled in a pot, removed, and dried:

> Then some nutmeg allspice and black pepper are added, and as much vinegar as is thought sufficient to give a sourish taste. All this is mixed with half the liquor in which the oysters are boiled, and put over the fire again. . . . At last the whole pickling liquid is poured into a glass or earthen vessel, the oysters are put into it and the vessel is well stopped to keep out the air. In this manner, oysters will keep for years, and may be sent to the most distant parts of the world.

Later, pickled oysters were shipped throughout the Midwest and even to California and England. When railroads were constructed, fresh oysters were sent to restaurants and grocery stores throughout the East Coast.

It was logical that oysters were among the first foods canned in New York. The sealable tin can was invented in England in the early nineteenth century. English immigrant Thomas Kensett arrived in New York about 1806; within a few years he had begun a canning business with his father-in-law, Ezra Dagget, also an English immigrant. They were among the first in the United States to hermetically seal tins of food—salmon, lobsters, oysters, meats, fruits, and vegetables. They were awarded the first U.S. patent for preserving food in 1825.

By the 1850s, many canning factories operated in New York City and in Astoria on Long Island. One firm, Wells, Miller & Provost, packed tomatoes in the city. The editors of the *American Agriculturist* claimed that canned tomatoes put up by this firm tasted as "nice sweet and fresh as if just picked from the vines." Canned goods were still expensive, and only the well-to-do could afford them. High-end restaurants adopted canned fruits and vegetables in order to serve their delighted customers out-of-season delicacies in the winter. The price of canned goods dropped dramatically after the Civil War, and by the 1870s, they were affordable to most New Yorkers and routinely sold in city grocery stores.

For the home canners, John L. Mason, owner of a metalworking shop on Canal Street, invented a self-sealing zinc lid and glass jar in 1858. The screw-on lid greatly simplified the canning process and made the jars genuinely reusable. It revolutionized fruit and vegetable preservation in the home. As the jars were easy to use and comparatively inexpensive to produce, their popularity soared. By 1860, Mason jars were shipped throughout the United States.

Food Transportation

During the colonial era, overland transportation to and from New York by wagon over dirt roads was slow at the best of times, and often impossible in bad weather. After the American Revolution, surveys were conducted to evaluate the possibility of constructing a canal that would link the Hudson River with the Great Lakes. The War of 1812 was a decisive factor in the final decision to construct the canal. It became apparent during the war that there was no easy way to move troops and supplies across the state to support military efforts. After the war, pressure to build a canal mounted, and construction finally began on July 4, 1817. Those who proposed and approved the Erie Canal's construction—and those who bought bonds to finance it—hoped that the canal would encourage settlement around the new waterway and that farms along the route would ensure an adequate food supply for New York's rapidly growing population.

As sections of the canal were completed, agricultural commodities, particularly wheat, began to travel southward with unprecedented efficiency. This was the beginning of a flood of grain from upstate New York that poured into the city, where it was milled into flour and then loaded onto oceangoing vessels for shipment to coastal cities in the eastern and southern United States, the Caribbean, and Europe. Likewise, most goods that were shipped westward through the canal came through New York City. The canal was completed in 1825, and by the late 1820s, hundreds of sailing vessels and fifty steamboats traveled up and down the river to and from New York City, while more than 1,400 ships arrived annually in New York Harbor from foreign ports. Within fifteen years of the canal's opening, more tonnage moved through the Port of New York than the combined tonnage of the nation's three other largest ports—Boston, Baltimore, and New Orleans.

The commercial success of the Erie Canal spurred on the construction of railroads. Tracks were first laid northward from New York City. This meant that dairy and produce farmers who lived north of the metropolis, but not on a navigable river, could ship fresh milk and produce into the city daily.

By the 1850s, railroads connected New York and Chicago, which greatly enhanced the transportation of agricultural goods to New York from the Midwest during the Civil War. Live cattle were soon shipped from the Midwest to New Jersey. They were shipped across the Hudson and herded daily through city streets to the Meatpacking District, situated in the area from West Sixteenth Street south to Gansevoort Street, and from the Hudson River east to Hudson Street. By 1900, more than 250 packing plants were operating in the district, but that was the industry's peak.

After the Civil War, the invention of the refrigerated railroad car in the 1870s permitted livestock to be slaughtered in Midwestern feedlots and then transported to New York. It was no longer necessary for live cattle to be shipped to New York and through its streets. The shipment of cheap dressed beef from the Midwest reduced the need for local butchers. In 1860, New York City had more than two thousand; only a few hundred survived in 1900. Butchers hoped that their customers' appreciation of the quality and flavor of their meats would breed loyalty, but shoppers readily passed up locally butchered beef and pork for cheaper cuts shipped in from the Midwest.

After the completion of the transcontinental railroad in 1869, agricultural goods—particularly fruit and vegetables—could be shipped from San Francisco to New York. Other railroads connected the city with the South. By the 1880s, truck gardeners in Virginia and North Carolina were shipping produce to New York; by 1899, Florida growers were shipping oranges and other citrus to the city by train.

The twentieth century saw the construction of all-weather roads and, eventually, the interstate system. The advent of long-haul trucks with roof-mounted refrigeration systems, in 1948, made it possible for refrigerated and frozen foods to be easily transported from even the most isolated communities to New York. The invention of shipping containers and the construction of container ships in 1956 made it easier for many foods—particularly fruit, vegetables, grains, coffee, chocolate, and meat—to be shipped from Central and Latin America, and in winter, shipments are particularly heavy.

Holidays and Celebrations

From its earliest days, New Yorkers enjoyed a range of secular, religious, and unusual holidays and relished the attendant food and beverage traditions associated with them. In colonial times, at least some residents celebrated the feast of Bacchus (March 16), Shrovetide or Carnival (typically forty days before Easter), Easter, Pinxter (Whitsuntide), May Day (May 1), Ascension

Day, Christmas, New Year's, Twelfth Night/Day (January 5–6), and Voor-bereiding ("preparation for the Lord's Supper," observed quarterly). Holidays were typically celebrated with revelers firing guns into the air, beating drums, and drinking excessive amounts of liquor. City officials passed regulations attempting to prevent these activities, but they failed.

Sinterklaas, or St. Nicholas Day (December 5 or 6), was also celebrated in New York, at least until the 1740s, when it was officially dropped from New York City's list of official holidays. It may have been dropped, but it was not forgotten. Washington Irving popularized the Dutch celebration of a completely fictional Saint Nicholas in his *History of New-York* (1809), which just happened to be published on St. Nicholas Day. He described the arrival of the saint on horseback on the Eve of Saint Nicholas, who was now identified as the patron saint of New York. John Pintard, a descendent of a Huguenot family that arrived in 1690, paid for the publication of a broadside with an illustration of a stern Saint Nicholas. Over the fireplace hung two stockings—one filled with goodies (perhaps toys, oranges, sugar plums, and "oley cooks"), the other, a stick.

Christmas was celebrated in the city in colonial times, but like other holidays, it was a time to fire guns into the air and drink. Drunkenness and rowdiness prevailed on the streets. Some of the shooting was purposeful. Historian Mary Booth, writing in 1860, reported that in colonial times, the day started with an exchange of presents; then, "the young men repaired to the 'commons' or 'Beekman's swamp' to shoot at turkeys which were set up for a target. Each man paid a few stuyvers for a shot, and he who succeeded in hitting the bird took it off as a prize." For those who celebrated Christmas (some Protestant denominations considered it to be a "Papist holiday"), the turkey was a dinner favorite.

From the early nineteenth century, efforts were underway to tame Christmas. The name "Santa Claus," a derivative of Saint Nicholas and Sinter-klaas, first appeared in print in New York in the 1770s and has been associated with Christmas ever since. The association of Christmas with a cozy family celebration complete with a large dinner was popularized by Washington Irving in his *Sketch Book* (1819). An acquaintance of John Pintard and Washington Irving was Clement Clarke Moore, an Episcopalian minister of Walloon ancestry. He wrote "An Account of a Visit from St. Nicholas" (1823), commonly known as "'Twas the Night before Christmas." He intentionally set the arrival of Santa Claus on Christmas Eve (although some early versions say New Year's Eve, not Christmas). The shift from Christmas to Christmas Eve avoided potential religious issues. Illustrator Thomas Nast, a German immigrant who arrived in New York in 1850, created the modern image of jolly old St. Nick, which first appeared in *Harper's Weekly* in 1862. By this time, many New Yorkers celebrated a less rowdy Christmas complete with presents for the children and a family dinner.

New Year's Day was the main secular holiday during the city's early years. Both the Dutch and English exchanged gifts. The holiday was also celebrated by visits to the homes of friends and acquaintances, where refreshments were served. Some celebrated New Year's by "going from House to House with Guns and other Fire Arms, and being often intoxicated with Liquor"—a practice that had existed at least since 1675. Laws were passed to prevent such displays, and the city police doubled their forces on these holidays, but the celebratory shooting continued until the 1840s. The custom of New Year's Day visits continued well into the nineteenth century. Here, from the 1830s, is an account of a round of such visits:

> We began at nine in the morning, and at five in the afternoon we ceased, having visited sixty-seven houses. In some cases, in consequence of the great number of "callers" in a house, we merely walked in and said "Happy New Year," or "Compliments of the Season," "Thank you, we dare not indulge," "Good-morning." At other houses, when the young ladies were especially interesting, a few minutes' conversation and a sip of cherry bounce or coffee, "Good-morning," and off to another house. Such was the routine of the young men, while the elder, having fewer visits to make, remained longer at their calls and indulged in the table, lavishly spread with crullers, doughnuts, cook-ies (New Year's cakes), pickled and stewed oysters, chicken, turkey, mince-pies, jellies, etc., and with wines and liqueurs.

On New Year's 1837, New York's mayor opened his house to the public. Gentlemen came, politely tendered their greetings, and left; a few drank "a single glass of wine or cherry bounce, and a morsel of pound-cake or New Year's cookies," reported diarist Philip Hone. Then the rabble showed up demanding refreshments. They devoured the beef and turkey, wiped their greasy fingers on the curtains, drank the mayor's liquor, and discharged "riot-ous shouts of 'Huzza for our Mayor!'" The police had to be called in to restore order. For many, New Year's was simply a day away from working and a day for drinking; by evening, the streets were frequently littered with casualties of the festivities.

For the upper classes, hostesses offered their visitors beverages, such as rare wines, cognac, bourbon, and, occasionally, champagne. An English visitor to New York City on New Year's in 1870 found that eggnog was "the peculiar beverage of New Year's day," but also served were apple toddy, milk punch, brandy smash, and mixed drinks, such as the popular Tom and Jerry, an eggnog-like mixed drink with eggs, sugar, rum, and brandy served hot. By the end of the nineteenth century, however, the temperance movement had followers, at least among some well-to-do New Yorkers. When the English writer George Sala visited the city on New Year's 1880, he was mainly offered coffee, bouillon, and chocolate, but no alcohol.

Over time, the celebration shifted to New Year's Eve, and the midnight glass (or more) of champagne became obligatory along with singing "Auld Lang Syne." Public celebration of the stroke of midnight were celebrated across the city, but beginning in 1904 these celebrations began to concentrate at Times Square; watching the ball drop at 11:59 p.m. on December 31 became de rigueur in 1907. The Times Square celebration became a national event with the advent of radio and a global event watched by millions after the arrival of television.

New holidays were added to the city's calendar after the American Revolution. After 1784, the Fourth of July, Independence Day, was celebrated annually in the city with fireworks, parades, entertainment, drinking, and food. In 1797, Joseph Delacroix, owner of the Vauxhall Garden, offered celebrants entertainment plus ice cream, punch, or lemonade (but no alcohol) for six shillings. In 1838, an English visitor named Frederick Marryat described the city's Fourth of July celebration:

> On each side of the whole length of Broadway, were ranged booths and stands, similar to those at an English fair, and on which were displayed small plates of oysters, with a fork stuck in the board opposite to each plate; clams sweltering in the hot sun; pineapples, boiled hams, pies, puddings, barley-sugar, and many other indescribables. But what was remarkable, Broadway being three miles long, and the booths lining each side of it, in every booth there was a roast pig, large or small, as the centre attraction. Six miles of roast pig! and that in New York City alone; and roast pig in every other city, town, hamlet, and village in the Union. What association can there be between roast pig and independence? Let it not be supposed that there was any deficiency in the very necessary articles of potation on this auspicious day: no! the booths were loaded with porter, ale, cider, mead, brandy, wine, ginger-beer, mint juleps, besides many other compounds.

Yet another new holiday was Thanksgiving. It had been celebrated in New England since the late eighteenth century. Many New Englanders moved to the city, and they introduced New Yorkers to all the trappings of their celebration. In 1830, New York was the first state outside of New England to declare Thanksgiving a state holiday. As one New Yorker wrote in the 1830s, "The Yankee Thanksgiving, with its turkey, cranberry sauce, mince, pumpkin apple pie and cider, found favor with the dames of knick-erbocker proclivities, who not to be outdone, had added the indigestible doughnut and cruller to the dyspepsia provoking list."

An unusual Thanksgiving celebration took place during the Civil War. When President Abraham Lincoln issued a proclamation declaring that Thanksgiving would be celebrated on November 24, 1864, George W. Blunt, a member of New York's Union League Club, proposed to lift the spirits of Union soldiers and sailors in Virginia by supplying them "with poultry and pies, or puddings, all cooked, ready for use." The Union League Club appealed to hoteliers, restaurateurs, bakers, and private individuals (with the means to do so) to roast twenty or more turkeys and chickens and send them to a central location so they could be shipped south.

Delmonico's, the city's most fashionable restaurant, contributed the services of its chefs to stuff and roast thousands of turkeys. These delicacies were packed up and sent by train, ship, and wagon all the way to Virginia. In just three weeks, the Union League Club collected more than $56,500 toward the purchase of 146,586 pounds of poultry. New York's Fulton Market supplied much of that and donated a $3,386 profit back to the fund. An additional 225,000 pounds of poultry was received as contributions, along with enormous quantities of other Thanksgiving dinner ingredients. Northern newspapers crowed about the feast. The *New York Herald* proudly announced, "A people in the midst of a bloody war, having tens of thousands of soldiers in the field, and war ships studding every sea, yet every day expanding into greater commercial importance, and celebrates its national elections, feasts, and holidays with peace and harmony."

New Yorkers prospered during the Civil War as government contracts poured in for manufacturing military hardware and constructing and resupplying ships. Jobs were readily available, and wages were high. Food was plentiful in the city throughout the war, and the city's wealth meant that its restaurants thrived. Women joined sanitary commissions, which helped wounded soldiers and their families. The well-to-do created the Union League Club in 1863 to support the war effort. As at the Century Club, the city's first, formed in 1847, the Union League's members were men. Clubs made it possible for members to drink, dine, and socialize among themselves without having to resort to the city's public restaurants and bars.

Thanksgiving and Christmas were connected by an invention of Macy's department store employees: the Thanksgiving Day Parade. In 1924, Macy's employees organized a procession that started on 145th Street in Harlem and ended in front of the Macy's store, on Herald Square in midtown. Traditionally, the last float of the parade carries Santa Claus, who officially kicks off the Christmas shopping season. Today, millions of visitors and television viewers watch the trademark giant balloons as they're marched down the avenues. Virtually all the restaurants along the parade route that are open are filled, but most New Yorkers view the parade on TV and eat Thanksgiving dinner at home with their families and friends.

Culinary Education and Organizations

By the mid-nineteenth century, increasing wealth in New York City meant that more families were able to hire domestics. The problem with many immigrant household servants, especially those from Ireland, was that they were unable to prepare the food that employers wanted. One solution was developed by Pierre Blot, a Frenchman who came to New York about 1855. He lectured on the culinary arts, and in 1863 published his first book, *What to Eat, and How to Cook It.* Two years later, he launched a cooking school called the Culinary School of Design and styled himself the "professor of gastronomy." His second book, *Hand-Book of Practical Cookery,* was published in 1867, and he followed it with a series of articles on culinary topics in *The Galaxy,* a monthly magazine. These gave him great visibility. With financial assistance from a daughter of the railroad magnate Commodore Cornelius Vanderbilt, Blot opened the New York Cooking School, America's first French cooking school. It mainly catered to wealthy women, who brought their cooks with them for training, and it lasted only a few years, but the idea for cooking schools reemerged after the Civil War, as more immigrants streamed into New York and the need for domestics and restaurant cooks swelled.

During the 1860s, a German immigrant, Gesine Lemcke, opened the Greater New York Cooking School on East Forty-second Street and another branch in Brooklyn. Her aim was to train cooks, butlers, and waitresses. When Lemcke died in 1904, her daughter became the principal, and the school continued to operate until 1934.

In 1873, the nation went into an economic recession that continued for several years. Many immigrants lost their jobs, and new employment was hard to find. Juliet Corson, a thirty-two-year-old librarian at the Working Women's Library in New York, became concerned about the plight of poor women in the city. Corson volunteered as secretary to the Women's Educational and Industrial Society of New York, whose purpose was to offer free vocational training for unemployed working-class women. She was asked to teach cookery, even though she had little experience or culinary knowledge; the hope was that her students might find jobs as domestics. Corson studied

German and French cookbooks and began offering classes in her home. In 1874, the society moved into a building that housed classrooms as well as free dormitories for unemployed women taking courses at the school. The following year, Juliet Corson began submitting articles on cookery for newspapers and magazines, and lecturing at various venues around the city.

Corson's cooking courses attracted the attention of middle- and upper-class women, and she decided to launch her own cooking school. In November 1876, she opened the New York Cooking School, with a sliding-scale tuition that made it affordable for women from every walk of life. The school offered a series of twelve lessons. Based on her lectures and experiences, Corson wrote *The Cooking Manual of Practical Directions for Economical Every-Day Cookery*, which presented her culinary philosophy—to make "the most wholesome and palatable dishes at the least possible cost." Corson's cooking school and lectures were so successful that she received inquiries from many cities, including Philadelphia and Boston, on how to start and manage a cooking school. She published *Cooking School Text Book and Housekeepers' Guide* (1879), which became the textbook for many schools in other cities, such as Boston and Philadelphia. It included a section on "Dietary for Schools," which delineated the foods and beverages students needed and made suggestions for breakfasts and dinners. Copies of the "Dietary" were reprinted by the secretary of the Interior and sent to schools around the country.

Harper's magazine proclaimed Corson to be "the benefactor of the working classes, for she teaches them how to make two dishes where formerly they made but one; and the friend of women, for she has shown them the way to a useful and honorable profession." Her efforts—and those of home economics professionals—led to the teaching of cookery in New York City's public schools.

During the twentieth century, other culinary schools opened in New York. One was launched by Dione Lucas, an Englishwoman born in Italy and brought up in France. She attended Le Cordon Bleu cooking school in Paris and opened a restaurant in London just before World War II. When the war broke out, she immigrated to New York where she opened the Cordon Bleu Cooking School at her restaurant in Manhattan. It offered lessons for "five dollars apiece" and "a course of forty-eight lessons for $192." The school's name was later changed to the Gourmet Cooking School, which she continued to run out of her various restaurants. Another culinary school was opened by cookbook author James Beard in his townhouse on West Tenth Street and later on West Twelfth Street.

Some older schools still in operation are Peter Kump's New York Cooking School, founded in 1975 and renamed the Institute for Culinary Education in 2001; the Natural Gourmet Cooking School, founded by Annemarie Colbin in 1977; De Gustibus Cooking School, launched at Macy's in 1980 by Arlene Feltman Sailhac; and the French Culinary Institute in Soho, founded by Dorothy Cann Hamilton in 1984 and later renamed the International Culinary Center.

In addition to culinary schools, city universities have developed academic food studies programs. New York University, for instance, launched the Department of Nutrition, Food Studies, and Public Health in the 1990s. It offers undergraduate, master's, and doctoral programs in food studies, culture, and food systems. The New School also has recently started an undergraduate food studies department, and other city universities have offered numerous academic courses of various aspects of food.

Many culinary organizations have been launched in New York. The Société Culinaire et Philanthropique was founded in 1865. It is the oldest culinary association in America; its membership includes chefs, cooks, pastry chefs, bakers, and butchers. It is headquartered in New York, and its "Salon of Culinary Art" is presented each year during the International Hotel/Motel & Restaurant Show at the Jacob Javits Convention Center. Les Dames d'Escoffier was launched in 1973 by Carol Brock, then Sunday food editor at the *New York Daily News*. An organization of professional women in the food and wine industry, the New York Women's Culinary Alliance, was launched in 1981 by Sara Moulton and Maria Reuge. The Culinary Historians of New York was founded in 1985 to stimulate and share knowledge about food history. Slow Food USA was launched in Brooklyn in 2000.

When cookbook author and cooking teacher James Beard died, Peter Kump, a former student of Beard's, raised funds to buy Beard's Greenwich Village townhouse. Along with others, including Julia Child and Jacques Pépin, Kump helped launch the James Beard Foundation, which is housed in Beard's former home. Since 1990, the James Beard Foundation has given awards for culinary excellence to chefs, journalists, and other culinary professionals.

World War II

The United States entered World War II in December 1941. Like many other Americans, New Yorkers with lawns and backyards planted "Victory Gardens," raising a large amount of vegetables. Tomatoes were planted in Rockefeller Plaza and penthouses often sported beans. New York families changed their eating habits as some traditional foods became unavailable and domestic servants left to join the army or take war-related jobs during war.

During the war, many New Yorkers volunteered or were drafted in the armed services, and many other soldiers and sailors came through the city on their way overseas. Canteens were set up for military personnel, and women volunteers prepared cakes and sandwiches that were consumed with coffee, milk, and fruit when available. One canteen in Brooklyn served fourteen thousand servicemen in a single month in 1942.

Rationing went into effect in 1942 and continued until 1947, and it became difficult for restaurateurs and homemakers to acquire all the beef, wheat, sugar, imported spices, wines, and other products that they wanted. Another serious problem was the shortage of workers. Women entered the workforce and soon dominated sales forces in grocery stores and food production industries and as waiters in restaurants, diners, and other eateries. Many employees worked overtime, and as there were few consumer goods on the market, they pocketed their salaries or dined in restaurants. The war years were particularly good ones for the city's restaurants. From 1939 to 1946, restaurant sales in New York quadrupled. When the war ended, restaurant profits soared even more: New Yorkers wanted to compensate for the hardships during the war, and many had money that could not be spent during the war.

Food Journalism

Food journalism was one reason the New York culinary scene took off after World War II. Previously, food articles in magazines and newspapers had supplied recipes and helpful hints and were often thinly veiled (or overt) promotions for new manufactured food products and the latest kitchen equipment. But as the twentieth century rolled on, some newspaper food writers became extremely popular and influential. Clementine Paddleford, a Kansas native with a degree in industrial journalism, became food editor at the *New York Herald Tribune* in 1936, having previously written for the *New York Sun* and *New York Telegram*. By the early 1950s, her columns reached twelve million readers, and in 1953 *Time* magazine named her "America's best known food editor." She was also a frequent contributor to *Gourmet*. Clementine Paddleford's book *How America Eats* (1960) is a collection of her columns on regional food.

Just before World War II, American food journalism went upscale when authors began writing about more sophisticated culinary matters. Some prominent U.S. writers traveled to and lived in France between World War I and World War II, and this period nurtured some classic reportage and books about food. A. J. Liebling, an alumnus of the Columbia School of Journalism, wrote a series of articles for the *New Yorker*, which he later compiled into his influential work *Between Meals: An Appetite for Paris* (1962), published a year before his death.

Czech-born Joseph Wechsberg emigrated to the United States in 1938. Having taught himself English, he talked his way into a job with the *New Yorker* just before shipping out to Europe with the U.S. Army. Wechsberg often profiled great French chefs Fernand Point and Alexandre Dumaine. Wechsberg also wrote the gastronomic memoir *Blue Trout and Black Truffles: The Peregrinations of an Epicure* (1953) and *Dining at the Pavillon* (1962), the story of New York's premiere French restaurant.

Food journalism took another step forward when Earle MacAusland launched *Gourmet* in January 1941. He knew little about culinary matters, so he handpicked an editorial staff of experts. They included Pearl Metzelthin, author of *The World Wide Cook Book: Menus and Recipes of 75 Nations* (1939); and Louis de Gouy, a New York chef, restaurateur, and cookbook author who became the magazine's "Gourmet Chef." MacAusland also hired James Beard, who had just published his first cookbook, *Hors D'oeuvre and Canapés* (1940). The distinguished food writers M. F. K. Fisher, Jane Grigson, and Joseph Wechsberg, among others, were early contributors to *Gourmet*. At first, the magazine's main focus was on French food, but the articles and recipes covered cuisines from all over the world. In addition to *Gourmet*, the upscale, glossy, New York–based food magazines include *Bon Appétit, Saveur,* and *Food and Wine*, which was launched by Michael and Ariane Batterberry. The Batterberrys later became publishers of *Food Arts*, a magazine for professionals. They also wrote *On the Town in New York from 1776 to the Present* (1973), the first attempt at a culinary history of New York City.

Nonfood magazines also began publishing serious articles and columns about food. *Vogue*, for instance, hired Jeffrey Steingarten as a columnist in 1989. His books include *The Man Who Ate Everything* (1996) and *It Must've Been Something I Ate* (2002). The *New Yorker* has continued to offer frequent food articles and publishes an annual Food Issue each November. Calvin Trillin, who joined the *New Yorker* staff in 1963, traveled around the country writing the "U.S. Journal" column, which was often about food. He has published a number of food-related books, including *American Fried: Adventures of a Happy Eater* (1974); *Alice Let's Eat: Further Adventures of a Happy Eater* (1978); *Third Helpings* (1983); and *Feeding a Yen* (2003).

John McPhee began writing for the *New Yorker* in 1965. His meticulously detailed prose lends itself to long, in-depth pieces. For the article "Giving

Good Weight," about the early years of New York City's Greenmarkets, McPhee spent time working on a farm and manning a farmer's stand in the city. McPhee's books include *Oranges* (1967) and *The Founding Fish* (2002), an examination of the natural and culinary history of shad.

When *New York* magazine was launched in 1968, Gael Greene joined the staff, serving as a restaurant critic until 2000 and as a columnist until 2008. She documented the city's expanding interest in food and the rise of its restaurant culture. Her book *Bite: A New York Restaurant Strategy* (1972) is a collection of articles about the city's most notable eating places; she later recounted experiences culinary and otherwise in her memoir *Insatiable: Tales from a Life of Delicious Excess* (2006).

Raymond Sokolov, a Paris-based correspondent for *Newsweek*, became the *New York Times* restaurant critic and food editor from 1973 to 1975. For more than twenty years, Sokolov wrote the column "A Matter of Taste" for *Natural History* magazine: he crisscrossed the country trying to capture traditional American foodways before they were lost forever. Some of these columns were later collected in *Fading Feast: A Compendium of Disappearing American Regional Foods* (1981). In 2006, Sokolov became founding editor of the "Leisure and Arts" section of the *Wall Street Journal*'s weekend edition and also served as its restaurant critic.

New York Times

No source influenced what New Yorker's ate more than did the *New York Times*. For more than seventy years, it has hired professionals to write about food. Professional food journalism took off when, in 1957, the *New York Times* hired its first food columnist, the Mississippi-born food critic and writer Craig Claiborne, who had trained at L'Ecole Hôtelière in Lausanne, Switzerland. Claiborne was among the first restaurant critics to dine at restaurants incognito, and he was the first newspaper writer to review restaurants using the star system. Claiborne continued to write for the *New York Times* on and off for the next thirty-five years. He would write or coauthor seventeen food books, including *The New York Times Cookbook* and his autobiography *A Feast Made for Laughter* (1982).

Florence Fabricant began writing a food column, "In Seasons," for the *East Hampton Star* in 1972 and earned praise from Craig Claiborne. By December 1972, she was writing for the *New York Times*, where she has remained a columnist ever since. She has written or edited ten cookbooks, including her latest, *The New York Restaurant Cookbook: Recipes from the City's Best Chefs* (2009). Another New York food columnist, Marian Burros, expanded the food-writing brand at the *New York Times* to include consumer subjects like food safety and government-related food programs. She has written nine cookbooks including (with Lois Levine) *Elegant but Easy Cookbook* (1984).

As culinary journalism, and especially restaurant criticism, became a mainstay of local and national newspapers, attempts were made to put some distance between the writers and food companies, restaurants, and advertisers. Some food journalists were no longer allowed to go on press trips or to accept free meals or merchandise. Newspaper writers had been reviewing restaurants for years, but the professional standards for reviewing were set by Mimi Sheraton of the *New York Times*. She describes her techniques in her memoir, *Eating My Words: An Appetite for Life* (2004).

Some of America's top culinary writers have been attracted to the *New York Times*. William Grimes arrived at the *New York Times* in 1989 and since then has written extensively about food, including restaurant reviewing. He is the author of five books, including *Straight Up or On the Rocks: The Story of the American Cocktail* (2002) and *Appetite City: A Culinary History of New York* (2009). Molly O'Neill, who had written for the *Boston Globe* and *New York Newsday*, began a ten-year stint in 1989 as a reporter for the *New York Times* and subsequently became the weekly food columnist for the paper's Sunday magazine. In 1995, she was the first food writer nominated for a Pulitzer. She is the author of four cookbooks, the most recent being *One Big Table* (2010). Her landmark article "Food Porn," in the *Columbia Journalism Review* in 2003, took a critical look at food journalism, and she edited the comprehensive tome *American Food Writing: An Anthology with Classic Recipes* (2007). Amanda Hesser began working as a reporter for the *New York Times* in 1997; she wrote restaurant reviews and also edited the Sunday magazine. Hesser left the *Times* in 2008 but has continued writing for magazines and for her website, food52.com. For her books *The Cook and the Gardener* (1999) and *Cooking for Mr. Latte* (2009), Amanda Hesser won Literary Food Writing Awards from the International Association for Culinary Professionals. Kim Severson wrote about food for the *San Francisco Chronicle* for six years before arriving in 2004 at the *New York Times*, where she covered everything from Girl Scout cookies and Jamaican beef patties to the fate of New Orleans restaurants after Hurricane Katrina. Severson has won four James Beard Awards for journalism. She also has published a number of books, including *The Trans Fat Solution: Cooking and Shopping to Eliminate the Deadliest Fat from Your Diet* (2004), *The New Alaska Cookbook: Recipes from the Last Frontier's Best Chefs* (2009), and a memoir, *Spoon Fed: How Eight Cooks Saved My Life* (2010). Severson is now the Atlanta bureau chief for the *Times*.

In September 1997, the *Times* revamped its "Living" section into a "Dining" section that appeared on Wednesdays. It included recipes, restaurant reviews (previously published on Fridays), reports on new food products, calendars of culinary events, and articles of local interest as well as wider-ranging pieces on food issues and happenings around the United States and the world.

Other New York newspapers, such as the *New York Daily News*, the *Village Voice*, the *New York Post*, and the *Wall Street Journal*, have also covered the city's food scene, reviewing restaurants and publishing articles about food trends.

Television Food

Television stations experimented with cooking shows during the early 1940s, but none stirred up much public interest. James Beard, a trained actor and opera singer, had hosted a series of fifteen-minute programs called *I Love to Cook!* for NBC in 1946; they aired after a variety show, *Elsie Presents*, introduced by a puppet version of Borden's Elsie the Cow. None of Beard's programs have survived, but Beard was reportedly awkward and ill at ease in front of the camera. Regardless of Beard's lack of telegenic skills, television programmers liked the idea, and other shows soon followed. Dione Lucas hosted the first national thirty-minute cooking show on CBS in 1948. Her programs, *To the Queen's Taste*, followed by *Dione Lucas's Cooking Show*, focused on French food, but her stern and somewhat forbidding presentation made French cookery seem complex and difficult. It was Julia Child's *French Chef* that launched food television in 1962.

Following Child's lead, other chefs, restaurateurs, and food personalities took to the airwaves, and cooking shows appeared on both commercial and the newly emerging public television stations. Their perennial popularity culminated in the creation of the Television Food Network in 1993 in New York City. At first it focused on instructional cooking shows—colloquially referred to as "dump and stir" programs. They were relatively inexpensive to make and formulaic in their construction; many such programs had already aired on other television stations. Several new programs were developed, featuring chefs and personalities such as New Yorker's Sara Moulton, Mario Batali, and Rachael Ray—all of whom went on to host their own programs. By 2001, the Food Network was reaching seventy-five million households, with some of the most affluent TV viewers in America. By 2013, the network was being watched in ninety-six million homes—virtually every American home that had a cable or satellite TV hookup—and its website had seven million users monthly. While the network's initial audience was primarily female, increasing numbers of men began watching its programs. Today, almost half the viewers of the Food Network are male.

The Scripps Networks Interactive and the Hearst Corporation launched the *Food Network Magazine* in 2008. This monthly magazine promotes and builds on the chefs and programs on the Food Network and Cooking Channel. The magazine had 1.1 million subscribers by the end of its first year and today reaches an estimated 5.4 million readers. The Food Network was so successful that in 2010 Scripps Networks Interactive, the owner of the Food Network, launched a second cable television channel, the Cooking Channel, which focuses on instructional programs.

Food Problems and Solutions

The New York food scene is not just about feeding the wealthy. It has also been about feeding those in need. The Humane Society of New York City began giving food to families of debtors in 1787. In 1791, it began offering food assistance to the poor. It officially launched a soup kitchen in 1802. The Humane Society printed up tickets that it sold to individuals and organizations, which, in turn, gave the tickets to the poor. When Congress passed the Non-Importation Act in 1808, trade with Great Britain was embargoed, and many New Yorkers became unemployed. Thousands sought help in the Humane Society's soup kitchen. This was only a small number compared with those who needed food assistance during the War of 1812. By 1815, their soup kitchen served seventy thousand New Yorkers.

Many societies were formed in the nineteenth century to assist immigrants or the poor in New York. The French Benevolent Society offered food assistance to indigent Frenchmen. The Irish Emigration Society, formed in 1841, offered assistance to Irish immigrants. The St. Andrew's Society of New York, formed in 1826, offered food assistance to immigrants from Scotland. When New York went into a major financial crisis during the 1870s, the society opened five stands to serve the poor. In the first three weeks of operation, they served 1,500 people. It became the model for subsequent soup kitchens in the city.

On October 24, 1929, the New York Stock Market crashed, beginning the Great Depression. During the next eleven years, hundreds of thousands of New Yorkers were out of work. By 1931, eighty-four bread lines operating in New York served eighty-five thousand people daily. Soup kitchens and missions fed tens of thousands more. Shantyvilles became common throughout the city. Many out-of-work New Yorkers became beggars; others tried to sell apples on the street. When President Herbert Hoover was asked about the

Free coffee at Bowery Mission for unemployed circa 1880. Courtesy of the Library of Congress. Reproduction Number: LC-DIG-pga-03183

massive number of apple vendors in New York, he replied, "Many people have left their jobs for the more profitable one of selling apples." In 1932, he reported that "the hoboes . . . are actually better fed than they have ever been. One hobo in New York got ten meals in one day." In the same year, thirty-two New Yorkers died of starvation and 110 from malnutrition, an estimated twenty thousand school children were reported to be malnourished, and tens of thousands more suffered from nutrition-related diseases.

Bernarr Macfadden, the vegetarian health guru, established a five-million-dollar foundation to launch penny restaurants. His first opened in December 1931. It was a cafeteria-style operation that served "cracked wheat, Scotch oatmeal, lima bean soup, green pea soup, soaked prunes, seeded raisins, whole wheat bread, butter, raisin coffee and cereal coffee." Each dish cost one cent. Macfadden said he charged for the food so that unemployed workers would not feel that they were on charity. His penny restaurants served 1,500 to 3,000 customers per day. There were no chairs, just counters where customers stood while eating. At the height, they served an estimate eleven thousand New Yorkers. Others opened similar operations. The Salvation Army offered meals for a nickel. Diners were given trays filled with food, such as corned beef and cabbage, potatoes, coffee, stewed prunes, and bread. Unlike Macfadden's restaurants, this one had tables and chairs. It served men and women of all ages, regardless of "race, creed or color."

Beginning in 1853, the New York's Children Aid Society began offering lunches for some students in vocational schools. In 1908, the New York City Board of Education instituted three-cent lunches for students. The Federal School Lunch Act, passed in 1946, established federally subsidized lunches for the nation's school children.

The Food Stamp Act, passed in 1964, offered federal assistance to qualifying low- or no-income people. Funded through the U.S. Department of Agriculture, it provided qualified individuals and families with stamps they could redeem in grocery stores and supermarkets. In 2008, the program was renamed the Supplemental Nutrition Assistance Program (SNAP), and the system has shifted from stamps to Electronic Benefits Transfer (EBT) cards that operate like credit or debit cards. In 2001, eight hundred thousand New Yorkers qualified for food stamps. Ten years later, this had reached 1.6 million people, or about one-quarter of all adult New Yorkers. An estimated 750,000 residents live in what are called "food deserts," areas where there are no grocery stores or supermarkets that sell fresh fruits and vegetables. Recently, large chains, such as Whole Foods, have agreed to open outlets in food deserts that will offer better quality foods at reasonable prices. Also, it is now possible to use EBT cards at most of the city's Greenmarkets.

Today, more than 1.4 million city residents and the homeless are food insecure. Many organizations in the city have focused on helping New Yorkers who do not have enough food. The New York City Coalition against Hunger was formed in 1983 by nonprofit soup kitchens and food pantries to coordinate the activities of the emergency food providers. Today, the coalition represents more than 1,100 hunger-relief groups working in the city. Programs are available for the homeless as well as the elderly who are unable to purchase or prepare their own meals.

At the other end of the spectrum are those New Yorkers who are overweight. In 2011, it was estimated that 25 percent of New Yorkers were obese, and this is projected to hit 51 percent by 2030. Recently, the city's health department with the encouragement and support of Mayor Michael Bloomberg, has launched a number of efforts to curb obesity. In 2006, New York City required chain restaurants to post calories of the foods that they served; this went into effect three years before this became a national requirement. In January 2012, the city health department launched a program, "Cut Your Portions, Cut Your Risk," to encourage overweight New Yorkers to eat less at meals. The city health department has also attempted to reduce the consumption of sugary sodas as a means of reducing obesity.

CHAPTER THREE

~

A Culinary Stew

Immigrants and Their Food

From the beginning of European colonization, New York's population embraced myriad groups that differed culturally, linguistically, religiously, and racially. In addition to American Indians, there were British, Dutch, Swedish, German, Irish, and French settlers; enslaved peoples were shipped in chains from Africa and the Caribbean. After the colonial period, immigration from abroad rapidly increased, as did migration from other regions of America. These groups have shaped the city—and its foods and beverages—for four hundred years.

While New Amsterdam was established by the Dutch, the majority of early European settlers were Walloons from what is today Germany, northern France, and Belgium. Peter Minuit, the first director of the West India Company's operation in New Amsterdam, was a Protestant refugee from what is today North Rhine–Westphalia in Germany. Walloons also settled at the Waelenbogt, or Walloon Bay, which is today in Brooklyn. Most New Amsterdam colonists understood Dutch, but Rev. Jonas Michaëlius occasionally preached in French to reach those whose primary language was not Dutch. In addition, slaves were brought to New Amsterdam within months of the community's founding, and they continued to be imported throughout the colonial period.

The Dutch population in New Amsterdam was never very large. When the fur trade petered out, immigration languished, and other Europeans were permitted to settle in the colony. In 1643, the director general of New Amsterdam estimated the total male population of the city and its surrounding area at between four and five hundred. New Amsterdamers spoke eighteen different languages and included a number of English settlers; some freed slaves; Jewish refugees from Pernambuco, the former Dutch colony in Brazil; and some Swedes, Danes, French, and at least one Italian. By the time English military forces captured the city in 1664, only about half of those in the colony were of Dutch lineage.

As part of the agreement that surrendered New Netherland to England, Peter Stuyvesant, the Dutch director general, convinced the English to grant the Dutch colonists ownership of their estates, which were especially vast along the Hudson Valley. As the English and others immigrated to New York, the Dutch sold small parcels of their land for high prices, thus making themselves wealthy. Their financial position helped create an aristocracy that continued to influence New York for more than two hundred years.

Precisely what early Dutch colonists in New Amsterdam ate is unclear. No descriptions of meals have been uncovered. Archaeological evidence indicates that New Amsterdamers ate bread (made from wheat or rye), milk, cheese, game, apples, and some beef and pork, as well as maize, squash, and beans. Corn was converted into porridge and mush. Pumpkins were commonly consumed as fruit.

Several later descriptions of upstate Dutch fare have survived. Peter Kalm, a Swedish-Finnish scientist who visited New York in 1749, reported that the Dutch along the Hudson typically breakfasted on bread, butter, cheese, and milk, and that dinner, usually served at midday, consisted of one main dish accompanied by a "great salad" dressed with vinegar.

Manuscript cookbooks authored by New Yorkers of Dutch heritage date to the late eighteenth and early nineteenth centuries but do not likely reflect what Dutch colonists ate before 1664. However, unlike other immigrant groups who wanted to assimilate into their adopted land, the Dutch in New York maintained many of their traditions, including their language, well into the nineteenth century. This was partly due to their common membership in the Dutch Reformed Church, which kept many traditions alive.

Dutch settlers continued to arrive in New York after 1664. These immigrants likely introduced culinary traditions that were emerging or popular in Holland, and they were likely the source for some "Dutch" culinary traditions popularized by nineteenth-century writers. Waffles (from the Dutch *wafel*), for instance, were first recorded in New York City by 1744, and they were such a hit that "waffle frolics" and "waffle parties" were enjoyed in the city for decades afterward. Coleslaw (*koolsla*, a cabbage salad) was first cited in 1794; doughnuts, which may have been of Dutch, English, or German derivation, were sold in a public market by a Dutch woman by 1796; cookies (*koekjes*, "small cakes" that were, in fact, very large) were mentioned in New York by 1808; and crullers (*krullen*, "curls") were consumed by 1820 and were frequently cited throughout the nineteenth century. Pretzels had been made in Europe by the Dutch and Germans by the late seventeenth century, but the word does not appear in print in New York until the 1820s. Many other Dutch favorites—*hutspot* (a dish of potatoes and vegetables, usually served with meat), *olykoek* (a deep-fried cake), and *oliebollen* (a spherical doughnut often studded with dried fruit and typically served on New Year's Day)— were likely introduced into New York at an early time but were not recorded until decades—or centuries—later.

New Yorkers of Dutch heritage influenced the city's culinary life throughout the nineteenth century. A mid-nineteenth century writer for *Harper's* reported that the gardens and farms of "Dutch Fraus" in Brooklyn provided cabbage, potatoes, turnips, and other vegetables to Manhattan's public markets. But Dutch traditions were fading. In 1881, Gertrude Lefferts Vanderbilt complained that Dutch Americans had given up their traditions, including the foods of their forefathers.

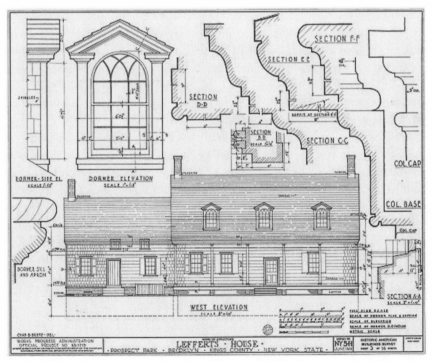

Lefferts's House, Prospect Park, Brooklyn. Courtesy of the Library of Congress. Reproduction Number: HABS NY,24-BROK,2-3

During the colonial period, each immigrant group contributed to the city's foods and beverages, but English settlers put down the deepest roots. Not only were English settlers most numerous, but also they continued to immigrate to New York in large numbers throughout the colonial period and long afterward.

English immigrants brought cookery books and recipe collections with them; English culinary styles came to dominate colonial New York's foodways and continued to do so well after the American Revolution. English cookbooks were imported into New York, and beginning in 1790, they were published in the city. Even after cookbooks authored by Americans began to be published in New York, English traditions continued to thrive, influencing what New Yorkers ate and drank. English-style pancakes, sweet and savory pies, tarts, sausages, puddings, rusks, roast beef, pastries, ketchups, dumplings, stews, soups, and condiments dominated New Yorkers' tables. These were accompanied by English-style beer, sweet wines from the Atlantic islands, and mixed drinks, such as possets and punches, that were popular in England.

English immigrants opened boarding houses, restaurants, and saloons, and established food businesses. English-born Richard Davies, who had founded the Canton Tea Company in New York, invented a popular mixture of teas that was marketed as "English Breakfast." Another English immigrant, Samuel Bath Thomas, opened a bakery called the "Muffin House" in New York in 1880. When his baked goods became popular, he formed the S. B. Thomas Company and began manufacturing "Thomas's English Muffins," a product that remains part of American breakfasts today.

Another English immigrant was William Loft, the son of a candy maker. In 1860, he opened a candy store in Manhattan, which developed into a chain that was a part of New York City life for 130 years. The company he and his son created eventually manufactured and sold more than 350 types of candies and was one of the largest candy store chains in America.

An English culinary import that became a perennial New York City favorite was the sandwich. Sandwiches first appeared in England in the 1760s. The sandwich concept migrated to New York, and recipes for them were published in the city by 1816. Virtually all early nineteenth-century American sandwich recipes were taken almost verbatim from British cookbooks. But Americans made the sandwich their own, and special sandwiches have become some of New York's defining foods—from hotdogs and hamburgers to the Reuben sandwich and pastrami on rye.

The British culinary influence may have predominated in early America, but other nationalities made contributions. Under British colonial control, immigrants from other countries were also permitted to settle in the city. More Dutch, Scandinavian, French, and German immigrants arrived. When the first census was taken in 1790, 33,470 people lived in Manhattan. Of these 2,250 were new immigrants from Germany, and 5,000 were (mostly Protestant) immigrants from Ireland.

Immigrants from abroad continued to move into the city. By 1825, Manhattan's population had reached 166,000. Immigration patterns changed in the 1830s as industrialization, revolutionary activity, crop failures, poverty, and religious persecution abroad drove waves of Europeans from their home countries. The first new wave of immigrants came from Germany.

German Immigrants

Germans had trickled into New York since the 1600s, but immigration picked up after the American Revolution. William Havemeyer, born in what is today Lower Saxony, started a sugar refinery in New York City. His descendants grew the firm into America's largest sugar-refining business, which would become known as Domino Foods. Another German immigrant, John Jacob Astor, came from a village near Heidelberg. He first went into the fur trade, where he made his first fortune. When he saw the potential profits in the tea trade with China, Astor jumped in, shipping furs to China in exchange for tea. This trade, begun in 1800, earned Astor a second fortune. He invested in Manhattan real estate, reaping huge profits when he sold the latter to a rapidly expanding city and made yet another fortune. He purchased property around his home on Broadway in downtown Manhattan, and here he built a block-square hotel called the Astor House. When it opened in 1836, it was the city's largest and most luxurious hotel, and its dining room served some of the city's finest French cuisine.

During the 1830s, the pace of German immigration increased due to a series of unsuccessful revolutions and agriculture failures in the southern and western parts of the country. Those immigrants who had already arrived in New York wrote home telling family and friends about life in America, thus creating a chain migration. By 1840, twenty-four thousand Germans lived in Manhattan; others crossed the East River and moved to Brooklyn Village and Williamsburg, where, by 1847, they comprised two-thirds of the entire population. In the 1840s, bad weather again destroyed crops in southern Germany, and a steep rise in food and beer prices led to widespread riots there that continued for months. Southern Germany, especially Bavaria, suffered yet another severe blow in 1848, when a revolution was brutally suppressed. More Germans fled to New York, and they continued to do so for decades afterward.

By 1860, the city was home to two hundred thousand Germans, and many lived east of Bowery and north of Division Street in Manhattan—an area that came to be called Kleindeutschland ("little Germany"), which was New York's first ethnic ghetto. As the immigrants became more affluent, they moved northward to the city's more fashionable neighborhoods, such as Yorkville on Manhattan's Upper East Side, Ridgewood in Queens, and Bushwick and Williamsburg in Brooklyn. By 1880, the number of Germans in New York had doubled again, forming almost one-third of the city's entire population. New York had more German-speaking people than any other city in the world except Berlin and Vienna.

Newcomers went into food-related businesses of one kind or another. Some opened hotels, boardinghouses, inns, and saloons. In 1854, a German immigrant set up a coffee and chocolate factory that also produced "German-style mustard." By 1855, two-thirds of the city's butchers were German, and German bakers outnumbered the Irish or Scots bakers who had previously dominated the profession. German immigrants ran the majority of the city's grocery stores from 1855 on; 75 percent of the grocers were from the Lower Rhine, particularly Hanover. By 1867, Germans had a near monopoly on the market-garden business supplying New York City.

Beer was the German national beverage, but the heavy, dark, British-style brews made in New York did not appeal to the immigrants. Brewing was an obvious career choice for the new arrivals, many of whom had followed this trade back home. German-owned breweries sprang up around the city to make the lighter lagers favored in the old country. Saloons owned or operated by Germans served the lager, and there German immigrants (only the men, of course) could socialize with their compatriots, eat a meal, and seek help finding work and housing.

Single German women had few employment opportunities; many became domestics or worked in boardinghouses. Domestic employees at least had the security of a roof over their heads and food to eat; they earned only about four to six dollars per month. The alternative was the factories, where working conditions could be horrendous. Domestics could also easily move from one place of employment to another as the job market was rapidly expanding. By 1855, about 15 percent of all domestics in New York City were German immigrants. Since these women cooked some, if not all, of the family's meals, their culinary traditions had some influence on their employers' way of eating.

German immigrants also found work in New York's rapidly growing restaurant scene. Some were cooks or chefs, while others worked as waiters in the city's best restaurants. Others opened small restaurants of their own, which were known for serving generous portions of food at low prices. In 1867, these were described as

> queer, dingy, rattle-trap dining-houses in which families of the Teuton race— men, women, and children—appear to spend a great deal of their time. The bar was piled with joints and manufactured meat adapted to the strong German stomach; enormous fat hams, not thoroughly boiled, for the German prefers his pig underdone; rounds of cold corned beef, jostled by cold roast legs and loins of veal; pyramids of sausages of every known size and shape, and several cognate articles of manufactured swine-meat. . . . [There were also] baskets full of those queer, twisted, briny cakes which go variously, I believe, by the names of *Pretzel* and *Wunder*; sardine-boxes piled upon each other . . . huge glass jars of pickled oysters, flanked by huge earthen jars of caviare. Raw onions in heaps give a tone to the combined odors of all these; and through this confusion of smells come powerful whiffs of the Limburger and Sweitzer cheeses, without which the *menu* of no German restaurant would be considered complete. . . . Conspicuously posted upon the walls are the *Weinlisten*, from which documents you gather that white wine is to be had at from one dollar and a quarter to three dollars per bottle, and red wine at from one dollar to four. The inevitable keg of *lager-bier* lies upon its slanting trestles, behind one end of the counter.

Auguste Ermisch, an immigrant from Mecklenburg-Schwerin, opened a restaurant at Nassau and John Streets in Manhattan. In 1873, his menu featured German bread, beef with macaroni, Vienna sausage with mashed potatoes and sauerkraut, wienerschnitzel, calf's tongue, lentil soup with bologna sausage, fish balls and red cabbage, dumplings, and even pumpkin pie. One of the more interesting items on the menu was "Hamburger steak," described in an article in the *New York Times* as "a beefsteak redeemed from its original toughness by being mashed into mincemeat and then formed into a conglomerated mass. This is very appetizing, but conscience compels us to state that it is inferior to the genuine article, which can also be had here in a very satisfactory condition of tenderness." Hamburg, or hamburger steak, was an inexpensive dish made by grinding scraps of beef left after butchering choicer cuts, such as Porterhouse steak or sirloin. This dish would become commonplace throughout the country within ten years; by the 1890s, hamburgers were sold by street vendors, who served them in buns for a convenient stand-up meal, thus creating the hamburger sandwich.

In Williamsburg, German immigrants Carl and Peter Luger opened a café, bowling alley, and billiards hall in 1887. After Carl died, the bowling alley and billiards hall were jettisoned and the establishment was renamed Peter Luger Steak House. In Manhattan, August Guido Lüchow, an émigré from

Hannover, went to work in a beer hall on Fourteenth Street in 1877 and, by 1879, had saved up enough money to buy the place. William Steinway, manufacturer of pianos, was a fan and frequent patron of the establishment, which became a favorite among New York's musical elite. As Lüchow's became popular it grew from a beer garden into one of New York's most fashionable restaurants.

German immigrants and their progeny, such as Charles Gulden, William Entenmann, and Richard Hellmann, opened food-related businesses. Charles Gulden, the son of a German immigrant, worked at his uncle's company, Union Mustard Mills and then in 1867 launched his own mustard company on Elizabeth Street in New York. By 1883, Gulden's product line included many different mustard varieties and other products. His spicy brown mustard has survived, although the company is now owned by ConAgra. William Entenmann, an immigrant from Stuttgart, Germany, opened a small bakery selling small cakes, breads, and rolls on Rogers Avenue in Brooklyn in 1898. His business thrived, and he expanded his product line. During the 1920s, the company moved to Bay Shore, Long Island. During the 1950s, it expanded sales throughout the Northeast and later throughout America; today, its brands are among the largest-selling pastries and donuts in America. Richard Hellmann, who arrived in New York City in October 1903, opened a deli on Manhattan's Upper East Side in 1905. On September 1, 1912, he began selling his store-made "Blue Ribbon Mayonnaise." Within fifteen years, his company was the largest mayonnaise manufacturer in the world. In 1927, Richard Hellmann sold his company; Hellmann's mayonnaise eventually became the most profitable brand in the product line of Best Foods, Inc., which today is owned by Unilever USA, headquartered in New Jersey.

The two world wars hurt German restaurants and many German Americans left the city. Most German restaurants closed. Lüchow's, one of New York's last prominent German restaurants, survived for decades before finally closing in 1986. The steakhouse that Carl and Peter Luger launched in Williamsburg, however, has survived, and other restaurants serving German-style food have opened around the city.

Irish Immigrants

Germans were only the first of several waves of immigrants to hit New York. The second was the Irish. Irish immigrants had been coming to the city since colonial times. Many came as indentured servants and some as convicts; still others were merchants, artisans, and shopkeepers who paid their own way. Most early Irish immigrants were Protestants.

Early Irish immigrants went into food-related businesses in New York. One successful Irish entrepreneur was John Hill, who opened the New Beef Steak and Oyster House in 1774. Another was William Niblo, who arrived after the American Revolution. He apprenticed at a coffeehouse and married the owner's daughter. In 1814, he opened the Bank Coffee House. In 1823, he purchased the grounds of a small circus, called "The Stadium," at the corner of Broadway and Prince Street. There he opened Niblo's Garden, the city's most fashionable resort, complete with a restaurant. In 1834, Niblo put up a theater, where plays and other entertainments were performed throughout the mid-nineteenth century.

Beginning in the early 1830s, Irish Catholics began to immigrate to New York. Most were poor, from rural areas; unskilled and uneducated, they were not prepared for the demands of the urban workplace. They were also Catholic in a mainly Protestant city, and they would face prejudice, poverty, and hunger for decades to come.

Some Irish immigrants opened eating establishments. Daniel Sweeney arrived in New York during the 1820s. He made money as a water vendor while learning the restaurant trade. In 1836, he opened a restaurant to serve middle-class workers in downtown Manhattan, offering oysters, roast beef, mutton, beans, pies, and desserts. It was an immediate success, and Sweeney later opened a hotel, which became a center for Irish immigrants during the following decades. Patrick Dolan, an Irishman who arrived in New York in 1846 and worked at Sweeney's restaurant, opened his own very successful restaurant in downtown Manhattan. Other Irish immigrants became importers. One of New York's largest importers of beer and wine was Thomas Mc-Mullen, who in 1852, published *Hand-Book of Wines, Practical, Theoretical, and Historical; with a Description of Foreign Spirits and Liquors*, one of the first books published in the United States on wine and how to make it.

When the Potato Famine hit Ireland in 1846, Irish immigration swelled to flood stage. In 1847, an estimated eighty-five thousand Irish men, women, and children departed for North America, many bound for New York. Decades after the Potato Famine subsided, the Irish continued to immigrate. By 1860, there were more than two hundred thousand of them in New York, forming about one-fourth of the city's total population. By 1890, more than four hundred thousand people of Irish heritage lived in Manhattan (and thousands more in Brooklyn and Queens). There were more Irish in New York than Dublin.

Many single women went into domestic service. In 1846, two-thirds of the domestic servants in New York City were Irish. Within a decade, 80 percent of the thirty-five thousand foreign-born domestics and waiters in Manhattan were Irish. Coming as they did from a famine-stricken land, these women were not necessarily able cooks, and they were unfamiliar with American food. Some, according to their employers, were unable to cook even potatoes properly by American standards: they "only half boil their potatoes, leaving the centre so hard, that it is called the bone of the potato." And they persisted "in bringing half-boiled potatoes to the table, notwithstanding our repeated orders to the contrary." But Irish kitchen help gradually became familiar with American food and its preparation, and they brought these skills and habits home to their families when they married.

Other Irish women became fruit and vegetable peddlers. They bought oranges, apples, and other groceries from middlemen and sold them on the streets. Those who were successful rented stalls in one of the city's markets. A few immigrants opened small hotels, and those who could afford to buy houses frequently turned them into boardinghouses.

Still others went into the grocery business, making their greatest profits in liquor sales. In a short period, Irish dominated New York grocery stores. Some gained economic prominence. Perhaps the most successful Irish immigrant grocer was Thomas Butler, who arrived in America in 1871. After working in hotels, he and a partner started a grocery store in 1882. They painted the shop front green and emblazoned their names on it in gold lettering. They sold their goods at low prices, and the public thronged to the store. Butler bought out his partner the following year and began to open more stores. By 1914, there were 235 Butler Grocery Stores. The chain continued to grow, reaching 1,100 stores in the New York area by the time Thomas Butler died, in 1934. Despite its Irish American ownership, and the fact that many of its customers were of Irish heritage, the chain did not sell any particularly "Irish" food products.

In Ireland, the diet of the rural poor was largely based on potatoes, oatmeal, buttermilk, some vegetables, and very little—if any—meat, which was simply beyond their means. The same was true of whiskey. In New York, food prices and alcoholic beverages declined throughout the nineteenth century. Irish immigrants, poor as they were, ate and drank well compared to how they had fared in Ireland. An observer noted in 1864 that Irish immigrants in New York bought cheap whiskey and cheap provisions, especially meat that "they have been accustomed to consider the luxury of the rich, and they go in for it accordingly. They eat meat three times a day, rudely cooked, and in large quantities. Whisky of an execrable quality, is plentiful and cheap."

McSorley's Old Ale House, which claims to be New York's oldest saloon, 2013. Courtesy of Kelly Fitzsimmons

Some Irish newcomers became waiters at New York City restaurants, while others opened working-class restaurants, especially oyster cellars. Many immigrants opened or worked in saloons. In 1851, Seamus O'Daoir, owner of a "porter house" on New York's Duane Street, wrote a poem for the *Irish American* promoting his drinking establishment and extolling the connection between the Irish and alcohol. Another enterprising immigrant, John McSorley, opened an alehouse for workingmen on East Seventh Street in 1854. McSorley's Old Ale House, New York's oldest continuously operating saloon, still serves ale, porter, and their famous liverwurst-and-onion sandwiches. Other Irish saloons served potatoes to go along with the alcohol.

Bars and saloons served as places of employment for Irish immigrants. Bartenders helped men find jobs and get a meal when necessary. Irish saloons were also places where men socialized and talked politics. In *Hungering for America* (2001), Hasia Diner observed that

> alcohol linked the Irish in America to the emotionally satisfying world of past memory and ushered them into a comfortable world of friendship with others like themselves. Above all, it heightened their Irish identity. In saloons, under the influence of alcohol, they declared their unswerving loyalty to Ireland, the place they had left but claimed still to serve, while they articulated a deep American patriotism.

Irish saloons became the core of Irish American political control over Tammany Hall, which dominated New York City politics until the Depression.

Irish immigrant Patrick J. Clarke became a bartender at a dingy saloon on Fifty-fifth Street and Third Avenue in 1902. Ten years later, he had saved enough money to buy the place. It was just another little neighborhood bar until 1945, when it was selected as the location for the Billy Wilder film *The Lost Weekend*, based on a book by Charles R. Jackson, who had done much of his writing in the bar. Celebrities discovered P. J. Clarke's, and it morphed into a restaurant, serving hamburgers, pies, and other dishes. Clarke died in 1948, but P. J. Clarke's survived and expanded to other locations in New York and in other cities.

Irish immigrants formed regiments in the New York militia, such as the Sixty-ninth, also called the "Irish Brigade." When the Civil War broke out in 1861, it was among the first units to respond to President Lincoln's call for volunteers to put down the rebellion. The "Fighting Sixty-ninth" served with great distinction during the war, and afterward it traditionally marched at the head of the city's St. Patrick's Day Parade, widely celebrated in New York since the nineteenth century. The day featured serious drinking and lavish meals featuring corned beef and cabbage, Irish stew, Irish soda bread, and colcannon (mashed potatoes with kale or cabbage).

Jewish Immigrants

The third wave of immigrants were Jews, initially from Germany and later from Eastern Europe. In 1654, when the Portuguese expelled the Dutch from Pernambuco, which is today in Brazil, some Dutch refugees, of whom twenty-seven were Jews, arrived in New Amsterdam. Eventually, after considerable debate among city leaders, Jews won the right to own property. Few Jews immigrated subsequently, but this changed suddenly with the advent of the first big wave of German immigration: an estimated eighty thousand of the Germans who began arriving in the 1830s were Jewish. Many settled permanently in New York—they were urbanites who had little difficulty adjusting to city life. Many ended up as butchers and bakers. For Passover in 1859, nine Jewish bakeries in New York used 2,200 barrels of flour making matzah, most of which was shipped to other communities.

During the 1880s, a new group of Jewish immigrants poured into New York City, fleeing political oppression, pogroms in Russia, crushing poverty in Eastern Europe, and the turmoil caused by the breakup of the Ottoman Empire. Unlike the earlier Jewish immigrants, the newcomers were largely poor, from rural villages; thus, many were unprepared for city life. They moved into tenement buildings in Manhattan's Lower East Side, which had previously been home to German immigrants. Many of these Eastern European were Orthodox Jews, and they strictly followed the laws of kashruth (Kosher dietary laws). Meats and some other foods had to be prepared according to these rules. To meet these needs, immigrants opened butcher shops, bakeries, restaurants, cafés, and cafeterias.

The meals prepared in these establishments (or at home) were simple fare. In addition to basic soups, stews, grain dishes, and the like, they included gefilte fish, pumpernickel and rye breads, challah, kreplach, latkes (potato pancakes), and blintzes (cheese-filled pancakes). Some Jews moved into commercial production of foods, such as bagels, which were sold by vendors on the streets of New York by the early twentieth century.

Many Jewish-owned businesses advertised that they were kosher, selling only kosher foods, wines, and liquors. But were they truly kosher? This issue perplexed New York Jews for decades. In 1887, the Orthodox synagogues in New York and other cities imported a rabbi from Vilna, Russia (now Lithuania), in part to regulate the kosher meat business. His efforts—and those of others—failed. In 1923, the Union of Orthodox Jewish Congregations launched a supervision and certification program for processed foods. It wasn't until New York State passed and enforced a Kosher Law in 1934 that this matter was, for the most part, resolved.

During the late nineteenth and early twentieth centuries, the vast majority of the city's pushcart vendors and door-to-door salesmen were Jewish; many moved up the retail ladder to open their own shops. By 1899, these included "140 groceries, 131 kosher butchers, 36 bakeries, 9 bread stands, 14 butter and egg stores, 24 candy stores, 7 coffee shops, 10 delicatessens, 9 fish stores, 7 fruit stands, 2 meat markets, 10 sausage stores, 13 wine shops, 13 grape wine shops, and 10 confectioners." Jewish grocers thrived throughout the early twentieth century. By 1938, there were almost ten thousand grocery stores that catered largely to the Jewish population in New York. In addition, about five hundred "appetizing stores," such as Russ & Daughters and Zabar's, specialized in prepared foods: pickled, smoked, and salted fish, such as lox, herring, and white fish, as well as dried fruit, nuts, pickles, breads, candy, and imported delicacies.

By comparison to other immigrant groups, most immigrant Jews drank little alcohol. In Jewish neighborhoods, saloons languished. As an alternative, two companies began manufacturing soda, which was well received in part due to its purported healthfulness. When the Sugar Trust's activities increased the price of sugar, Jewish soda manufacturers shifted to make seltzer (plain soda water), referred to as "Jewish champagne" and labeled the "staple

Diversity of sausages and other products for sale in a New York deli, 2013. Courtesy of Kelly Fitzsimmons

beverage of Yiddish New York." By 1907, there were more than one hundred Jewish seltzer manufacturers in New York. A Jewish candy store owner in Brooklyn, Louis Auster, has been credited with inventing one of the city's most iconic beverages, the egg cream. Despite its name, this classic fountain drink contains only soda water, milk, and chocolate syrup.

Jewish immigrants found employment in New York City, and many thrived economically. Those who had often gone hungry in their homelands could now enjoy foods that had been the province of the upper classes there. As Hasia Diner notes, "The formerly poor started to eat *blintzes*, *kreplach*, *kasha-varnitchkes*, *strudel*, noodles, *knishes* and more importantly, meat every day."

Jewish restaurants opened throughout the city. Ratner's, in Manhattan, was founded by Jacob Harmatz and Alex Ratner in 1905. It was a kosher dairy restaurant, where no meat was served. At the height of its fame, Ratner's would serve ten thousand meals per week. Other early and notable kosher restaurants included Steinberg's on the Upper West Side of Manhattan and Garfield's in Brooklyn. Neighborhood cafés and coffeehouses flourished on the Lower East Side, some of them catering to intellectuals—writers, poets, and artists. The Garden Cafeteria, a dairy restaurant on bustling East Broadway, was the most famous of these.

Like their non-Jewish German counterparts, Jewish immigrants also opened delicatessens, which eventually became sit-down restaurants. Following the laws of kashruth, these offered only meat, fish, and pareve (neutral) foods; a typical selection featured chicken soup, corned beef, gefilte fish, lox, knishes, pastrami, chopped liver, tongue, and garlic pickles. Some delis made their own beef sausages—salami, bologna, and frankfurters—but most found it cheaper and easier to buy from Isaac Gellis, a Jewish immigrant from Berlin, who opened a kosher sausage company on Essex Street shortly after the Civil War. Other companies, such as the Williamsburg Genuine Kosher Meat Products Company in Brooklyn and the Hebrew National Kosher Sausage Factory on the Lower East Side, later provisioned Jewish delis. Jewish delis also popularized old-country breads, notably rye and pumpernickel.

Gradually, as secular Jews and non-Jewish diners became steady customers, Jewish delicatessens expanded their menus to include cream cheese and farmer cheese to spread on bagels and bialys, herring in cream sauce, blintzes, and cheesecake. Of course, these establishments lost their kashruth-observing patrons in the process.

Some Jewish delis became iconic New York establishments. Joel Russ, a Jewish immigrant from what is today Poland, began his career in 1907 selling Polish mushrooms, which he carried on his shoulders. He saved up enough money to buy a pushcart and then a horse and wagon. In 1914,

Russ & Daughters appetizing store, Manhattan, 2013. Courtesy of Kelly Fitzsimmons

he opened his first store on Orchard Street on the Lower East Side and expanded his offerings to include salmon and herring. His business would eventually become Russ & Daughters, which is still one of New York's premier appetizing stores.

Louis Zabar, a Jewish refugee from Ukraine, started selling smoked fish in Brooklyn in 1934; he later moved the business to the Upper West Side of Manhattan. Still family owned and run, Zabar's now offers a full range of gourmet foods and kitchenware at its single vast store on Broadway at Eightieth Street, and smoked fish is still a huge part of the business.

During the Depression, deli owners had a difficult time selling their relatively expensive meats and imported products. Mogen Dovid Delicatessen Corporation, a trade association, encouraged Jewish deli owners to appeal to a wider audience and to keep their prices moderate; they published a periodical for deli owners that included a list of suggested prices for standard deli items. Many Jewish delis sell kosher meats but do not otherwise adhere to the laws of kashruth, including closing the store for the Sabbath. Some notable Manhattan delis past and present are the Carnegie, the Second Avenue Deli, the Stage, and Katz's.

Food played an important part in the Jewish communities in New York. As Hasia Diner wrote, "Food drew Jewish men and women to the streets. In the immigrant and first American-born generations, Jews lived in relatively

Katz's Deli, on Houston Street, Manhattan, 2013. Courtesy of Kelly Fitzsimmons

compact Jewish neighborhoods. The provision of food to Jews by Jews enhanced the sense of community."

By 1910, more than 1.2 million Jews lived in New York, and this number continued to increase; by the 1920s, the Jewish population of the city was nearly two million. This immigration stopped in 1924 but picked up again in the 1970s, when the city became the destination of choice for thousands of Soviet Jews fleeing relentless oppression. Many moved to Brighton Beach, Brooklyn, now dubbed "Little Odessa." Today, New York is home to about one hundred thousand Russian Jews, more than any other place in the world. Russian restaurants, cafés, clubs, and bars have proliferated in the area, and neighborhood shops supply imported specialty items from Russia. One immigrant from Odessa, Tatiana Varzar, opened a small restaurant on the boardwalk in Brighton Beach that grew into Tatiana Restaurant, one of the most popular eating establishments and nightclubs in the neighborhood.

Italian Immigrants

Although Italians lived in New York since colonial times, they were few in number. Some Italian immigrants became prominent in the early nineteenth century. Ferdinand Palmo, who arrived in New York in 1808, opened Palmo's Garden on Broadway near Duane Street. Its restaurant, the Café de Mille Colonnes, was filled with gilded columns and huge mirrors. Palmo hired Italian musicians for the band at the restaurant, which quickly became one of the city's hot spots. In 1844, he opened an opera house that specialized in Italian opera.

According to the 1850 census, fewer than four thousand people of Italian heritage lived in the United States. In the 1850s, Italian immigration picked up momentum. By the 1860s, Italian foods such as spaghetti, macaroni, and vermicelli were manufactured in the city, and merchants imported Chianti and other Italian wines.

Italian immigration surged after the Civil War. Most of the newcomers were from poverty-stricken areas of southern Italy, and they came to New York seeking economic opportunities. They became street vendors and gardeners. Italian commission merchants established themselves in the peanut business, hiring their fellow Italian immigrants as pushcart peddlers to sell the nuts. By 1870, there were several hundred Italian peanut vendors on the streets of New York. Some moved up the retail chain by buying carts and hiring others to operate them, or by setting up stationary stands. Some also returned to Italy and recruited others to come to America, guaranteeing them jobs as peanut vendors. Some Italians hired in this way returned home after they had made enough money; most, however, encouraged their families to immigrate to America, thus creating another chain migration.

Immigrants mainly lived in tenements south of Greenwich Village in what would become Little Italy. Where they could, they kept chickens, goats, and on occasion pigs in their tenement basements; for those lucky enough to live in a house, backyard gardens were the norm. Others lived or worked on small farms around the city where they grew fruits, vegetables, and herbs commonly used in Italian cooking: these included certain types of lettuce, Savoy cabbage, tomatoes, eggplant, onions, asparagus, beans, potatoes, broccoli, celery, peas, thyme, parsley, mint, basil, garlic, and oregano. These were marketed only to Italian immigrants at first, but eventually these items caught on with New Yorkers of other ethnic groups.

Some Italian food products were unavailable in New York, so Italian-owned businesses imported olive oil, Parmesan and other cheeses, sausages, anchovies, pastas, and coffees. These were supplied to Italian American grocers, who introduced them to other New Yorkers. By the 1930s, Italians ran 10,000 grocery stores, 875 butcher shops, and 1,150 restaurants in the city. Many of the city's other restaurants hired Italian chefs, waiters, and kitchen help. Italian cookbooks were published in New York beginning in 1911. Italian foods were popularized through festivals, such as the Feast of San Gennaro, which has been celebrated since 1926 along Mulberry Street in Little Italy. New dishes based on Italian heritage emerged; for example, spaghetti and meatballs, a combination not traditionally served in Italy, became an American mainstay.

Italian immigrants opened fish markets and introduced New Yorkers to types of seafood they hadn't appreciated before. Few New Yorkers, for instance, ate tuna—it was considered too oily, its flesh too dark. In the autumn of 1897, the *New York Times* published an astounding saga of an Italian fishmonger who had bought a nine-hundred-pound tuna for nine dollars at Fulton Market. "About his store that night a changing group made up of old women, old men, young girls, and small boys with bulging eyes worshiped at the shrine. The old people spoke of fish in their day in far-off Italy, and revealed the secret of the wonderful sauce. To this last the young girls paid careful attention." Within two decades, New Yorkers began to eat canned tuna, which by the 1940s, became the nation's most consumed fish.

Italians also opened ice-cream parlors, quick-lunch establishments, and restaurants. Many were highly rated, such as Morelli's in Little Italy. Others were identified as "spaghetti joints"—usually very small establishments in cellars. One was described in 1891 as "lit by a smoky kerosene lamp. A little bar is in one corner, and narrow, wooden benches, black with use, run around the walls and are fastened to them. Here five cents will buy a plate of maccaroni [sic], a bit of toast, and a cup of coffee."

By the 1930s, Manhattan had about six hundred Italian restaurants, while Brooklyn had three hundred and the Bronx another two hundred and fifty. Most remained small "hole-in-the-wall" joints with sawdust on the floor and few refinements of décor or service. They served big bowls of macaroni and spaghetti, and pizza with tomato sauce and cheese. At the other end of the Italian restaurant spectrum were restaurants such as Monetta's on Mulberry Street, Barbetta's on West Forty-sixth Street, and Sardi's near Times Square. Sardi's served both Italian and French cuisine, and was (and remains) a popular theater crowd hangout in the Theater District. Whether large or small, these restaurants popularized common Italian foods.

Italian immigrants also started factories that produced Italian foods. Macaroni had been known in America since the late eighteenth century, but it was considered an exotic luxury. The Atlantic Macaroni Company began operating in 1897 and La Rosa Macaroni Company in 1914. Emanuelle Ronzoni formed the Ronzoni Macaroni Company in 1915. It specialized in farina macaroni, farina spaghetti, and *pasta all'uovo* (egg noodles). Along with La Rosa, Ronzoni became one of the largest pasta makers in America. Yet another business was launched by Joseph Kresevich and his wife Angela, immigrants from Trieste, Italy, who started the Stella D'Oro Biscuit Company in 1932.

In time, Italian foods and dishes reached all levels of New York society. By the late ninetieth century, spaghetti had become a mainstream dish. Pizza was sold in Little Italy by 1902. Lombardi's Pizzeria, which opened in 1905, still stands on the corner of Spring and Mott Streets. Pizza was eaten mainly by Italian Americans until after World War II, when returning GIs who had served in Italy sought out dishes they had enjoyed overseas. Pizza was on its way to becoming one of New York's (and America's) favorite foods. Still, as late as 1956, the *New York Times* had to define pizza as "a circular mixture of dough, cheese, sauce and Italian lore." New York–style pizza—a thin crust with a thin layer of sauce—remains the city's favorite pizza.

Italians had a greater influence on New York culinary scene than did many other immigrant groups. As historian Richard Hooker said, their cookery "was strange enough to interest Americans but not so different as to be unacceptable or difficult." Italian food has continued to thrive in New York, especially as chefs and restaurateurs such as Lidia Bastianich and Mario Batali have created Italian food empires. In 2010, Lidia Bastianich, her son Joe Bastianich, and Mario Batali opened Eataly, a fifty-thousand-square-foot emporium devoted to Italian food and drink. New Yorkers have accepted

Italian food with open arms, whether it be homemade lasagna layered with locally made mozzarella and ricotta; "a slice" from a neighborhood pizza joint, folded in two and dripping with oil; or an elegant repast fragrant with truffles and complemented with fine Tuscan wines.

Chinese Immigrants

Chinese immigrants arrived in New York City beginning in 1855, when a census included thirty-eight Chinese men. When construction began on the transcontinental railroad in 1863, an estimated ten thousand Chinese laborers helped build the western portion, and Chinese cooks came along to prepare their meals. With the railroad's completion in 1869, the Chinese population—and the delights of their culinary repertoire—spread eastward across America. By 1873, more than five hundred Chinese lived in New York City, in the area that would become Chinatown. Even after Congress passed the Chinese Exclusion Acts in 1882, Chinese continued to migrate to New York from the West Coast, and illegal immigration continued through Canada. New York's Chinese population steadily increased.

Racial discrimination prevented Chinese immigrants from employment in many professions; restaurants were an exception. Chinese restaurants opened in Chinatown, and initially they mainly served the immigrant population. Like many ethnic restaurants, they served more than cheap comfort food; they also helped immigrants to assimilate, became gathering places for new arrivals, and occasionally functioned as aid societies, lending money when necessary and helping people find work.

Few New Yorkers ventured into Chinese restaurants except out of curiosity. One brave soul reported in 1891 that a Chinese restaurant on Mott Street served rice, stewed pork, pig's feet, duck, chicken, boiled cabbage, onions, bamboo shoots, celery, beans, soy sauce, and tea. Special party menus included pigeon, sea worms, bird's nest soup, muscles, and rice wine. The observer of this restaurant may well have seen chop suey, which was described by the *Brooklyn Eagle* as a combination of "pork, bacon, chickens, mushroom, bamboo shoots, onion, pepper." Others reported that chop suey contained mushrooms, parsley, cornstarch, water chestnuts, bean sprouts, seaweed, and many other ingredients. There was no agreed-upon definition, and each establishment made it with whatever ingredients were available. The only thing clear about chop suey was that it originated in America, although it was based on Chinese culinary traditions.

By the late 1880s, chop suey joints were popular in New York. A writer in *Leslie's Illustrated* warned in 1896 that "an American who once falls under

Port Author Restaurant, Chinatown, during Chinese New Year's celebration circa 1890s. Courtesy of the Library of Congress. Reproduction Number: LC-DIG-ggbain-00025

the spell of chop suey may forget all about things Chinese for a while, and suddenly a strange craving that almost defies will power arises" and "he finds that his feet are carrying him to Mott street." A 1915 description of these chop suey establishments noted that non-Chinese diners found the food "really toothsome and gratifying." But the author, who had traveled extensively in China, also pointed out that the food had little in common with the food actually served in China. Chinese Americans rarely ate anything like it, either. One wrote in 1902 that "there is a great deal of pork in it, and it is too greasy. It is made more to suit American tastes." Other Chinese Americans regarded chop suey as "a culinary joke at the expense of the foreigner."

By 1900, New York's Chinatown had more than one hundred restaurants. Their basic menu was fairly set: chop suey, chow mein, egg foo young, and a noodle soup called yat gaw mein, or "yakaman." Egg rolls probably didn't appear until the 1920s and fortune cookies, an American invention, not until the 1940s. These dishes, although based on home-style village food, had been relentlessly adapted to American tastes. By the 1930s, Chinese restaurants, such as the Bamboo Forest on MacDougal Street and the Chinese Delmonico's on Pell Street became popular.

The Chinese immigrants themselves, whether at home or in restaurants, clung steadfastly to the traditional fare from whatever region or country they had come from. They imported products from China and created their own market gardens, which supplied home kitchens and Chinese restaurants. They ate mainly rice, vegetables, fish (frequently salted), shrimp, other seafood, fowl, special herbs, and pork. They drank tea, eschewed dairy products, and rarely consumed sugar. They stir-fried, braised, or steamed their food in woks, and they ate with chopsticks.

Chinese restaurateurs intentionally moved out of Chinatown, where competition was severe and few non-Chinese were willing to eat. By 1910, more than half of the Chinese-owned restaurants in New York were located outside Chinatown. After World War I, Chinese restaurants expanded in size and number as their foods became more acceptable to their non-Asian neighbors. The Chinese immigrant population of New York increased again after World War II. In 1958, the city had more than three hundred Chinese restaurants, of which thirty were in the Times Square area alone. By 1960, only fifty of the nearly six hundred Chinese restaurants in New York were located in Chinatown.

By 1988, the 781 Chinese restaurants in New York City employed more than fifteen thousand workers. New immigrants brought other culinary traditions with them. Unlike earlier arrivals, who were mainly Cantonese, the new immigrants came from Sichuan, Hunan, and other regions. Some had lived in other countries before arriving in New York. Restaurants specializing in Chinese regional cuisines from Peking, Sichuan, and Hunan opened around the city. By the twenty-first century, the city had an estimated half a million residents of Chinese heritage. The Chinese restaurant business continued to grow and prosper, in part because of a demand for inexpensive Chinese food and the continued inflow of Chinese immigrants willing to work for low wages. At the other end of the economic spectrum are trendy upper-class Chinese restaurants offering traditional and innovative Chinese fare. New Yorkers seem to have unlimited appetites for the foods of China.

Greek Immigrants

When Greek immigrants arrived in America in the late nineteenth century, they wanted the foods that they remembered from back home. Many immigrants went into the food service business. Beginning in the 1890s, Greek immigrants in New York established stores that imported and sold Greek wines, cheese, olive oil, black olives, dried fish, figs, and many other foods. These operations subsequently expanded to Chicago, Boston, and other large northern cities. Other Greek immigrants opened candy stores, fruit stands, ice-cream parlors, bakeries, and coffeehouses.

Many Greek immigrants became street food vendors, selling whatever potential customers would buy. When zoning and licensing laws made it more difficult to operate pushcarts, Greek vendors bought coffee shops and small restaurants. By 1913, at least two hundred of these "third-class" restaurants served customers on Seventh Avenue alone. A few upscale Greek restaurants opened on Sixth Avenue. There, according to one observer, "soup, roast lamb, potatoes, salad, Greek pudding and bread may be secured for thirty-five or forty cents." Greek immigrants soon dominated the city's corner diners. Usually their food was very similar to that of other neighborhood restaurants; one distinctive characteristic of the Greek diners was their use of paper cups that featured the Parthenon. Greece is a coffee-loving country, and many Greek immigrants opened coffeehouses. After World War II, especially during the 1960s and 1970s, more Greeks immigrated to New York, particularly to Astoria in Queens, Bay Ridge in Brooklyn, and Washington Heights in Manhattan. The city became home to more than two hundred thousand people of Greek heritage. Greek businessmen purchased coffee shops and hired the new immigrants to operate them. Others launched restaurants, many of which served Greek foods, while others opened pizza parlors.

Tom's Greek diner in Brooklyn, 2013. Courtesy of Kelly Fitzsimmons

Slaves from Africa and Migrants from the South

Enslaved Africans had been brought to New York since colonial days. By 1700, slaves and freed slaves comprised an estimated 14 to 21 percent of the city's entire population. Most slaves lived with families, and many ended up as cooks. Freed slaves established small communities that were later incorporated into New York. When the British army left New York at the end of the American Revolution, three thousand freed slaves left with them. When the first census was taken in 1790, out of a total population of 33,470 people living in Manhattan, 2,369 were slaves.

Slavery was outlawed in the state in 1837, and many African Americans ended up as street vendors. Others worked as cooks and waiters in the city's restaurants. When the Civil War ended in 1865, African Americans from the South began to migrate into the city; some took jobs as cooks and servants in private homes, schools, and hotels. Many worked as cooks in the city's booming restaurants, and their cooking abilities were highly praised by observers.

A wave of African Americans into the city increased after 1903 and reached its peak in the 1920s, when tens of thousands of African Americans moved in, seeking jobs in factories. Many ended up in Harlem, which at the time was occupied by Irish and Jewish immigrants and squatters. During the 1920s and 1930s, West Harlem became the center of the "Harlem Renaissance." Nightclubs such as the Cotton Club featured the greatest African American entertainers and supplied their patrons with beer and other alcoholic beverages even during Prohibition. The Cotton Club menu included Chinese dishes, such as "Chinese soup," moo goo gai pan, and egg foo young; other items included baked oysters Cotton Club, filet mignon, broiled live lobster, steak sandwiches, crabmeat cocktails, and scrambled eggs and sausage. Although the Cotton Club was segregated—only whites were admitted as customers—other Harlem clubs were integrated, providing an opportunity for African Americans and whites to socialize.

African Americans brought their culinary traditions with them when they came north. Edna Lewis, who was born in Virginia, arrived in New York during the Depression. In 1949, she became the cook at Café Nicholson, a restaurant opened by a friend on New York's well-to-do Upper East Side. Café Nicholson became a gathering place for literary greats including Tennessee Williams, William Faulkner, and Truman Capote, as well as other New Yorkers in the arts. Lewis became known for her perfectly roasted chickens and her lofty soufflés. In 1957, Lewis left the restaurant and worked at various food-related jobs, including catering. Although Lewis wrote notable cookbooks, such as *The Edna Lewis Cookbook* (1972) and *The Taste of*

Country Cooking (1976), she continued to work in New York restaurants, most notably as chef at the venerable Brooklyn restaurant Gage and Tollner. In 1995, Edna Lewis received the first Living Legend Award from the James Beard Foundation.

In the 1960s, some African American culinary traditions were popularized under the rubric of "soul food," and by 1964 Harlem became known as "Soul City." One African American, Sylvia Woods, became particularly associated with "soul food" in New York. Woods, who was born in Hemingway, South Carolina, moved to New York in 1941 and married Herbert Woods. In 1962, the couple bought a luncheonette, which they named "Sylvia's." They served hamburgers and French fries as well as foods traditional in the South, such as fried chicken, ribs, hot cakes, corn bread, collard greens, black-eyed peas, candied yams, and rich desserts. Six years later, they moved to a larger restaurant on 126th Street. Sylvia's became a tourist attraction, drawing visitors from all over the world. In the 1990s, Woods launched Sylvia Woods Enterprises, supplying canned soul food to supermarkets. A consultant recommended that "Sylvia's of Harlem—Queen of Soul" be placed on the product labels, and thereafter Sylvia Woods was called "the Queen of Soul." She wrote two cookbooks: *Sylvia's Soul Food: Recipes from Harlem's World Famous Restaurant* (1992) and *Sylvia's Family Soul Food Cookbook* (1999).

Yet other African American culinary traditions were espoused by the Nation of Islam, which forbade many of the traditional African American foods, especially pork, but retained a fondness for sugary desserts and well-cooked vegetables. Its culinary hallmark became the bean pie, akin to pumpkin pie but filled with sweetened, spiced, mashed kidney beans.

Hispanic Immigrants

Puerto Rico was acquired by the United States through conquest during the Spanish-American War (1898). During World War I, America needed soldiers, and to acquire them, Congress passed the Second Organic Act in 1917, granting Puerto Ricans U.S. citizenship, which gave them freedom to travel freely between the island and the United States. This plus Congress's limitation of immigration from other countries, encouraged Puerto Ricans to migrate to New York, particularly East Harlem in Manhattan, south of the Gowanus Canal in Brooklyn. By the late 1920s, there were an estimated 150,000 to 200,000 Puerto Ricans living in New York, and they were served by more than 125 restaurants and 200 bodegas and colmados (neighborhood grocery and convenience stores).

Puerto Ricans continued to migrate to New York during the Depression. This turned to a flood after World War II and reached a peak in 1953 when seventy-five thousand people left the island. The mostly rural, unskilled immigrants settled predominantly in the northeastern part of Manhattan, which is known as El Barrio or Spanish Harlem. This migration continued, and by 1964, more than 10 percent of New York's total population was of Puerto Rican heritage. Puerto Ricans organized social, cultural, and sports clubs that often sponsored public festivals. The Puerto Rican club Los jíbaros (the Puerto Rican peasants) organized festivals that highlighted the preparation of foods like *chicharrones* (fried pork rinds), *tostones* (twice-fried green plantains), and *arroz con dulce* (coconut milk rice pudding).

In El Barrio, Puerto Ricans strived to maintain their food habits. *Carnicerías* (butcher shops), *cuchifritos* (snack stands), and bodegas brought Puerto Rican flavors to the neighborhood. In the 1950s, Puerto Ricans owned and supported food stalls in the covered food market that they baptized La Marqueta. This market became like a piece of the Caribbean in Manhattan, where they sold yuca and other root vegetables, *yautía* (underground stem of a plant of the genus *Xanthosoma*), plantains, green bananas, *culantro* (long-leaf cilantro), fruits, *gandules* (pigeon peas), avocados, and *maví* (bark used to make a slightly alcoholic drink).

Prudencio Unanue, a Basque who moved to Puerto Rico when he was seventeen, immigrated to New York and, in 1928, opened a small firm in New York to import products like olives, olive oil, and sardines from Spain. In 1936, Unanue founded Goya Foods, which sold rice and beans in bulk in La Marqueta and supplied bodegas with a wide array of foods for the Puerto Rican table: dried codfish, tropical fruit syrups, papaya and guava preserves, chorizo sausages, anchovies, sardines, spices, and cans of prepared foods like *pasteles* (savory plantain and green banana cakes) and *mondongo* (tripe soup). Goya has expanded and diversified according to the changes in migration trends and as the new generations lack the skills to prepare traditional foods. Now Goya is a large food importer and processing company that is the leader in its market. In spite of the large size of the company, family members still serve in key positions.

Hispanics are currently one of New York's fastest-growing immigrant groups. Dominicans mainly settled in Washington Heights in Manhattan or in Queens. Many have gone into operating bodegas and small restaurants catering to the city's Hispanic population. Few Mexicans lived in New York prior to 1980, but since then, the Mexican population has increased several fold. More than six hundred Mexican-style restaurants have opened, and some offer specific Mexican regional styles. In addition, taco trucks prowl the streets.

Japanese Immigrants

Few Japanese immigrants arrived in New York prior to the 1950s. In 1882, Congress passed the Chinese Exclusion Acts, which also restricted immigration from Japan. In 1908, the United States and Japan concluded a gentleman's agreement in which the United States would not officially halt Japanese immigration, but the Japanese government agreed to deny visas to laborers who wanted to emigrate to America. The few Japanese restaurants established in New York prior to World War II catered almost exclusively to Japanese ex-pats and visiting tourists from Japan, although there were exceptions such as the Miyako on West Fifty-eighth Street and the Daruma on Sixth Avenue. To attract a wider clientele, they offered sukiyaki and other Americanized dishes.

During the early 1950s, this began to change as Japanese officials connected with the United Nations arrived in the city. Japanese markets in New York began to sell raw fish for sashimi and sushi to resident Japanese nationals, but raw fish was also bought by some "Caucasians who have tasted and liked this speciality," reported a Japanese market owner in 1954.

By the late 1950s, Japan had recovered from the devastation of World War II, and its economy was booming. At the time, many American corporations were headquartered in New York City, and Japanese businessmen flocked there, opening offices managed by Japanese nationals. These professionals demanded authentic, high-quality Japanese food, not the made-up American dishes identified as "Japanese," and they could afford it. Japanese chefs and sushi masters were imported to feed their compatriots. New restaurants opened, manned by sushi professionals, and their Japanese customers invited New York counterparts to share in Japanese food. Japanese cuisine is complex and subtle, but what received the most attention from their colleagues were sashimi—sliced filets of raw fish—and sushi—vinegared rice topped with raw fish (among other things). Before then New Yorkers did not eat raw fish, and it seemed unlikely that most would ever sit down to a meal of raw seafood.

This began to change in the 1960s. Craig Claiborne, the *New York Times'* food editor, discovered Japanese food in 1961. Two years later, he cautioned that raw fish was probably still "a trifle too 'far out' for many American palates." By 1965, he described New York City as "a metropolis with a growing public enthusiasm for the Japanese raw fish specialties, sashimi and sushi." Two years later, he noted that "gastronomically there has been no phenomenon in recent years to equal the proliferation of Japanese restaurants, East Side, West Side and up and down the town."

Recent Immigrants

The Immigration Act of 1965 liberalized U.S. immigration law, making it easier for people from other countries to move to America. Jet air service made travel easier, swifter, and more affordable. New York became a major destination city for immigrants. In 1970, 18 percent of the city's population was foreign born; by 2010, it was 40 percent. Prior to 1970, most immigrants hailed from Europe; after that date, they were mainly from the Caribbean, Latin America, South and East Asia, the Middle East, and Africa. White flight began, and the city's racial composition changed. By 1990, Asians made up 7 percent of the city's total population, Hispanics about 25 percent, and African Americans slightly more, but of the last group, five hundred thousand were from the Caribbean, particularly Haiti and Jamaica.

Asian immigrants have included Koreans, Filipinos, and Indians. Korean immigrants settled in enclaves in Flushing and Elmhurst, Queens. Beginning in the 1970s, Korean immigrants began to retail produce, groceries, and fish. They soon operated 90 percent of the city's produce stores. By 2000, the metropolitan area was home to more than two thousand Korean-owned produce retail stores. Most have been very successful, but in 1988 Korean greengrocers in African American neighborhoods have run into ethnic conflicts and boycotts. Recently, food trucks selling Korean tacos have become popular on New York streets. Korean restaurants line West Thirty-first to West Thirty-third Streets, which is now called Koreatown, and Chef David Chang, the son of Korean immigrants, has achieved culinary stardom with his Momofuko restaurant group.

Filipinos began to immigrate to New York after 1970. Filipino restaurants have opened particularly in Queens and Brooklyn, and in the East Village in Manhattan. They serve traditional Filipino fare, such as *bangus* (a boneless baby milkfish), *adobo* (the Filipino national dish), *arroz caldo* (rice porridge), and Spam fried rice. Some opened specialty food stores in Manhattan. Many have settled in Flushing, Queens, where a Filipino fast-food chain, Jolly Bee, just opened a franchise.

Small numbers of Indians lived in New York prior to World War II. Indian migration picked up after the war. They were diverse: they adhered to different religions (Hindu, Muslim, Christian, Buddhist, Sikh, and smaller groups such as Biharis and Jains), castes, and classes. Many were vegetarian. Indian immigrants came from different regions of India and had different culinary traditions. Some opened spice stores and restaurants on Lexington Avenue between Twenty-sixth and Twenty-ninth Streets, which was soon called "Little India." Others opened grocery stores in those neighborhoods where Indian immigrants lived. These sold a variety of spices, basmati rice, flours, cans and jars of spicy pickles, sweets, snacks, and fresh vegetables. In the 1990s, Indian restaurants began to open in Flushing, Long Island City, and Jackson Heights, Queens, where many Indian immigrants lived. Some restaurants focused on specific Indian cuisines, such as those from Punjab, Gujarat, Bengal, or South India. Most served regional variations of dishes, such as rice, curries, Indian breads, Indian *lassi* (a yogurt-based drink), roti, samosas, tamarind sauce, and tandoori chicken. Some Indian restaurants were run by Jews and served kosher Indian food. Others were fast-food operations, called "curry in a hurry" outlets. Still other Indians opened pizzerias and other non-Indian fast-food operations. Smaller numbers of Pakistanis and Bangladeshis have followed similar patterns.

The first significant number of early Arab immigrants began arriving in the 1880s. They hailed initially from Lebanon and Syria, and most were Christian. After 1970, immigration from Arab countries picked up. This second wave of Arab immigrants included many Muslims. In 2010, there were an estimated 370,000 Americans of Arab heritage living in the New York area. The center of the Arab community in the city is a section of Atlantic Avenue in Brooklyn, where Arab restaurants, grocery stores, bakeries, and other shops are concentrated.

Arab Americans (along with Jewish Americans) popularized the falafel, which is usually made from fried ground chickpeas, fava beans, or the combination of the two, and other vegetables. These combinations are usually stuffed into pita bread. Falafels and stuffed pita bread have been sold by street vendors in New York for years and have recently become a favorite of many of the city's food trucks.

One unusual group has been Afghan refugees who began arriving in New York after the Soviet occupation of Afghanistan in 1979. Many have become food vendors; others have opened ethnic restaurants; and still others have opened up fast-food chicken establishments. Kentucky Fried Chicken chain was probably founded by an Afghan immigrant, and many Afghans are owners of these outlets today.

Ethiopians and Eritreans arrived in New York beginning in the 1960s, and some opened Ethiopian restaurants. Ethiopians introduced New Yorkers to *wat*, a thick stew, and *injera*, a large flatbread made from teff. Eritreans introduced New Yorkers to similar dishes (typically spicy hot) as well as their interpretations of Italian dishes. During the 1980s, Senegalese began immigrating to New York. They were followed in the 1990s by Guineans, Malians, Ghanaians, Nigerians, Ivory Coasters, and peoples from other African countries. Many were street vendors, but others opened grocery stores in Harlem, Clinton Hill, University Heights, Flatbush, and the Bronx. These sold specialty foods imported from West Africa. During the early twenty-first century, entrepreneurs began opening restaurants. Many serve traditional foods of their home countries, such as *cheb*, *mafe*, and *yassa*. Others have gone into the food delivery services, which today is dominated by West Africans.

Peoples from the West Indies (mainly Jamaica, Barbados, Trinidad, and Guyana) arrived in New York after 1964. Many ended up working in restaurants or as street vendors. Their culinary traditions have just begun to influence mainstream New York. Common Caribbean dishes include callaloo (edible leaves of various plants used as greens or in making thick soups), chicken, beef or goat patties, curried goat, fungi, Jamaican patty (pastry that contains various fillings and spices and is often sold, surprisingly, in pizza joints), peas and rice (peas or beans and rice), and roti (a round flat bread); patties and stews are now common foods sold by street vendors and food trucks. Many Caribbean foods are sold in Brooklyn on Labor Day at the Caribbean Day Parade, which claims to be the largest parade in the world with an estimated two to three million people participating and watching.

Some West Indians, especially Jamaicans, are Rastafarian, members of a quasi-religious group whose dietary precepts incline them to vegetarianism (some Rastas eat fish but not shellfish). The approved foods, called "ital," are pure, natural, and unprocessed; they are supposed to enhance "Livity," or life energy. Consumption of alcohol is strongly discouraged. Rastas have opened restaurants in New York neighborhoods where large numbers of them have settled, including Crown Heights and Bedford-Stuyvesant in Brooklyn, the north Bronx, and around Laurelton and Cambria Heights, Queens.

During the 1960s throughout the 1970s, many Haitians emigrated to the United States. An estimated four hundred thousand people of Haitian ancestry now live in New York, especially in Flatbush and East Flatbush in Brooklyn and Springfield Gardens in Queens. Many Haitian Americans work in New York grocery stores, restaurants, bakeries, and bars. Haitian Americans have begun to influence mainstream American foodways through street vendors and small restaurants, mainly in areas where large numbers have migrated.

It isn't just that immigrant groups have moved into New York and started selling traditional or modified culinary treats from their homelands. The city creates opportunities for groups to interact in ways that they might never have in their points of origin. Groups and individuals have learned from others, and what's frequently offered on restaurant menus or on the family table show signs of these interconnections. Although many restaurants purport to offer "authentic" foods and beverages (and some do), it is more common that immigrants have added nontraditional styles and dishes to their culinary repertoires.

Jamaican-born Cheryl Smith, chef and co-owner of the Global Soul Restaurant in Brooklyn. Courtesy of Kelly Fitzsimmons

CHAPTER FOUR

From Garden to Grocery

A Tour of Markets, Vendors, and Other Food Sellers

Early European colonists in New York grew, raised, and prepared much of their own food in their yards and farms. Houses had kitchen gardens and chicken coops. Cows and pigs were often allowed to roam freely. As the city grew, urbanization decreased room for gardening and farming at the tip of Manhattan; farmers and dairymen moved northward on the island or to Long Island or New Jersey, where they supplied the city's expanding population. Days were set for farmers to bring in their goods to sell to city residents. Others imported and sold specialty items, such as spices, sugar, tea, chocolate, coffee, wine, and spirits from Europe and the Caribbean, and other foodstuffs from other North American colonies. Still others, such as butchers and bakers, retailed food directly to city residents. Street vendors, farmers' markets, and grocery stores provided a complex distribution system for a wide variety of foodstuffs that New Yorkers enjoyed—and continue to enjoy today.

Street Food

Starting during the colonial days, vendors hawked their wares on city streets. They sold an incredible array of products, including many foods and beverages: milk, buns, clams, fish, strawberries, radishes, potatoes, sweet potatoes, onions, muffins, gingerbread, corn, oysters, soda, baked pears, chestnuts, peanuts, tea rusks, and even horseradish, to name just a few. Potatoes were grown in western Connecticut and were brought by sloop to New York City, where they were sold by men pushing wheel barrels for twenty-five to fifty cents per bushel.

African American women and children sold baked pears from glazed earthenware dishes that were filled with homemade syrup. They also vended steaming-hot "hot corn" from pails. They were sold in its green husk, which provided a no-expense container. According to a writer in 1808, corn was sold abundantly in the fall. Vendors provided salt to customers, and the hot corn made for "very pleasant eating." To attract buyers, some vendors shouted out, "Hot corn, hot corn, here's your lily white hot corn; hot corn, all hot; just come out of the boiling pot!" Others called out,

> Hot corn, hot corn——
> Here's your lily-white corn;
> All you that's got money
> (Poor me that's got none)
> Come buy my lily hot corn,
> And let me go home.

On Saturdays, vendors flocked to Canal Street west of Broadway, where they sold fish, oysters, and clams, which they had caught or gathered themselves. The "clam man" distinctive cry was,

> Here's clams, here's clams, here's clams to-day,
> They lately came from Rockaway;
> They're good to roast, they're good to fry,
> They're good to make a clam pot-pie.
> Here they go!

Water was crucial for everyday life in the city. Vendors acquired water from springs on the island and brought it twice daily via cart for those in the city. The quality of water was particularly important for brewing tea, so New York City erected a tea-water pump over the spring at Chattam and Roosevelt Streets. Vendors acquired water from this (and later additional) pumps and sold it on the streets, yelling out, "Tea water! Tea water! Come out and get your tea water!" To go with the tea were rusks (dried biscuits) that were sold by bakers' boys who yelled out, "Tea ruk, ruk, ruk, tea ruk."

Fruit and vegetables were seasonal treats. Cherries were favorites in June and July. Apples were sold in the fall and winter, and as many of the sellers were Irishwomen, they soon acquired the sobriquet "Apple Marys." Peaches sold in the summer. Each vendor had their own cries: "Penny apiece! bananas and peaches!" "Pe-e-e-eaches! Pe-eaches! Fi-i-i-I've cents a quart!" "'E-e-ere you are! Delaware peaches, nice 'n' ripe! o-o-o-only five cents a bushel!"

Farmers who kept cows on the outskirts of the city drove around with milk carts and sold their beverage at from six to ten cents a quart. Others carried pails filled with milk, scooped it out of their large pails, and poured it into containers provided by customers. The pails themselves were open at the top and were exposed to dust and sweat. As immigrants flooded into the city during the nineteenth century, the demand for milk increased. Distributors carried several gallons at a time by employing a wooden yoke "three feet long chiseled out and smoothed to fit over the shoulders and the back of the neck, with nicely rounded arms extending over the shoulders. A light chain or a rope was suspended from each arm with a hook at the end. With this yolk across his shoulders the carrier stood between two pails or other containers, and by stooping forward attached the hooks to the vessels; then straightening up, the weight of the vessels rested on his shoulders." As they walked along the streets, they shouted, "Here's Milk, Ho!"

Other vending businesses were based on nuts. Vendors selling chestnuts was a common sight in New York until the native American chestnut tree was wiped out by a fungal disease in the late nineteenth century. Old World chestnuts have been introduced into America, and roasting chestnuts were common on city streets, particularly about Christmas time.

Many sold peanuts, which were low cost, and all sellers had to do was roast them. By 1787, a small trade in peanuts was carried on between Charleston and New York. The unshelled peanuts were sold by a few vendors, who roasted them at their stalls and sold them to passersby. Englishman Henry Wansey enjoyed roasted peanuts on his tour of the United States in 1794. He found them unusual enough to take a supply home to England, where he served them to guests. On January 23, 1803, a letter written by "Jonathan Oldstyle," the pen name of Washington Irving, appeared in New York's *Morning Chronicle* complaining about the "crackling of nuts" at the Theater on Park Row, then New York City's only theater. Irving later reported, presumably humorously, that college students enjoyed "pea-nuts and beer, after the fatiguing morning studies." Peanut shells continued to be a nuisance throughout the nineteenth century.

The peanut vending business in New York escalated into a big business after the Civil War. In 1867, Thomas Rowland of Norfolk, Virginia, bought peanuts from farmers and shipped a small batch to an Italian merchant, also called a "pardone," who hired Italian immigrants to sell the consignment. The pardone equipped the vendors with a pushcart and a bag of peanuts on credit. Later, this model was expanded into a wide variety of goods. The peddlers were required to sell a certain quantity of goods within a given period of time or their carts were taken away and they were refused further supplies.

Vendors returned 25 percent of their sales to the pardone and pocketed the remaining 75 percent. By 1870, several hundred vendors sold food through this system. Jewish and Greek immigrants followed a similar pattern, selling other merchandise, and those three large immigrant groups controlled the vending trade until the 1920s.

A similar vending operation was launched by pecan growers. During the Civil War, many Union soldiers became familiar with this kind of nut while in Louisiana, Texas, Mississippi, and other areas where they grew. After the war, the pecan trade from the South to New York picked up. By 1867, pecans were sold in New York markets from December through April. R. C. Koerber began shipping pecans from Texas to New York City on a large scale in 1884. Three years later, he sold twenty thousand pounds, and in 1890 more than one hundred thousand pounds. Not all were sold by street vendors—they were also supplied to restaurants, hotels, and groceries.

In 1870, an author claimed in a *Harper's* magazine article that vendors generated only "a few shillings' worth" of sales. However, vending could be a lucrative business. In 1887, a house on Mulberry Street in New York City was sold at auction to an Italian who bid more than twenty-four thousand dollars. Much to the surprise of those at the auction, the buyer was a street vendor who operated a peanut stand on Park Avenue. He paid cash on the spot. Another vendor, John Courtsounis, a Greek immigrant who came to the United States in 1901, sold roasted peanuts on the street outside Columbia University. He made enough money to pay for his sisters and brothers to come to America and to open a restaurant.

The majority of vendors during the second half of the nineteenth century were Irish, Italian, and Jewish immigrants, but there were also African Americans and even a few Chinese (who sold pineapple candy and cigars). A writer for the *New York Tribune* reported in 1869 that "they furnish impromptu dinners and breakfasts for a shilling; prepare oyster-stews while you take out your pocket-book, and bake waffles while you determine the time of day. They dispose of frozen custards and sour milk, sweetened, for ice cream; soda-water without gas; lemonade without lemons." A reporter writing for *Scribner's Monthly* reported in 1870 that street vendors

> mainly sold fruit, apples, peaches, chestnuts, candy, cakes and pies, soggy yellow buns, and frightful red tarts, sweetmeat-stand, with its jars and boxes and heaps of many-colored confectionery, sticks and caramels and lozenges, and round, rough cakes, red, white, or yellow, of a cocoa-nut sweet-stuff peculiarly characteristic of New York candy-stands, and "ice-water, one cent a glass." Here is an old man calmly compounding red lemonade in a huge tin pan; and

yonder is a soda-water stand with its green marble urn, its company of inverted glasses, and its array of richly colored syrups in bottles generously large. Here is a basket of rough-coated pine-apples, and a burly woman with gold ear-rings converting the imperfect ones into piles of juicy slices, which a bit of ice keeps cool and fresh. There is a long stand with a green heap of uncut water-melons and a tempting array of red-fleshed, black-seeded halves and quarters.

Some vendors targeted juveniles. They dispensed mead, spruce beer, cakes, and ginger pop. Others catered to the needs of first-generation immigrants. For some groups, street food became an important way of retaining their ethnic identity. Pushcart peddlers selling old-country foods played a particularly important role for many immigrants in the late nineteenth century. Still others revised foods from the old country to create popular foods that attracted a large number of New Yorkers. Although there were few Mexican Americans in New York at the time, three foods—tamales, frijoles, and chili con carne—became well known. Chili con carne—a Tex-Mex invention—became a popular street food in New York in the 1880s and was sold in restaurants by the following decade. The popularity of the tamale on the streets of New York was spurred on by the Mexican Food Corporation, which employed white-clad street vendors selling tamales wrapped in corn husks and shouting, "We are the boys of the hot tamale." The success of this tactic was attributed to the exotic nature of the tamale at that time. The upper class considered tamales a "Bohemian eatable"; one tea party host invited "ten Hot Tamale men" to serve tamales (along with another such Bohemian treat, the Frankfurt sausage) to his guests. Tamales and chili con carne were sold on the street until the early 1920s, when they were no longer exotic, and cheap restaurants began selling them, such as the Chili Villa on West Forty-ninth Street.

For immigrants, who were familiar with European street vendors, street sales were a logical venture. They did not need to be highly skilled or fluent in English; many immigrant vendors operated in areas dominated by their own language group, spoke the language of their customers, and sold foods that immigrants preferred. There were plenty of opportunities—legal and otherwise—to sell food on the streets of New York. More important, the city's traditional system of supplying residents with food—that is, retail grocery stores and public markets—were hard pressed to meet the challenge of feeding the city's rapidly growing population, which increased from 391,000 in 1840 to 2.5 million in 1890.

Not everyone was impressed with the vendors or their cries. A reporter in 1855 referred to them as ruffians who, in the most dirty way, peddle oysters from an old wagon at one cent each. Their furniture consists of stentorian lungs, from which the most ear-splitting cries disturb the peace of every street and the temper of all the denizens, a pail of nasty water, a soda-water bottle of vinegar and another of a ferocious compound called pepper-sauce, and a box of salt, pepper, and street-dust mixed. Buying and selling only the cheapest oysters in the dirtiest way, they offer many spoiled ones—very likely to be productive of disease, and otherwise engender and minister to ill-health.

City officials tried to regulate street vendors beginning in 1691 when a city ordinance forbade the vendors from operating until two hours after the opening of the city's public markets. In 1707, the city tried to completely ban all vendors, but it didn't work. This wasn't much of a problem until the mid-nineteenth century when immigrants began to flood into the city. In the late nineteenth century, New York City officials instituted a law requiring pushcart vendors to relocate every thirty minutes. Most vendors ignored the law except when a policeman was sighted, in which case they moved their pushcarts in a circle and repositioned them within a few feet of where they had been. The law was difficult to enforce in the crowded neighborhoods filled with recently arrived immigrants, such as the Lower East Side. The law was rescinded in 1915.

Another solution was to establish open-air pushcart markets, which forced vendors into specific areas. The first was established on Hester Street in 1886. The most famous and popular open-air pushcart venue was Paddy's Market. It stretched on both sides of Ninth Avenue between Thirty-fifth and Forty-second Streets with sometimes as many as two hundred pushcarts. The Irish, Italian, French, Middle Eastern, and Greek vendors sold produce, breads, meat, fish, poultry, spices, coffees, and teas. Many more open-air markets were established, but they did not prevent other vendors from operating on busy streets.

Yet another solution was licensing vendors. The City Bureau of Licenses was created, and vendors were required to obtain licenses. This was strongly supported by food retailers, such as grocery stores and restaurants, who believed that street vendors took business away from them and that streets and sidewalks filled with vendors discouraged their customers. Rather than complain about the competition, owners argued that the congestion caused by street vendors made it difficult for emergency vehicles, such as fire engines, to navigate the city.

Exposés about the food vendors sold frequently appeared in newspapers and magazines. Vendors acquired fruit and vegetables, claimed one, from the refuse from docks, railroad yards, auctions, and wholesale markets, where broken boxes and rotten food were discarded. The fruit was small and often defective, and the food was sold in unsanitary conditions, at least so said those writing exposés.

The continuous clamor generated pressure for the city to study vendor problems. A Pushcart Commission was appointed in 1906. They found that Jewish, Italians, and Greek immigrants made up 97 percent of more than four thousand legal pushcart vendors. The Italians sold fruit and vegetables; the Greeks, fruit and ice cream; and the Jews, the largest group of vendors, sold a much larger, more diverse array of foods and beverages. These vendors mainly operated on the streets and sidewalks of Manhattan and in the Jewish neighborhoods of Brooklyn, such as Brownsville. The commission found that many pushcart vendors often had to bribe police, other city officials, and store owners in order to operate. If payoffs were not made, arrests often followed. In 1904 alone, more than five thousand vendors were arrested for obstructing sidewalks and streets and for failure to move their stands every thirty minutes as then required by city ordinance. Some were unusual arrests—like the one where it was said that a whistle on a peanut cart bothered a local church. Little evidence was found of health hazards with the food sold by the vendors—in fact, the commission found fewer problems with street vendors than with grocery stores: vendors had no ability to store food and therefore had to buy small quantities of fruit and vegetables daily, while grocery stores usually bought large quantities and kept them for longer periods of time. Contrary to what merchants claimed, the commission found that open-air vendor markets increased business for local stores.

The commission offered few solutions to the problem of congestion on the streets and sidewalks of New York, and during the next few years, the number of vendors increased dramatically. In 1913, the city designated vending areas, such as streets with access to the Manhattan, Williamsburg, and Brooklyn Bridges in hopes of reducing the number of vendors in Manhattan.

The U.S. Department of Agriculture (USDA) examined New York vendors in 1925. It found that the ethnic composition of the vendors had changed: 63 percent were Jewish, mainly immigrants from Eastern Europe; 32 percent were Italian; and the remaining were German, Irish, African Americans, and others. An estimated one million Manhattanites were dependent on these vendors for all or part of their food. The Italian vendors usually sold peppers, cheese, garlic, nuts, and olives; Jewish vendors typically sold fish, onions, potatoes, cabbage, carrots, pickles, soda, halvah, knishes, chestnuts, pretzels, and ice cream. The report also found few sanitary problems with New York City street vendors—in fact, vendors received fewer violations from the Health Department than did grocery stores and stalls at large farmer's markets. The main exception, according to the report, was the fish sold by street vendors, which was, according to the report, a "menace to health." The report recommended that sanitary conditions be strictly enforced to protect food from flies, dust, and insects. This was especially a problem for those foods that were typically not washed after purchase, such as candy, bread stuffs, pretzels, dried figs, and unshelled nuts.

A more serious problem for vendors was sparked by the arrival of automobiles in the city. Vendors who operated in the streets caused traffic delays, especially during rush hours. In 1918, the city declined to issue more licenses, and it began to strictly enforce existing laws; many vendors went into other occupations or moved to other cities. The number of legal street vendors dropped from almost 6,000 to 2,383 in 1920. The city established the Department of Public Markets to give more supervision to vendors. During the 1920s, reporters lamented the loss of the city's iconic street vendors, such as those selling hot tamales, apples, pretzels, hot dogs, and hot corn. Enforcement was one reason for the decline; a sharp decline in immigration was another: Congress passed laws restricting immigration, and in 1924, it virtually ended all legal immigration.

One of the new hot spots in the street food world in the 1920s was orange juice. Orange growers in California and later Florida launched national campaigns to encourage Americans to drink orange juice. They targeted one campaign directly at children, whom they encouraged to open juice stands. Orange juice took off when vitamin C was popularized, and orange growers convinced Americans that they needed orange juice every day. On New York streets, vendors acquired oranges and juiced them while customers waited for the fresh drink. New Yorkers Robert T. Neely and Orville A. Dickinson thought that selling orange juice was a great idea. They formed Nedick's Orange Juice Company in 1913. Named for the first three syllables of their last names, it later expanded into a fast chain that sold a wide variety of foods and beverages along with their iconic orange drink. The Nedicks chain folded in the 1980s, but vendors continued to sell fresh squeezed orange juice until the price of oranges escalated to the point where a small cup of fresh squeezed orange juice cost more than customers were willing to pay for a street beverage.

Despite the laws and complaints, the number of street vendors exploded when the Depression hit. In 1930, it was estimated that there were 7,900 street vendors on city streets, and as the Depression deepened, many more prowled the streets. Vendors, many of whom were not licensed, clogged the streets and often sold defective products and preyed on unsuspecting tourists, giving the city a bad name. When New York City was selected as the site for the 1939 World's Fair, Mayor Fiorello LaGuardia decided that the streets needed to be cleaned up. He created indoor markets where vendors were located. This worked for a while—until vendors took once again to the streets.

Changes in immigration patterns again altered the ethnic composition of street vendors, their offerings, and the types of foods that New Yorkers eat. The Immigration and Nationality Act amendments passed Congress in 1965, and the Immigration and Reform Act, passed in 1986, lessened restrictions on immigration from Asia, particularly China, the Caribbean, Central America, and Africa.

Succeeding mayors tried to restrict them by making vendors acquire a permit from the health department and pay retail tax. In their application they had to provide a list of food to be served and agree to pay retail tax. As the number of permit seekers exceeded the number of available permits, they were distributed via a lottery, a practice that continues today. During the 1990s, Mayor Rudy Giuliani tried to close more than one hundred streets to vendors and tried, unsuccessfully, to force vendors into pushcart markets. Other restrictions include that carts must be at least ten feet from the crosswalk and twenty feet from any doorways.

Pushcart vendors provided the less affluent the opportunity to sample different ethnic foods, and to this day immigrant vendors still offer foods like "coco helado" (water ices) and button-sized Hong Kong–style teacakes on the streets of New York.

Motorized vending vehicles plied New York City streets as early as the 1920s. Good Humor ice-cream trucks lured children with their sleigh bells, and beginning in the 1950s, soft-serve ice-cream vans, such as Mister Softee, rolled along or parked near schools and playgrounds, their siren song a maddeningly repetitive recorded jingle. Beginning in the late 1990s, food trucks began to proliferate in the city. Some of the pioneers of this resurgence sold coffee, desserts, or both, but they were soon joined by young entrepreneurs offering an array of ethnic specialties: Chinese dumplings, Belgian waffles, wienerschnitzel, fish tacos, and Margherita pizza. Coming full circle, artisan ice-cream makers now park their sleek vans in upscale neighborhoods and sell their premium treats in respectful silence.

During the last decade, food trucks have become fixtures on New York City streets. There are even some areas designated for food trucks. In 2010, when Central Park's Tavern on the Green closed, selected food trucks were permitted to lease space behind the building; they were even granted liquor licenses. With just a fraction of the overhead costs required by a

Street Vendors in Manhattan, 2013. Courtesy of Kelly Fitzsimmons

brick-and-mortar restaurant, a food truck also has the advantage of mobility. The operator can go where people are known to gather, putting word out via Twitter and Facebook to inform customers of that day's location. Some city restaurateurs, though, feel that food trucks are taking business away from them and have tried to restrict their growth through increased regulation. The New York City Food Truck Association (NYCFTA) was formed in January 2011 to represent food truck operators. In the same year, *Zagat's New York Restaurant Guide* began to rate food trucks.

Public Markets

For more than two hundred years, public markets were the primary retail and wholesale food sources for most New Yorkers. Financed and regulated by the city, public markets were originally scheduled events held in fields. Market days made it possible for city residents to buy goods carted in by local farmers. Hogs and cattle were so numerous in New Amsterdam by 1641 that city officials set specific days for livestock to be driven into the city and sold to other farmers or city residents.

The first public market was established in 1648, when Peter Stuyvesant created an outdoor market between Whitehall and Broad Streets on what was then the East River. It was initially scheduled for Mondays, but

Food truck in Manhattan, 2013. Courtesy of Kelly Fitzsimmons

in 1656, it was changed to Saturday, when "the people from the country bring various wares, such as meat, bacon, butter, cheese, turnips, roots, straw, and other products of the farm to this City for sale." Two years later, the first meat market was opened; rather than selling live animals, it sold butchered meat.

The first market house was constructed in 1676. It was located in what was then a shallow valley at Maiden Lane and the East River. As it was located in a wetland, the Dutch called it Vlaie, meaning swamp. The name was later Anglicized, and the place became known as the "Fly market." By 1680, sloops transported food down the Hudson as well as across the East River from Long Island and across the Hudson from New Jersey.

Goods were also sold through public auctions, or "vendues." As an English visitor, Sarah Knight, reported in 1704, "They have Vendues very frequently, and make their Earnings very well by them, for they treat with good Liquor Liberally, and the Customers Drink as Liberally and generally pay for't as well, by paying for that which they Bidd up Briskly for, after the sack has gone plentifully about, tho' sometimes good penny worths are got there."

During the early eighteenth century, New York sported five markets along the East River at the ends of streets. These were originally open-air markets, but large buildings were eventually constructed. The market hall on Broad Street housed vendors as well as serving as a location for balls, dinners, and meetings. The markets were officially open two days a week, although some vendors in them sold goods every day except Sunday.

Depending on the season, poultry and game, including wild geese, ducks, and other waterfowl, were plentiful. In the spring and autumn, pigeons were so abundant that, in 1754, one penny would purchase six. All meat, fish, and fruit was sold through public markets until 1763, when a poulterer set up shop near City Hall. Milk was the exception: it was sold almost exclusively by street vendors. Markets were well supplied, mainly by farmers in New Jersey and on Long Island. City authorities inspected the markets, and if they found vendors selling underweight products or impure food, the vendors were fined and food was occasionally destroyed. On the eve of the American Revolution, an English visitor reported that the city's four markets were well provisioned.

Two markets were abandoned after the American Revolution, but three new ones were constructed along the East River. Farmers brought their products to these markets on specified days, and their customers—housewives, employees, servants, or slaves—picked up what was needed. By 1807, the city's markets were closed on Sundays but open the other six days. The markets were abundantly supplied in season with an incredible diversity of game, meat, and seafood. They sold eight game animals (bear, deer, raccoon, groundhog, opossum, squirrel, rabbit, and hare)—some dead, others alive; five amphibious creatures, such as turtles; fourteen different shellfish; fifty-one different species of birds; and sixty-two different types of fish. Hucksters in the market sold vegetables and fruit. The novelist James Fenimore Cooper accurately proclaimed in 1828 that "it is difficult to name fish, fowl, or beast that is not, either in its proper person, or in some species nearly allied to it, to be obtained in the markets of New-York."

Unusual game remained an important part of the city's public markets for decades. Thomas DeVoe, a butcher at the Jefferson Market, reported in his book *The Market Assistant* (1867), that "every item of human food [is] sold in the Public Markets," including venison, elk, caribou, reindeer, black-tailed deer, mule deer, moose, antelope, pronghorn antelope, bighorn sheep, rocky mountain goat, hares, rabbits, guinea pigs, squirrels, black bears, raccoons, lynx, opossums, groundhogs, porcupines, skunks, beavers, otters, badgers, muskrats, and many, many more.

Vendors and wagons typically arrived at the markets at 3:00 a.m. on weekdays but 2:00 a.m. on Saturday, the busiest market day. In some cases, the farmers had begun their journeys the previous afternoon, traveling up to thirty miles from Long Island or New Jersey and then waiting for the ferry across the East River or the Hudson. By 7:00 a.m., the markets were sufficiently stocked, but supplies continued to arrive for the next few hours, creating massive traffic jams as wagons waited to unload their produce and customers fought to enter, shop, and then leave with their purchases.

The earliest customers at the markets were those who shopped for hotels and restaurants, such as the Fifth Avenue, St. Nicholas, Brevoort, Metropolitan, Astor, Hoffman, St. James, and Delmonico's. They selected the "choicest beef, the fattest mutton, the freshest cutlets, the earliest fruits and vegetables; for the reputation and patronage of their houses depend upon the excellence of their table," proclaimed a New York reporter in 1869. After these buyers had made their rounds, prices dropped somewhat. Then came shoppers from well-to-do and middle-class households, who bought the meat, fish, fruits, and vegetables required for the coming week. After 2:00 p.m., prices dropped steeply as stall owners tried to clear out their inventory; the customers at this hour were the proprietors of boardinghouses, street vendors, and others more focused on price than on quality.

As the city's population grew, more public markets were built. By 1867, there were eleven in the city; the two largest and most important were Washington and Fulton Markets. Washington Market was opened in 1812 on the west side of lower Manhattan, on Washington Street between Fulton and Vesey Streets, and later expanded to the surrounding area. In 1867, it consisted of a series of rectangular buildings constructed around a circular building with a small cupola on top. The market, which included many stalls, stores, and extensive warehouses, was touted as the largest market in the United States—some said the largest in the world. And it was indeed massive, with more than five hundred stalls and three thousand vendors. About thirty thousand people were estimated to earn their livelihood there. In a time before refrigeration, New Yorkers had to buy their food frequently. The Washington Market alone served about one hundred thousand customers daily during a busy season, such as Christmas. Customers came from all over the region to purchase their groceries. It was estimated that Washington Market provided for at least two million people. In addition, foods were packaged at Washington Market and transported to other states, including California.

Washington Market sold a wide variety of produce. Early in the season—in April and May—fruits and vegetables came from Bermuda and the Carolinas. In the high season for local produce—late summer and early fall—more than six hundred wagons from New Jersey, Long Island, and western New York came to the market daily with fresh farm products. The most important fruit sold in the markets was the apple, which arrived from upstate New York at the beginning of October and disappeared by the end of November. During these

General view of Washington Market, 1877. From "How New York is Fed," Scribner's Monthly 14 (October 1877): 729. Courtesy of Kelly Fitzsimmons

two months, New Yorkers purchased half a million barrels (each containing about 225 apples), and most of these were sold through the public markets or by street vendors. The second most important fruit was the peach, which came in from New Jersey, Delaware, and Maryland. During their two-month season, an estimated twenty thousand bushels of peaches were sold daily. Other fruit with significant sales were pears, grapes, and berries.

Washington Market was known for its meat, poultry, and game, and observers marveled at the variety and quantity. In 1828, an observer reported seeing canvasback ducks from the Susquehanna; venison from New Jersey, Long Island, and the Catskill mountains; grouse from Hempstead, on Long Island; snipe from the Newark meadows; and partridges from Bull Hill along the Hudson River. An 1839 visitor to the market found "three hundred head of deer, with quantities of bear, rackoons [sic], wild turkies [sic], geese, ducks, and every variety of bird in countless profusion." Once railroads connected New York with the Midwest, in the 1850s, meat could be transported from as far away as Kansas and Illinois. "The best beef, mutton, veal and lamb the country affords are displayed upon the stalls," wrote a marketgoer in 1869. "Those roasts and steaks, those hind-quarters, those cutlets, those breasts with luscious sweet-breads, would make an Englishman hungry as he rose from the table."

Fulton Market, on the east side of Manhattan, was established in 1820. Initially, it sold a wide variety of goods. As one observer reported, it was

> a butcher's store, a fruiterer's stall, an oyster-counter, a coffee shop, a poultry-yard, and a fish-monger's establishment. It is every thing in one—a magnum not in parvo, but a magnum in magna. It is one vast repository for the sale of every article of diet you could fancy from a lamb-chop up to a "steak for two," from a shrimp up to a lobster, from a cup of coffee up to the largest table d'hote fare you could pick out.

But Fulton Market was best known for its fish and seafood. An 1828 visitor found a profusion of cod from Newfoundland; lobster, catfish, flounder, eel, mussels, and clams from the Long Island Sound; and softshell crabs from Baltimore. The oysters came from Blue Point, Long Island; the York River and Chincoteague Island in Virginia; and Chingarora in Raritan Bay, New Jersey. By 1853, it was estimated that there were more than a thousand vessels engaged in bringing in oysters to the New York markets.

Exterior of Fulton Fish Market. Courtesy of the Library of Congress. Reproduction Number: LC-DIG-ppmsca-12798

A separate fish market was constructed at Fulton Market in the 1831; right on the docks, it could receive fresh seafood straight off the boats. From the Fulton Fish Market, fish and seafood were packed and shipped out via railroads and ferries to a radius of four hundred miles. By the 1860s, two hundred schooners and smacks plus smaller oyster boats supplied the Fulton Market with "cod, halibut, haddock, herring, mackerel, blackfish, bluefish, smelt, weak fish, and white fish, eels, porgees, sea bass, striped bass, trout, sturgeon, sheep's head, flounders, and many others too numerous to mention." Fish and seafood were brought in from a five-hundred-mile radius around the city. In addition, freshwater fish from the Great Lakes were shipped to the city via the Erie Canal and railroads. During the "R" months, some 250,000 oysters were eaten every day in New York, and about 25,000 daily during the remaining months of the year. Most came through the Fulton Market.

The Fulton Fish Market thrived both as a wholesale outlet serving restaurants, hotels, and fishmongers and as a retail operation, selling directly to New Yorkers. Some stalls sold seafood to be eaten on the spot; Dorlon's oyster bar, one of the more popular, served patrons well into the night. It was started in the 1840s by Alfred P. Dorlon, who worked at his father's stall wholesaling oysters. Dorlon and his brother later opened an oyster stall of their own and placed a few tables out front, where people could eat oysters. Over the next ten years, Dorlon's expanded to become one of New York's most fashionable oyster bars. It was described in the late 1860s as plainly furnished, without tablecloths or carpets. As to the patrons, "No opera, soiree, fashionable palace, can boast of a more fashionably dressed and distinguished company. Fastidious ladies, who at home dwell in splendid boudoirs and sit in perfumed chambers, take Dorlan's [sic] on their way from the opera, for a stew or a saddle-rock roast." The "men of wealth, and women of society; fastidious scholars, and authors of renown" who ate at Dorlon's had to stand in line waiting their turn. The business survived until 1888, when the Fulton Fish Market became seedy and well-to-do customers took their business elsewhere. Also, the oysters in New York Harbor and Long Island Sound were overharvested, and the price of oysters skyrocketed.

As early as 1857, New York City newspaper editorials advocated closing downtown markets. Their arguments initially focused on congestion: if the markets closed, thousands of carts and wagons would be removed from the streets, permitting other businesses to move in. During the following decade, more newspapers and magazines criticized the chaos, disorder, shabbiness, and filthiness of the city's markets. The buildings were in disrepair, and customers complained that vendors were not only rude but also guilty of fraudulent practices and that other crime was rampant in the markets.

Thomas DeVoe became the city's superintendent of markets in 1871. He was well aware of the problems confronting public markets, and he energetically launched reforms. New buildings were constructed at some markets, while others were renovated. But it wasn't enough. Demographic trends were against the existing public markets. Most were located at the southern end of Manhattan, but during the mid-nineteenth century, prosperous New Yorkers moved northward on the island, as immigrants and the poor moved into lower Manhattan. The immigrants were better served by pushcart vendors who charged lower prices than market stallholders. The well-to-do continued to send their servants down to fetch food from the markets, but as grocery stores, butcher shops, and specialty stores moved uptown, it became easier to shop locally.

There were other reasons for the decline of particular public markets. One reason for the success of the Fulton Market had been its proximity to the Brooklyn ferry terminal. Brooklynites who worked or shopped in Manhattan passed by or through the market. After the completion of the Brooklyn Bridge, in 1883, foot traffic dropped off because the bridge exit was blocks away from the market. Shops and grocery stores opened around the access roads leading to the bridge. The Manhattan and Williamsburg Bridges took even more customers away from Fulton Street. By 1912, the only market surviving on the site was the wholesale fish market.

Public markets stopped generating profits for the city and gradually became a liability. In 1899, Deputy Controller Edgar J. Levey said that it was time for the city to "go out of the public market business." Several markets were closed, but the Washington Market survived; it was rebuilt in 1884 and renovated twice during the early twentieth century. Its retail building was finally closed in 1956, and the wholesale operation survived a few more years. The block on which the market stood was eventually incorporated into the World Trade Center.

As public markets closed, the city needed a wholesale market to supply restaurants, hotels, and grocery stores with fresh produce, meat, and other products. In 1962, ground was broken for the New York City Terminal Market at Hunt's Point, in the Bronx. The site offered easy access to rail, truck, and ship transport without disrupting traffic and was easy for buyers to reach as well.

The Fulton Fish Market survived through the twentieth century. Additional buildings were constructed in 1936, and one building was replaced in 1939. But it was downhill from there. In the 1970s, fishing boats ceased landing their catches at the market, refrigerated trucks becoming the best mode of delivery. In 2005, however, the Fulton Fish Market was relocated to Hunt's Point.

Interior of Public Market New York City, 1948. Courtesy of the Library of Congress. Reproduction Number: LC-DIG-ppmsca-12798

Greenmarkets

During his tenure as mayor in the 1950s and early 1960s, Robert F. Wagner supported a farmer's market at City Hall that featured the eight "Miracle Gardens," which were developed on formerly litter-strewn vacant plots around the city. In 1970, the privately funded Council on the Environment of New York City was created as a policy organization to write reports about environmental issues in the city. It evolved into an agency that actively supported worthwhile efforts to improve the environmental quality of the city.

In October 1973, John L. Hess, a columnist for the *New York Times*, commended the city of Syracuse for permitting farmers to sell their goods on one city street every Tuesday. This article was read by Barry Benepe, a forty-eight-year-old urban planner, who convinced one of his colleagues, Bob Lewis, that New York City should have a farmers' market as well. With support from the Council on the Environment of New York City, they worked for three years, acquiring the necessary permits, locating a site, and convincing farmers to give the new market a try.

In July 1976, their efforts bore fruit when the Greenmarket opened on a dirt lot surrounded by a fence on Second Avenue and Fifty-ninth Street. Seven plant, vegetable, and fruit growers trucked in their farm produce from

Long Island, New Jersey, and the Hudson Valley on Saturdays. Television news picked up the story and gave the Greenmarket visibility. A few months after it opened, the city convinced Benepe and Lewis to move the operation downtown to Union Square. At the time, the parking lot surrounding Union Square Park was a hotbed of drug dealing. Around the square, businesses were faltering and stores were closing. With the city's support, the Green-market thrived, and the neighborhood followed suit, becoming a center for upscale restaurants and other businesses.

The city's second Greenmarket opened in Brooklyn, at the intersection of Atlantic and Flatbush Avenues; others followed elsewhere in the city. To-day, there are fifty-four farmers' markets serving all five boroughs. Some are seasonal, open only during the growing season, while others operate all year round. Some markets are open two days a week, others just one; the Union Square Greenmarket operates four days a week throughout the year.

The Council on the Environment of New York City changed its name to GrowNYC in 2007. It supports the city's Greenmarkets, builds com-munity gardens, and encourages recycling. In 2011, GrowNYC initiated a new program, placing receptacles at Greenmarkets to collect produce scraps for composting. The compost is used on urban farms and garden projects throughout the city.

GrowNYC, a recycling program for vegetable matter, at the Union Square Greenmarket, 2013. Courtesy of Kelly Fitzsimmons

Retailing

Retailing of food developed slowly in the city over the course of the seventeenth century. During the Dutch period, the West India Company maintained a store that sold goods, including imported food and beverages, to the colonists. Ships entering the harbor often sold their goods right off the wharf or moved their goods to warehouses, where they were sold directly to customers.

Breweries and bakeries wholesaled their products to taverns but also sold directly to customers. From the earliest days, city government tried to regulate these artisans and require that they sell their goods at reasonable prices. Bread was regulated after 1649, and at least some bakers were charged with violating regulations. The content and weight of breadstuffs were monitored, as were the prices that bakers could charge. Since the cost of ingredients and the mandated minimum weights of certain items meant that sometimes the baker could not make a profit, so bakers figured out ways to trim their costs by using cheap grain and fillers and selling bread that was under the legal weight. In 1681, baker David Provoost was brought up on charges for "having bad breed not fitt for Sale." He was let off with a warning, but other prosecutions followed.

New York law required butchers to operate through public markets, but in the 1840s butchers began to open freestanding stores. As many New Yorkers preferred buying their meat and poultry from a shop rather than trying to navigate the large, overcrowded public markets, the law was changed. Shops specializing in fish and seafood soon opened in the city as well.

From colonial times, small stores sold specialty goods, such as spices, tea, chocolate, or coffee, that were not typically sold by street vendors or in public markets. Small stores emerged in the mid-eighteenth century, selling imported products—spices, coffee, tea, chocolate, pickles, fresh fruit (oranges, lemons, and mangoes), figs, cooking oil, olives, ketchup, capers, herrings, and walnuts, as well as pickled anchovies, lobsters, and oysters. Confectioners sold sugar plumbs, sugar candy, "Jarr Raisins and Cask ditto; Currants, Figgs and Prunes; Almonds in the Shell; Cloves, Mace, Cinnamon and Nutmeg; Ginger, Black Pepper and Allspice; Dry Citron by the Box or smaller quantity; West India Sweetmeats of all Sorts; Preserves of all Sorts, such as Currants, Jellys, Quinces, Grapes, Strawberries, Raspberries, Damsons, Peaches, Plumbs and sundry other sorts," noted an eighteenth century advertisement.

Grocery stores selling both perishable and nonperishable foods appeared in the late eighteenth century. By 1817, the city had an estimated 1,500 family-owned grocery stores, many owned by Irish immigrants. Most sold wine or spirits, particularly rum, which is where they made their profits. They were often located in the basements or attics of boardinghouses or tenement buildings, and they served as gathering places for immigrants to meet and socialize. By the mid-nineteenth century, family-owned grocery stores far outnumbered the stalls in public markets.

Specialty stores focused on particular products, such as imported tea. The Great Atlantic Tea Company was founded by George F. Gilman and George H. Hartford around 1860. It was similar to other retail stores of the time. Gilman, the owner of a leather company, also dabbled in shipping interests. He imported small consignments of tea, which he sold to wholesalers. Hartford was his assistant. Hartford convinced Gilman that they would make more money if they cut out middlemen and retailed the tea directly to the public. Gilman and Hartford opened a retail tea shop in New York City and also began selling tea by mail; they eventually named their business the Great American Tea Company. Sales were good enough that Gilman and Hartford started buying tea in larger quantities, which enabled them to cut their expenses and set their retail prices even lower, underselling other grocers. They expanded their line to include coffee and other luxury products.

By 1865, the partners had five small stores in New York City, thus creating America's first grocery chain. The completion of the transcontinental railroad in 1869 made it possible for the company to receive shipments of tea and other specialty goods from Asia via San Francisco and then ship them by train throughout the country. Hartford and Gilman began to open stores across the nation, and to reflect the newly bicoastal operation, they changed their firm's name to the Great Atlantic & Pacific Tea Company, subsequently shortened to A&P. Over the next few decades, the A&P stores gradually augmented their inventory to include a full range of groceries.

The early success of the A&P was condemned by independent grocers, who attacked the company for its predatory pricing and the resulting destruction of small family-owned businesses. Despite such criticism—or perhaps because of it—A&P built more stores and expanded their product lines. It quickly became America's largest grocery chain as it opened stores throughout the United States. By 1925, A&P had more than fourteen thousand stores across the United States.

Other entrepreneurs, impressed by A&P's early success, started their own chains. The Jones Brothers Tea Company was founded in Scranton,

Pennsylvania, in 1872 by Cyrus, Frank, and Charles Jones. When the Jones brothers expanded their chain to New York, they changed its name to Grand Union Tea Company, soon shortened to "Grand Union." In 1883, Bernard H. Kroger began a chain-store operation in Cincinnati. Two German immigrants, brothers Charles and Diedrich Gristede, opened their first grocery store in New York in 1891; Gristede's grew into an upscale chain with stores in New York's wealthier neighborhoods.

Italian immigrant Luigi Balduchi sold bananas in Greenpoint from 1915 until 1925 when he and his wife Maria opened a produce stand there. Twenty years later, they moved to Greenwich Avenue in Manhattan and eventually sold upscale meat, fish, bakery goods, and other products. By the late twentieth century, it had expanded into a small chain that proclaimed itself to be the premier destination for food lovers.

Another Italian immigrant Nicholas D'Agostino and his brother launched a market by Italian immigrants in 1932 on Eighty-third Street and Lexington Avenue. They opened additional stores, and today the company operates thirteen supermarkets in New York City. Nathan Glickberg opened a small fruit and vegetable stand on West Seventy-fourth Street in Manhattan in 1933. In 1954, he moved his operation to Broadway and renamed it Fairway Market. The company expanded during the 1980s but ran into stiff competition. Today, it is a small chain with five stores in the New York metropolitan area that concentrate on specialty items. One of Fairway's competitors was started by Mike Citarella as a fish market in Harlem in 1912. In 1941, he moved the store to Columbus Avenue. In the 1980s, the company expanded its offerings to include specialty meat, prepared foods, pastry and produce, and other gourmet food. Another upscale specialty food retailer was launched by Giorgio DeLuca and Joel Dean in Soho in 1977. Nine years later, Dean & DeLuca moved to Broadway and Prince Street. It has opened additional stores in New York and other sites.

Supermarkets

In 1930, Michael J. Cullen, the son of Irish immigrants, opened a grocery store he named "King Kullen" on Jamaica Avenue in Queens. He stocked more than a thousand basic food products at prices that undercut those at local markets. There was also free parking in lots adjacent to the store, drawing in customers in cars. Encouraged by the success of the first location, Cullen quickly opened more stores, and by 1936 fifteen King Kullen stores served Queens, the Bronx, and Long Island. King Kullen undercut the prices at traditional chain and independent grocers by at least 10 to 15 percent, making up the lost profit through high sales volume. In the New York metropolitan area, supermarkets generated annual sales in excess of fifteen million dollars during the Depression.

The Depression hit just as Cullen debuted his first King Kullen store, and it helped make his business model a success. Price became the number 1 factor for consumers in deciding where to shop. Beginning in the mid-1930s, many grocery chains closed their smaller stores and opened supermarkets. Independent grocers were unable to follow suit, however, and thousands went out of business in New York City during the late 1930s and early 1940s. World War II slowed the growth of supermarkets, as wartime restrictions halted the construction of stores, foods were rationed, and many food processors concentrated on military contracts. Before the war, almost all grocery store clerks had been young men; as they enlisted and left their jobs, women filled their places. When the war ended, women continued to work in supermarkets and made up a majority of their employees.

Supermarkets thrived in New York during the 1950s and 1960s. A&P remained America's largest food retailer until 1975, when it ran into financial reversals, as did other large chains in the city. This decline was largely due to increased competition in the city. Small grocery stores, bodegas, and delis cut into supermarket business, as did larger supermarkets outside of the city that were accessible by car.

During the early 1970s, alternative food-distribution systems emerged, such as food coops and community-supported agriculture (CSA). In 1976, the first Greenmarket was established in Union Square, selling foods grown, raised, and prepared locally, which was defined as within two hundred miles of the city. Eventually some 120 more Greenmarkets opened around the city, and these, too, reduced sales at city supermarkets. Specialty grocery store chains, such as the Gourmet Garage, the Garden of Eden, and Union Market, have attracted a wide following in the city. Fresh Direct, an online grocery service, opened in 2002. In 2005, Whole Foods, a supermarket chain that emphasizes "natural and organic products," opened a store on Union Square and subsequently other stores elsewhere the city.

Delicatessens

Yet another retail operation is the delicatessen. German immigrants imported European specialty foods, such as European wines and brandies, Westphalia ham, Magdeburg sauerkraut, Gruyère cheese, German poppy-seed oil, pasta from Italy, and fish from the Netherlands. These items were sold directly to restaurants and delicatessens. According to Artemas Ward, chronicler of the nineteenth-century grocery trade, the first delicatessen opened on Grand Street in New York City around 1868. Delicatessens were patronized by German Americans, of course, but they also attracted passersby who were enticed by the window displays of foreign and "fancy" foods. Delicatessens sold cooked, ready-to-eat meats, sausages, poultry, and fish, as well as cheeses, teas, mushrooms, caviar, olive oil, pickles, and other imported goods.

Delicatessens filled the gap between butcher shops, which mainly sold uncooked meats, and general grocery stores, which offered bulk and packaged goods and liquor. Originally, deli customers purchased the prepared food products and took them elsewhere to eat, but as delicatessens thrived and expanded, some made a place for customers to sit down and eat in the store, particularly at lunchtime.

Delicatessens remain an important cultural component of New York, but the term is used much more loosely today. As other new groups of immigrants—Italians, Greeks, Puerto Ricans, West Indians, Chinese, and Koreans—moved into the city, many found that "deli" ownership proved an excellent entry point. While some delis today still specialize in cured meats, pickled fish, and other Old World specialties, most sell a general line of packaged and prepared foods. Deli owners from newer immigrant groups, though, often include their native favorites; for instance, Korean American–owned delis frequently sell kimchi and a few other Asian delicacies, while West Indian proprietors offer savory turnovers called "patties."

Today, New York's marketers and food retailers offer home cooks and restaurateurs a wide selection of local and imported produce, meats, fish, seafood, spices, poultry, grains, and prepared foods. Most are available year round, although the quality often depends on the season and the food miles that the products must travel to reach the city. Likewise, New Yorkers have a vast choice when it comes to beverages to which we now turn.

CHAPTER FIVE

~

Drinking in the City

During New York's colonial period, most people quenched their thirst with plain water. Clean water was plentiful in springs, lakes, and rivers throughout much of Manhattan, Staten Island, Long Island, and the Bronx, but in New Amsterdam, at the tip of Manhattan, the fresh water supply was limited. The Dutch colonists collected rainwater in cisterns and shallow wells, but there wasn't enough for their needs. Deeper wells were dug, but there still was not sufficient fresh water for drinking, cooking, brewing, and washing, or for watering the ever-growing herds of livestock. Residents who were able to traveled north, beyond the city's walls, to collect fresh water from springs.

Under English colonial rule, wells were systematically dug, and in 1688 a public well system was established. Still, problems persisted as the population grew: wells became polluted not only with seepage from privies, garbage heaps, and cemeteries but also with effluent from commercial operations such as hatters, dyers, and starch makers. During the next century, several solutions were tried to solve the water problem. For cooking, New Yorkers boiled or filtered their water before they used it. Some believed that adding alcohol to water would purify it. Those who could afford the cost paid carters who brought water into the city—presumably from rural springs, but buyers could never be sure where the water came from.

Yet another solution was to buy bottled spring water from upstate. In 1820, Dr. Darius Griswold began bottling water at Saratoga's Congress Springs. He stuck with the business for just a few years before leasing the bottling rights to Dr. John Clarke and Thomas Lynch in 1823. Saratoga Mineral Water, the first commercially successful bottled water in the United States, was shipped to New York City and then distributed to other eastern cities. Other bottled waters soon followed.

Despite these efforts, yellow fever, cholera, and other waterborne diseases ravaged the city again and again. The well-to-do usually headed out of the city during summer, when such epidemics typically struck. It was the poor who suffered the most. Medical opinion of the day placed the blame on the poor themselves—for eating fresh fruit, especially watermelons, and drinking bad water.

Health and economic concerns finally convinced the city government to embark on a massive project that would bring fresh water to Manhattan via an aqueduct. The Croton River north of the city was dammed, reservoirs were built, and a forty-two-mile aqueduct was constructed. The project began in 1837; when it was completed five years later, New Yorkers celebrated with parades and fireworks. Private houses were connected directly to the system, so the homes of the wealthy had running water and indoor privies for the first time. The less privileged continued to draw water from public taps for decades to come, but at least it was safe to drink. During this same period, the city began to construct a sewage system that piped raw sewage into the bay, which at least helped protect some of Manhattan's fresh water.

The Founding Beverages

It was not by choice that water was the most common drink in colonial New York; even water acknowledged as pure was considered a distant second best to alcoholic beverages. Alcoholic beverages were thought to be more nutritious, and there was a class stigma associated with drinking water—after all, only the poorest of the poor had no alternative. The Dutch and English preferred beer, and breweries were established within a decade of the city's founding. Colonists also liked their wine and brandy.

Even before the arrival of hard liquor in the colony, alarms were raised regarding the amount of alcohol consumed by city residents. William Kieft, who became the director general of the colony in 1638, believed that "much mischief and perversity is daily occasioned by immoderate Drinking." One-quarter of all the buildings in New Amsterdam, he claimed, were "grog-shops or houses where nothing is to be got but tobacco and beer." He passed a law preventing the sale of beer during religious services, although he encouraged the sale of beer through the Dutch West India Company's store, the profits of which helped fund the colony.

Concluding that the production of alcohol could be used to generate in-come for the city (and himself), Kieft established the colony's first distillery on Staten Island. Then he concluded that the production of alcohol could be used to generate income for the city. When he made a disastrous decision to go to war against the Indians in 1643, money was needed to pay for the war. Betting that an excise tax on beer would be a good revenue source, Kieft imposed the tax of $1.20 per cask. Tapsters (tavern owners) who refused to pay the tax were shut down and their beer confiscated and given to soldiers. This tax, however, did not raise enough revenue to cover the colony's war expenses, and Kieft was recalled home to Holland.

Peter Stuyvesant, Kieft's successor, maintained the beer tax and imposed a fee of two cents on each wine jar sold. These taxes did not affect home brew-ers, merchants, or really anyone else. They did not apply to the state-owned brewhouse, nor to the sale of wine and brandy by the colonial government. These generated more revenue for the Dutch West India Company than did anything other than the fur trade.

Stuyvesant forbade excessive drinking at night and any drinking at all on Sunday, but his edict went "unobserved." In 1648, he passed another ordinance to regulate and license "Taverns, Alehouses and Tippling places" within the colony. The result was that by 1654 a large number of illegal establishments were serving beer and wine. Shortly thereafter, rum began to be imported into New Amsterdam; its consumption increased after the city's conquest by the English. Rum was distilled in New York by the end of the seventeenth century, and the industry grew quickly. By 1768, New York had seventeen distilleries producing half a million gallons of rum annually.

New York's upper classes preferred mixed drinks, which appeared in many guises. Flips (beer sweetened with sugar, molasses, dried pumpkin, or honey and strengthened with rum) had become popular by 1690. Possets, made from spiced hot milk and eggs combined with ale or beer, evolved into eggnog and other beverages. Syllabub—spiced milk or cream whipped to a froth with sweet wine or cider and sugar—was a spirituous drink for festive occasions. Shrubs, composed of citrus juice from imported oranges, lemons, and limes mixed with various spirits, were popular drinks before the War of Independence, as were hot toddies (made of liquor, water, sugar and spices) and cherry bounce (made from cherry juice and rum). The most popular mixed drink was punch, usually composed of rum, citrus juice, sugar, and water, with myriad variations. Milk punches, made with egg yolks, sugar, rum, and grated nutmeg, were also common for parties and balls. There were iced punches for summer and hot punches for winter. Sangaree, a mixture of wine, water, sugar, and spices, was an Anglo-American version of sangria, a common drink in Spain.

Alcoholic beverages were often mentioned in newspapers of the day, and they even occasionally inspired poetry of sorts. In February 13, 1744, the *New York Gazette* published "A Receipt for All Young Ladies That Are Going to Be Married, to Make a Sack Posset." The recipe likely originated in England, but it was widely reprinted in America:

> From famed Barbados, on the Western Main,
> Fetch sugar half a pound: fetch sack from Spain,
> A pint; and from the Eastern Indian coast
> Nutmeg, the glory of our Northern toast;
> O'er flaming coals together let them heat,
> Till the all-conquering sack dissolves the sweet;
> O'er such another fire let eggs, twice ten,
> New born from foot of cock and rump of hen;
> Stir them with steady hand, and conscience pricking
> To see the untimely fate of twenty chicken;
> From shining shelf take down your brazen skillet;
> A quart of milk from gentle cow will fill it;
> When boiled and cooled, put milk and sack to egg,
> Unite them firmly, like the triple League;
> Then covered close, together let them dwell
> Till Miss twice sings, *You must not kiss and tell.*
> Each lad and lass snatch up their murdering spoon,
> And fall on fiercely, like a starved dragoon.

To support New York's fondness for alcoholic beverages, the number of taverns and other places serving and selling them increased rapidly. By 1773, the city had "396 licensed taverns and many illegal groggeries that sold alcohol." Rum and whiskey were the beverages of choice for the lower classes—they were cheap, and they had more of a kick than the more expensive beer and wine. By the mid-1820s, New York State had 1,129 distilleries, and New York City alone had more than 1,600 "spirit sellers," who sold whiskey for thirty-eight cents a gallon.

According to one British observer, this abundance of sellers and low price meant that "the people indulge themselves to excess, and run into all the extravagancies of inebriety." He concluded that "the friends of humanity would rejoice in the establishment of an adequate check to an evil of such dangerous consequence in a country which promises to become eminent in greatness and power." Despite concerns, New York City headed in precisely the opposite direction. Many immigrants, who began arriving in the 1830s, went into brewing and distilling. By 1855, more than five hundred German and Irish immigrants were brewers and distillers. Many more immigrants went into selling beer and spirits. By the middle of the nineteenth century, Manhattan alone had an estimated five thousand liquor stores and taverns.

Hot Beverages

The Dutch were importing tea to New York by about the middle of the seventeenth century, and it soon became the city's hot beverage of choice. Throughout the eighteenth century, tea consumption steadily increased, at least among the ladies of society. Good tea required good water, and in colonial times a thriving business was launched selling "tea water" from particular springs. Garardus Comfort, a cooper, owned a house with a well. He began distributing Comfort's Tea Water some time before 1741. Special tea water pumps were identified, and vendors began selling tea water from pumps and from vendors on the streets. By 1774, it was estimated that three thousand families got their household drinking water from the "tea water men."

Some took the tea-drinking habit to extremes. In 1734, a New Yorker wrote, "I am credibly informed that tea and china ware cost the province, yearly, near the sum of £10,000; and people that are least able to go to the expence, must have their tea tho' their families want bread. Nay, I am told, often pawn their rings and plate to gratifie themselves in that piece of extravagance." In 1762, William Smith, writing in his history of New York, noted bitterly that "our people both in town and country are shamefully gone into the habit of tea-drinking." Indeed, New Yorkers loved their tea. It was sometimes served at meals but especially in "the afternoon, as in England," as a coffeehouse owner reported. Tea gardens, also called pleasure gardens, were also launched in New York by the mid-eighteenth century.

In 1773, the British parliament imposed a tax on the sale of tea in the colonies. Every schoolchild knows how Bostonians responded with the Boston Tea Party on December 16, 1773. Less well known is the similar drama that played out in New York. In April 1774, two ships—the *Nancy* and the *London*—entered New York Harbor at about the same time, both carrying tea. The tea consignee to the *Nancy* sent a note to the captain, reporting that the city's populace was "violently opposed" to the landing or vending of the tea and "that any attempts in us, either to effect one or the other would not only be fruitless, but expose so considerable a property to inevitable destruction." The *Nancy* returned to England without unloading its tea. The captain of the *London* claimed that there was no tea onboard, but when the ship was searched, it was found to contain eighteen chests of tea. The Sons of Liberty, disguised as Indians, threw the tea into the harbor and threatened the captain, who set sail to England at his earliest opportunity. Among those Americans, tea drinking stopped during the War for Independence in part to show support for the revolution and also because it was difficult to import due to the British blockade. The exception was New York loyalists, who consumed it when it could be obtained.

After the war, tea drinking again became fashionable among the city's well-to-do, and tea-drinking occasions regained their former glory. Now tea could be acquired directly from China rather than through the British or Dutch. Robert Morris, a Philadelphia merchant and a signer of the Declaration of Independence, saw a great opportunity. It was time to cut out the middlemen in Europe and trade directly with China. Morris joined with others to outfit a ship, the *Empress of China*, which sailed out of New York on February 22, 1784, and returned fifteen months later with a cargo mainly of tea. When this tea was sold, each investor netted thirty thousand dollars (equivalent to about 1.6 million dollars today). Other ships made the journey to China as well, and soon a thriving business between New York and China was underway and fortunes were made in the trade.

Afternoon tea was served at most restaurants and boardinghouses, and tea leaves were sold by specialty shops. By 1860, there were sixty-five retail tea shops in the city. James Geery at 119 Mulberry Street, at the corner of Bayard Street, was widely known for the excellence of his teas. J. Stiner & Company had a thriving business in importing and selling tea; they opened additional shops, thus becoming one of America's first chain-store retailers. By 1867, it operated ten stores. Another tea shop was launched by George F. Gilman and George H. Hartford, who imported teas, coffees, and other products. Gilman and Hartford opened a retail tea store in New York City and also began selling tea through the mail. Their business would eventually evolve into the A&P grocery store chain.

Tearooms became common in New York during the late nineteenth century. These were largely owned, operated, and frequented by women, who saw these establishments as good alternatives to the saloons where men congregated. While a tearoom did not necessarily revolve around afternoon tea—most were ladies' lunchrooms, homey or elegant—tea was an important item on their menus. Tearooms became particularly popular during Prohibition as alternatives to the speakeasies, and they went out of fashion after Repeal in 1933.

Coffee arrived in New York not long after tea. In 1696, Lieutenant John Hutchins opened a coffeehouse called the King's Arms; it became the unofficial headquarters of English émigrés in New York. The first floor of the two-story wooden structure had a coffee bar and booths; the second floor contained rooms for public and private meetings. For years, it was the city's only coffeehouse. The Exchange Coffee House, probably located at the foot of Broad Street, opened by 1730. The Merchants Coffee House, at the end of Wall Street, opened in 1731. It promptly became the premier coffeehouse in New York; during the British occupation of the city during the Revolutionary War, it was the venue for auctioning off captured American vessels. In 1784, the Bank of New York was launched in the Merchants Coffee House, and it continued to be the place where public meetings were held and business deals were consummated until it burned down in 1804.

Several other coffeehouses were opened, the most important being the Tontine Coffee House at the corner of Wall and Water Streets, which opened in 1793. After the Merchants Coffee House burned down, the Tontine Coffee House became the most prominent in the city. Typically, coffeehouses sold hot chocolate and food as well as coffee and tea; in 1808, some added a new beverage—soda water.

Compared with making tea by simply pouring water over tea leaves, brewing coffee was a complicated process, which was one reason it took a while for coffee to catch on in New York. At first, unbranded, green coffee beans were sold from open barrels, scooped out by the customer or grocer and then weighed and priced. One New Yorker observed that exposed to air, odors, and dust, the beans, "from long transit and resting in the small stores, became tough and tasted as much of codfish and oil as [they] did of coffee." New Yorkers roasted the coffee beans at home and ground them as needed. Coffee roasting was an art, and roasting beans in a pan over a fireplace or even with a coffee roaster was unpredictable. For those who were skilled roasters, the coffee was flavorful and aromatic. For those less skilled, beans were scorched or underroasted and did not develop their full flavor. Home roasting of the beans often produced an acrid brew that had to be camouflaged with milk, cream, and sugar.

Tea, however, was more expensive, and coffee had a greater caffeine payload. In addition, tea had a lingering feminine association, while coffee quickly became the more "manly" choice. New Yorkers began to consume ever-increasing quantities of coffee, and the city became the center of America's coffee trade. By the early nineteenth century, supply could not keep up with demand. Coffee prices jumped from 42 cents per pound in 1810 to $1.08 in 1812. At the time, coffee was mainly grown on the Arabian Peninsula and on a few Caribbean islands, but as fortunes were made in the coffee trade, more plantations were established in Brazil and the Dutch colonies of Java and Sumatra. As they began to be imported into the city, coffee prices started to fall—to thirty cents per pound in 1823 and bottomed out at eight cents seven years later. While this decline in price hurt coffee producers, it was a boon to consumers. New Yorkers became hooked on coffee. When the federal government abolished import taxes on coffee in 1832, its consumption jumped even more. New York averaged three pounds of coffee per person in 1830; by 1840, this reached more than five pounds; and nine years later, it topped out at eight pounds. Coffee had surpassed tea as the city's hot beverage of choice.

Roasted coffee was also sold at retail in New York, but if it sat in the store for very long, it lost its flavor. New York inventor and manufacturer Jabez Burns addressed a key problem in coffee roasting—the fact that the beans rested directly on a hot surface, where they could quickly scorch. In 1864, Burns devised a screwlike device to keep the beans moving as they roasted. The equipment was too bulky and expensive for home use, but it was ideal for large-scale coffee-roasting operations.

Counterfeit and adulterated coffee was a common problem throughout the nineteenth century. In one 1881 study, Francis Thurber, a New York City grocery distributor, deplored "the adulteration of coffee and the vast scale on which it is practiced" and noted that despite what was being sold in many grocery stores, "a primary requisite for making a good cup of coffee is, of course, coffee." Thurber's efforts and those of others enticed newspapers to examine coffee adulteration; newspapers such as the *New York Times* alerted readers to these problems by publishing articles with headlines such as "Poison in Every Cup of Coffee."

Despite initial concerns with the stimulating qualities of coffee and tea, temperance advocates eventually concluded that these beverages were at least good alternatives to alcohol. Temperance coffeehouses, or "temperance drinking saloons," were opened to counter the ubiquitous bars and taverns. The coffeehouse offered a place where people could socialize without being tempted by strong drink. As one observer commented, "A coffee-house is a liquor saloon without liquor. It is a place where a workingman can get a well-cooked meal at a cheap rate, where he can read his newspaper and enjoy his game of chess or draughts without being preached at. It is the saloon, less the saloon's evil concomitants."

Growth of Bars and Grogshops

The precise origin of the word "bar," meaning a place where liquor is served, is obscure. Some historians have suggested that it emerged from the grog-shops commonly found in seaports in the eighteenth century, or in taverns.

Others believe that bars started in various kinds of retail stores, such as groceries, barber shops, and bakeries, where liquor was sold for off-premise consumption as a side business. Over time, the retail businesses declined and liquor became the main attraction. Spirits were stored in barred cages to prevent unauthorized access. When customers arrived, the proprietor opened a small window in the bars above the counter and poured drinks from a small selection of bottles. Early establishments had only a few common mugs used by all customers. Counters initially were just small wooden planks, but as time went on, the counters were enlarged to accommodate more drinkers, and the counters were renamed "bars." From their humble beginnings bars increased in size and attractiveness, the range of drinks they served diversified, and their accouterments became more refined.

New York's City Hotel, built in 1794, had a bar room off the lobby with a "liquor cage" so that the alcohol could be locked up when the bar was closed. The early nineteenth century saw a proliferation of great hotels in New York and such bars were de rigueur. Over time, bars were upgraded into much larger rooms with long hardwood (mahogany or oak) counters often adorned with intricate carving. Elaborate mirrors, more woodwork, and an impressive display of liquor bottles formed the "back bar" facing the drinkers. Counters sported brass foot rails and sometimes handrails, designed to accommodate standup drinking.

As bars became popular, a new profession emerged—the bartender. The first publicly acclaimed bartender was Orsamus Willard of the City Hotel. According to a British naval officer who stayed at the hotel in 1826,

> The entrance to the house is constantly obstructed by crowds of people passing to and from the bar-room, where a person presides at a buffet formed upon the plan of a cage. This individual is engaged, "from morn to dewy eve," in preparing and issuing forth punch and spirits to strange-looking men, who come to the house to read the newspapers and talk politics.

Willard, who lived at the hotel, was identified by another British visitor as a man "who never forgets the face of a customer." Willard served traditional wines, brandies, and spirits—but also concocted inventive assortments of mixed drinks. His most famous and popular beverage was the mint julep, which consisted of "four or five stalks of unbruised mint" combined with ice, brandy, water, and sugar. For his celebrated apple toddy, Willard rolled apples in wet brown paper and buried them "in live embers till they are thoroughly roasted and quite soft; then a fourth part of apples, a fourth part of brandy, a fourth part of water, a lump of ice, and the whole to be rich with a fourth part of sugar, makes the agreeable compound." His slings had a ratio of one-third rum, gin, or brandy to two-thirds water, sweetened with sugar and spiced with nutmeg. When Willard added bitters to the sling, it became a cocktail, as described by another English visitor.

The Metropolitan Hotel, which opened on Broadway in 1852, also had a fashionable bar. Its most prominent bartender was a man named Jerry Thomas, who about 1851 settled in New York, where he operated the first of his four bars, all of which received wide acclaim. In 1858, he tended bar at the Metropolitan Hotel, where he was particularly known for his flamboyant manner of mixing drinks, a style that would continue to be the model for future bartenders. Then Thomas did what no other bartender had done: he started writing down his recipes for publication. Commissioned by the New York publisher Dick & Fitzgerald, he assembled a collection that would be published in 1862 as *The Bar-Tender's Guide; or How to Mix Drinks*. For sophisticated New Yorkers the cocktail soon achieved stardom.

Swill Milk

Another important beverage in New York was milk. Shortly after New Amsterdam was founded, the Dutch imported cows, and dairy farming became an important occupation on the island of Manhattan. Unfortunately, the growth of the human population outpaced that of their dairy herds, leading Reverend Jonas Michaëlius to complain that milk "cannot here be obtained" except at "very high price." He urged the Dutch West India Company to send more farmers and dairymen to the colony. The Dutch complied, and the colonists were again able to enjoy an abundance of milk and other dairy products, as they had in the old country. Herds of dairy cattle flourished in New Amsterdam and in the Dutch settlements that grew up in Brooklyn.

In colonial days, many New York families kept their own cows. Some enterprising individuals tied cows to stakes in city streets and fed them garbage and then drank—or sold—the milk. Property owners charged for the privilege of herding cows on their streets. According to dairy historian John Dillon, "The disposition of the manure was a provision of the lease contract," and at the time there was an unlimited demand for manure to fertilize Manhattan's farms and gardens.

As the city's population grew, the demand for milk increased, and the business of distributing it became more profitable; dealers multiplied and competition became intense. In the 1820s, some ambitious New York City dairymen adopted a British system that exploited another popular beverage—beer—to support milk production. Eager to maximize profits from their operations, brewers built cow barns adjacent to their breweries. Mash, or slop—the watery by-product of brewing with grain—was siphoned from the brewery directly to cows' mangers through wooden chutes. By the 1830s, an estimated eighteen thousand cows in New York City and Brooklyn were being fed almost exclusively on brewery mash. Brewers saved money by not having to cart away the waste, and they enjoyed substantial profits from the sale of milk. They made additional profits by selling the cow manure to farmers, and when the cows died, they sold the carcasses to butchers.

Robert M. Hartley, the founder of the New York Temperance Society in 1829, investigated the city's brewing and distilling industries and concluded that milk production was one of their main profit centers. In fact, he concluded that the profits generated by the dairy operations were so substantial that, if they were eliminated, New York's alcohol industry would collapse. Hartley's investigation of the dairies generated some shocking discoveries: the dairies were poorly managed and badly kept, and the cows were frequently diseased—some to the point that they could not stand and had to be winched up for milking. The milk from brewery and distillery dairies was low in butterfat and extremely thin, with a pale bluish cast. Brewers and distillers (as well as other milk distributors) were known to adulterate milk to make it appear wholesome. They stretched it with water; brightened it up with powdered chalk, carrot juice, and annatto; broke in raw eggs for creaminess; and even sweetened the milk with molasses so children would ask for it.

Hartley suspected that poor quality and adulterated milk was the primary reason for New York City's steep increase in infant mortality during the 1830s. He launched a campaign against "swill milk" or "slop milk," publishing a series of pamphlets and articles opposing its sale. In 1842, he compiled his views in America's first book about milk, An Historical, Scientific, and Practical Essay on Milk, as an Article of Human Sustenance.

On the take from brewery and distillery owners, city officials ignored his campaign, and the number of breweries exploded in New York during the 1840s and 1850s, and so did the number of dairies. But Hartley's efforts had raised an alarm and caught the interest of newspapers, which began investigations of their own into the atrocious conditions in the dairies. In 1847, the New York Tribune reported on "one of the largest and filthiest swill milk stables and urged the city to act." Yet another series of exposés ran in the New York Evening Post during the early 1850s; newspaperman John Mullaly collected these articles in a book, which was published in 1853. The newly launched New York Times began featuring articles on swill milk in 1854. In 1858, Frank Leslie's Illustrated Newspaper "declared war" on the brewery dairies of Manhattan and Brooklyn. The first article, "Startling Exposure of Milk Trade of New York and Brooklyn!" reported that the stables surrounding the distilleries were "disgusting," "dilapidated and wretchedly filthy." The controversy heated up and turned violent when one of the newspaper's reporters was murdered while developing a story.

Despite the barrage of exposés, lectures, pamphlets, books, and newspaper and magazine articles, the sale of swill milk continued unabated. The brewing and distilling industries were just too ingrained in the municipal political system to permit anything more than superficial modifications to be mandated. It was not until 1896 that the city required milk purveyors to be licensed, established standards for milk, and hired inspectors to examine milk to ensure that dealers complied with the law. Large milk companies could more easily comply with these requirements, while many of their smaller competitors were driven out of business by the burden of the new regulations. But the end result was a relatively safe milk supply for the city.

The campaign against swill milk encouraged pure food laws in New York City and State. For almost three decades, national legislation was blocked by liquor industry lobbyists and those politicians on the take from the industry. This changed in 1906 when Upton Sinclair, a relatively unknown novelist, published *The Jungle*, an exposé of the meat industry in Chicago. Within months, the Pure Food and Drug Act and the Meat Inspection Act passed Congress.

Lager Beer

New Amsterdamers planted barley and wheat and brewed their own beer at home. The Dutch writer David Pietersz de Vries reported that "our Netherlanders raise good wheat, rye, barley, oats, and peas, and can brew as good beer here as in our Fatherland, for good hops grow in the woods; and they who make it their business can produce enough of those things, as everything can be grown which grows in Holland, England, or France." The first brewery opened in 1633. Oloff Stevensen van Cortlandt, progenitor of one of the city's most prominent and wealthy families, later acquired the brewery and enlarged it. Additional other breweries were established by other families as the city's population increased. In addition, large casks of beer, such as Bass ale, were imported.

During the early nineteenth century, beer production in New York declined in part because of the deteriorating quality of the city's water. German immigrants had opened new breweries in New York—the first as early as 1834. City brewers, who generated almost five hundred thousand dollars (more than one billion dollars today) in annual sales at the time, complained to the city government about the inadequate water supply. This concern, and others, encouraged the city to embark on a massive project to bring water to Manhattan from upstate via the Croton Aqueduct.

George Gillig had served apprenticeships in breweries in Bavaria before he immigrated to New York in 1836. Four years later, he opened a brewery on Lexington Avenue in 1840; he was reportedly the first New Yorker to brew lager beer, which was lighter bodied, less bitter, weaker, and fizzier than other beers and ales traditionally consumed in the city. Still, lager beer was popular among German immigrants from southern Germany, and Gillig opened two more breweries, one in Williamsburg, the other in Staten Island.

Other early German brewers included Joseph Doegler and Frederick and Maximilian Schaefer. Doegler, a Bavarian, arrived in New York in 1843 and began working in a brewery. He purchased Gillig's brewery in 1853. The Schaefers purchased the Sebastian Sommers brewery in New York City in 1842; six years later, they began marketing a lager beer under their own name. Franz Ruppert, who had come to New York from Göllheim, Germany, sometime before 1842, launched what would eventually become the Jacob Ruppert Brewing Company with his brother in Turtle Bay (in Manhattan on the East River) in 1851.

By 1854, New York had "twenty-seven breweries, and many of them, such as Turtle Bay, Gilley's, and Schaefer's, brew more than ten thousand barrels, of thirty gallons each, of lager beer in the course of the year," reported the *New York Tribune*. These breweries produced eighty-five thousand barrels, equivalent to thirty million gallons, which were distributed by two thousand retail outlets, independent of large hotels and restaurants. Other German breweries opened in Williamsburg in Brooklyn. By 1872, there were seventy lager breweries in New York.

The main outlet for lager beer was saloons owned or frequented by German immigrants. They also served German-style food, and some establishments provided a free lunch to those who bought beer. Lunches at German-owned saloons included foods like blutwurst, sausage, sardines, herring, ham, pig's feet, rye bread, hamburgers, roast beef, corned beef, onions, pumpernickel bread, salads, cheeses, crackers, bologna, and pretzels. At first it was just those saloons that catered to immigrants that served lager beer, and only Germans who drank it, but this soon changed. As lager beer rolled out of the local breweries, New Yorkers began flocking to places that served it. Other city saloons and bars soon jumped on the lager wagon. In September 1855, the *New York Times* reported that "a very large portion of the inhabitants of the City of New York, who a few months since, were in the habit of drinking one or more glasses of rum, gin or brandy, every day, are now using about the same number of glasses of lagerbier instead." Lager beer was an improvement, according to a reporter for the *New York Herald* who believed that the "increase in the use of lager beer will do more to overthrow drunkenness and rowdyism, and to establish good order on their ruins than all the labors and the efforts" of temperance advocates. By the 1860s, an estimated three to four thousand establishments sold lager beer in Manhattan alone, with many more in surrounding communities, and it was estimated that more than half of their patrons were not German immigrants. As one observer reported in the 1870s, "New Yorkers ran mad after it, and nothing was spoken of or drunk but Lager, or Logger beer, as it was more usually called."

In addition to serving beer in bars and saloons, many brewers set up their own beer gardens—large halls planted with trees and flowers; sometimes part of the ceiling or a wall could be opened to let in the sun in good weather. These beer gardens could hold as many as three to four thousand people at a time. Some were family oriented; others catered to the less-affluent immigrants. The largest beer garden in New York was the Atlantic Garden, reported a popular writer in 1872, an "immense room with a lofty curved ceiling, handsomely frescoed, and lighted by numerous chandeliers and by brackets along the walls. It is lighted during the day from the roof. At one side is an open space planted with trees and flowers, the only mark of a garden visible." The Atlantic Garden contained a restaurant, "several bars, a shooting gallery, billiard tables, bowling alleys, and an orchestra." Another observer wrote that there were "dense clouds of tobacco-smoke, and hurry of waiters, and banging of glasses, and calling for beer, but no rowdyism."

Beer gardens served a variety of functions other than drinking. They were social centers, concert halls, eating establishments, and athletic fields; civic, religious, and organizational meetings were held in them as well. Beer gardens were not just for German Americans; mainstream New Yorkers and immigrants from elsewhere frequented them as well.

Wine

Colonial New Yorkers imported a variety of wines, such as canary, port, sherry, and muscadine. Sack (fortified white wines from Spain and the Canary Islands) and hock or Hockheimer (German white wines) were also common by the late eighteenth century. Frequent hostilities between England and France during the colonial period made it difficult for New Yorkers to import French wines, but after the Revolutionary War, French wines were sold in the city. Particular favorites included claret, a dark French Bordeaux, Burgundy, and Champagne. Specialty wine stores opened. A Swiss-born sea captain named Giovanni Del-Monico sold his ship in 1824 and with the proceeds opened a wine shop in the city. His customers were mostly French-men and other European immigrants or foreign visitors. To maximize profits, Del-Monico imported casks of wine and did the bottling himself, but he wasn't satisfied with the business. He sold his wine shop in 1826 and returned to Switzerland to visit his family. There, he convinced his brother Pietro, a pastry chef, to return with him to New York and open a café and pastry shop. He sold his business and later with his brother opened Delmonico's res-taurant, which stocked French and other wines. By the 1830s, all high-end restaurants in the city served a wide range of imported wines.

Specialty stores, such as Acker Merrall & Condit that opened on Cham-bers Street in 1856, sold a wide range of imported wines to restaurants and well-to-do New Yorkers. (Acker Merrall & Condit has survived and claims to be the oldest wine store in America.) German immigrants sold wines from Germany in saloons, bars, beer gardens, and restaurants, and Italian immigrants imported and sold wines from Italy in grocery stores and Ital-ian restaurants. Jewish immigrants produced kosher wines that were sold in New York by the 1880s. California wines were sold in New York by the late nineteenth century, and New York State wineries began selling wine in the city shortly thereafter. Both tended to be cheap wines that targeted immigrant communities.

Wines continued to be imported, but an English visitor to America in 1878 reported that it was "very expensive, and it is only once in a while that it appears on the tables even of the rich—so seldom that it cannot be called a custom. Sherry, port, claret, madeira, and champagne are rare luxuries, and only appear on festive occasions, or in the houses of epicures and wealthy foreigners." Five years later, another British visitor, George Sala, was assured by Americans that "the custom of wine drinking would speedily fade out altogether from good society in America" due to the temperance movement.

The Temperance Movement

The temperance movement began in the late eighteenth century and slowly picked up steam in New York State during the early nineteenth century. The movement's popularity was understandable. According to one Brit-ish observer, the easy availability and low price of alcohol meant that "the people indulge themselves to excess, and run into all the extravagancies of inebriety." Temperance crusaders estimated that three-quarters of the crime and pauperism in New York City was related to liquor consumption.

The temperance movement in New York took off in the 1830s, when ad-vocates joined forces. They faced one very serious problem. If New Yorkers were not to drink alcoholic beverages, what would they drink? Public water fountains were constructed after the completion of the Croton Aqueduct in 1842; later, temperance and other groups funded the construction and maintenance of "ice-free" water fountains—particularly in public parks—where people could drink water without expense. Temperance advocates also encouraged restaurants to offer glasses of water to patrons when they sat down.

Yet another solution popped up from scientists. In the 1700s, they discovered that carbon dioxide was the source of the bubbles in natural springs, as well as the "fizz" in beer and champagne. By 1800, beverage manufacturers had discovered that they could produce their own fizzy water by adding a solution of sodium bicarbonate, thus creating carbonated water. However, the carbonation process was more commonly accomplished under high pressure using sulfuric acid, and manufacturing carbonated water this way was more difficult and dangerous. Workers could be seriously burned by the acid, and containers of charged soda water sometimes exploded. In 1809, Benjamin Silliman, a Yale chemistry professor, and a partner purchased costly soda-making equipment and opened two retail soda-water outlets, one at the City Hotel and the other at the Tontine Coffee House. He sold Ballston water (from an upstate spa), soda, or seltzer (plain carbonated water), which was made on the premises. An Irishman, George Usher, may have beaten them to it.

Soda water continued to be part of the New York beverage scene, especially after easier and safer ways of producing it were invented. By the mid-nineteenth century, vendors sold seltzer and ginger pop, spruce beer, mead, and other goodies. One New Yorker wrote about the soda vendors in the mid-nineteenth century:

> Their locale was almost universally designated by a sign, on which, for the mead and beer, was delineated a bottle with a stream of liquor pouring from it into a tumbler at its side, with a uniformity of outline and of curve that would have done credit to a geometrical draughtsman. The ginger pop was designated in a very different manner, being totally devoid of any illustration of convenience or economy; inasmuch as two men were portrayed as fulfilling the regulations of a duel, being placed opposite to each other and each extending a bottle, from which emanated a stream of liquor propelling a cork, which was as the bullet of a pistol.

During the late nineteenth century, soda fountains emerged. The temperance movement supported them as an alternative to bars. Plain soda was cheap at two cents per glass; with flavorings it cost a nickel, which virtually everyone could afford. On Wall Street stood Delatour's soda-water stand,

and during the summers Delatour dispensed drinks to long lines of custom-ers. Soda fountains competed to offer the most flavor selections. One offered thirty-two different syrups, eight kinds of mineral water, and soda water. By 1891, New York had more soda fountains than it had bars.

A large variety of flavorings and ingredients were combined with soda. During the 1880s, a popular specialty was made with chocolate syrup, cream, and raw eggs mixed into soda water. In poorer neighborhoods, a less expen-sive version of this treat was created called the Egg Cream (made without the eggs or cream), which remains an iconic New York beverage.

Most temperance advocates concluded that these worthwhile alternatives to alcoholic beverages were not enough to rid the city of excessive drinking. They turned to stronger measures.

Prohibition

Despite widespread support for Prohibition in upstate New York, most New Yorkers strongly opposed it. Liquor was an important business in the city: an 1897 survey of the borough of Manhattan found a ratio of one liquor distributor to every 208 residents. Saloons were also an important base of support for Tammany Hall's political machine, which had controlled the city government since 1854.

During and after the Civil War, even more saloons and bars opened, and there was no shortage of customers. One of the few victories of the New York temperance movement was achieved in 1866 when, prompted by temper-ance advocates, the city banned the sale of liquor on Sunday. This caused Germans immigrants to rally, proclaiming, "Liberty and Lagerbier!" Others just crossed the Hudson River to New Jersey, where there were plenty of breweries, beer gardens, and saloons open on Sundays. Still others went to saloons and bars that continued to serve alcohol on Sunday despite the new law. Ignoring this law set a precedent and served as a model for responding to legislation restricting alcoholic consumption that continued right up to— and through—Prohibition in the 1920s.

By 1870, Manhattan had 7,071 licensed suppliers of liquor and probably an even greater number of illegal establishments. The free lunches offered on bar counters were a strong draw for workingmen—all they had to do was buy a drink, and they could eat their fill. Hot lunches were served from 11:00 a.m. to 3:00 p.m. A choice of "pea soup, chowder, bean soup, lamb stew, beef stew, pork and beans, etc." was offered by one New York saloonkeeper. "There were some ten plates of cold lunch besides, consisting of bologna, liver sausage, spiced fish, pickled herring, smoked or shredded fish, sliced

cabbage, onion, bread pretzels, potato salad, radishes, etc." Free lunches en-
sured that customers acquired the habit of drinking liquor at noon, and this
helped to develop a regular clientele for saloons and bars. Moreover, the food
served at saloons was often salty, which increased the desire to drink more
alcohol, which, of course, was where the bars made their profits.

The New York State legislature tried to restrict drinking in 1896, when it
passed the Raines Law, banning the sale of liquor on Sunday. But the law had
a good-sized loophole: alcohol could be sold with meals in hotels with more
than ten rooms. Within months, hundreds of "Raines hotels" were in operation, and many of these also served as brothels. Other drinking establishments began reopening on Sundays, but the authorities usually ignored them
provided they kept a low profile. A survey of Manhattan and Bronx saloons
in 1908 found that 5,000 of the 5,820 legal saloons served alcohol on Sunday. This should have given Prohibition advocates an inkling of problems
to come, but little attention was paid to enforcement at the time—or later.

The Anti-Saloon League, the main national lobbying organization for
Prohibition, considered New York City the "liquor center of America," and
their literature cited statistics proclaiming that *every week* people in the city
consumed 75,000 quarts of gin, 76,000 quarts of brandy, 100,000 quarts of
champagne and wine, 498,000 quarts of whiskey, 33 million quarts of domestic beer and ale, and 300,000 quarts of assorted other alcoholic beverages. If
accurate, New Yorkers—and visitors—were downing an awful lot of alcohol.

Despite strong pro-drinking forces in New York City, the Eighteenth
Amendment, which outlawed the manufacture, sale, transportation, and
importation of alcohol in the United States, became the law of the land
at the stroke of midnight on January 16, 1920. The National Prohibition
Act, commonly known as the Volstead Act, had an immediate effect: the
consumption of liquor dropped off immediately. Saloons disappeared, never
to reopen. Public drunkenness sharply declined, and hospitals dealt with far
fewer of the medical problems associated with drinking and alcoholism. Still,
it remained fairly easy to acquire alcohol all through Prohibition in New
York. The main alcohol distributor became the speakeasy, a shady operation
usually located in a dark and poorly ventilated cellar or a hidden back room.
It supposedly acquired its name because customers spoke quietly about such
places in public and when inside so as not to alert the authorities. Customers
achieved admission only after proper scrutiny by guards who checked out all
comers by eyeing them through a peephole in the door. The liquor at speakeasies, sold at inflated prices, was of dubious origin and notoriously harsh,
foul tasting, and sickening.

Prior to Prohibition, saloons, bars, and other drinking establishments were stocked with the products manufactured by commercial breweries, distilleries, and vintners, whose practices were regulated. The alcohol served in speakeasies, however, was made by amateurs; "bathtub gin" was not just a figure of speech. Spirits were sometimes made with poisonous wood alcohol. Imported liquor was available but only at extremely high prices, and a lot of what was sold as imported spirits was actually domestic bootleg liquor poured into fancy bottles with fake labels. Customers never knew where their drinks came from or what they were made from. In one year alone, the deaths of 625 New Yorkers were directly attributable to ingesting poisoned alcohol and another 1,200 to alcohol-related causes.

The major flaw in Prohibition was enforcement. The federal government allocated only 4.75 million dollars for enforcement throughout the United

New York City Deputy Police Commissioner watching agents pour liquor into sewer following a raid during the height of Prohibition. Courtesy of the Library of Congress. Reproduction Number: LC-USZ62-123257

States, and only 129 federal enforcement agents were assigned to New York City. The framers of the Eighteenth Amendment assumed that local and state police would also uphold the law. But many state and local agencies lacked the trained manpower to do so; nor did they have the ability to deal with the wave of organized crime that Prohibition engendered.

New York City police were particularly lax in enforcing the liquor ban. The New York State legislature passed the Mullan-Gage Act on April 5, 1921, which made violations of the Volstead Act also violations of state law, requiring state and local police to enforce federal law. According to Samuel Hopkins Adams, a writer for Collier's, "Restaurants, private houses, blind tigers, and the hip pocket of the casual wayfarer were raided with a disconcerting impartiality. A baby carriage, even, was held up and found to harbor a bottle which did not contain milk." During the first two months after the passage of the Mullan-Gage Act, four thousand New Yorkers were arrested for violating it; however, less than five hundred were indicted, only six were convicted, and not one received a prison term. When Al Smith, an ardent opponent of Prohibition, became governor of New York in 1923, the bill was repealed.

From that time on, the city's police generally declined to arrest anyone as long as liquor distributors were unobtrusive and bribed them and city officials on time. The lack of effective enforcement gave speakeasies free rein, and by 1922 there were an estimated five thousand illegal booze joints in the city. When organized crime began centralizing the illegal manufacture, distribution, and retail sales of liquor, money and power flowed to the crime syndicates. As New Yorkers increasingly flouted Prohibition, a generation came of age with little respect for the law.

Wealthier New Yorkers never felt that the Volstead Act was intended for them anyway; people with plenty of cash had no problem securing bootlegged wines, liquors, brandies, or any other alcoholic beverages throughout the Prohibition era. They socialized with their peers at private cocktail parties throughout Prohibition. The urban middle class also had access to alcohol through speakeasies, and if they chose, they could (and did) experiment with apparatuses required for making bathtub gin. It was the working class and the poor who suffered most during Prohibition. The favored drink of less-privileged Americans—beer—was almost unobtainable: the raw ingredients were bulky, brewing required a lot more space than distilling or concocting spirits, and the finished product came in big wooden barrels, much harder to conceal than glass bottles. In rural areas, the time-honored art of moonshining went into high gear, with tens of thousands of illegal stills turning out "white lightning." Many minority groups in New York City, such as Italian and Jewish immigrants, did not believe that drinking was immoral, and they did not believe it should be illegal. They also knew that fortunes could be made providing liquor, and many bootleggers and underworld bosses came from these groups.

In 1929, the New York City police commissioner estimated that the city had thirty-two thousand speakeasies—double the number of all establishments serving alcohol (legally or otherwise) prior to Prohibition. Others said that the commissioner's estimate was far off— there were really one hundred thousand speakeasies in the city. Mabel Willebrandt, the U.S. assistant attorney general responsible for prosecuting violations of the Volstead Act, commented on the lawlessness in New York's speakeasies: "It can not truthfully be said that prohibition enforcement has failed in New York. It has not yet been *attempted*."

As the violence of organized crime increased, newspapers, magazines, radio programs, and movie-theater newsreels kept Americans, even in rural areas, apprised of the latest murders, shootings, and arrests associated with illegal alcohol. Prohibition agents earned $1,800 per year, and New York City police officers even less. Both could supplement their income substantially by accepting bribes, and many did. As enforcement efforts faltered, Congress stepped in and passed the Jones Act, which greatly increased the penalties for violating the Volstead Act. The first conviction was a felony, with a maximum penalty of five years imprisonment and a ten-thousand-dollar fine. Even with such harsh provisions in place, enforcement couldn't keep a lid on the liquor trade. The Jones Act did alienate many prominent Americans, and opposition to Prohibition strengthened. In 1929, Pauline Sabin, a wealthy and politically well-connected New York socialite who occasionally sipped alcoholic beverages, formed the Women's Organization for National Prohibition Reform. In less than a year it counted more than one hundred thousand members; by 1931, its membership had reached three hundred thousand; and by the time of the presidential election in November 1932, it had more than 1.1 million members.

Despite growing opposition to the Volstead Act, widespread disregard for its provisions, and the associated violent crime and corruption, the Eighteenth Amendment might not have been repealed had it not been for the Depression. Republicans had strongly associated themselves with Prohibition, while many Democrats, especially Catholics, Jews, and those of Irish, Italian, and German origin, strongly opposed it. When the New York stock market crashed in 1929 and the economic system collapsed, the Republicans, who had controlled Congress since 1919 and the presidency since 1921, were blamed. In November 1932, President Herbert Hoover lost his reelection bid and the Democrats swept into power with large majorities in both houses of Congress. President Franklin Delano Roosevelt, former governor of New York, pledged to get the economy moving again, and repeal of Prohibition was part of his plan. Roosevelt and his allies presented repeal as a means of generating revenue. Reinstating the excise tax on the sale of liquor was thus one argument for ending Prohibition. Others argued that repeal would relaunch industries that had once employed hundreds of thousands of Americans. Still others believed that repeal would help put an end to the burgeoning crime generated by the illegal production and sale of alcohol. On February 20, 1933, the U.S. Congress approved the Twenty-first Amendment repealing Prohibition. The Amendment was ratified by enough states, and on December 5, 1933, the "noble experiment," as it was called, ended. Throughout the city, countless toasts were raised to repeal.

Beverage Diversity

Since Prohibition, New Yorkers have enjoyed a diversity of beverages. New York coffeehouses thrived during the 1960s, when they were frequent gathering places for poets, writers, beatniks, and counterculture, but later they began to disappear. They were not resurrected in New York until the arrival of Starbucks, Stumptown Coffee, and other premium coffee vendors.

The commercial production of wine began in New York State in the nineteenth century, and California wineries exported wine to New York beginning by the early twentieth century; these wines tended to be generic, cheap, and low quality and thus were the perfect beverage for the poor and alcoholics. They found few customers among the middle- and upper-class New Yorkers, who, if they drank wine, continued to consume imported wine from Europe.

Ironically, legal wine consumption skyrocketed during Prohibition. Wineries legally supplied wine to Catholics and Jews who consumed it for religious reasons. For everyone else, wineries manufactured nonalcoholic grape juice with instructions on how to convert it into wine. It was legal to make wine at home, and many New Yorkers gave it a try. The homemade stuff filled a void during Prohibition, but with repeal, wine consumption plummeted as other alcoholic beverages became available again.

As fine French restaurants flourished in New York City, so did the sale of imported European wines. Specialty wine shops, such as Acker Merrall & Condit (founded in 1856), Sherry-Lehmann Wine & Spirits (founded in 1934), and Astor Wines & Spirits (founded in 1946), broadened their selections and increased their supplies to meet the needs of restaurants and well-to-do New Yorkers. During the 1960s, California wines came of age, equaling and sometimes surpassing French vintages. New York State wines also improved, and both are now regular offerings in restaurants and liquor stores.

Growing interest in wine led the *New York Times* to assign a weekly wine columnist, Frank Prial, in 1972. In 1976, Kevin Zraly first offered his comprehensive wine course at Windows on the World, the restaurant on the 107th floor of the World Trade Center; the course is still offered, now at a midtown hotel. Today, wines are imported into New York from around the world and around the country, and New Yorkers are enthusiastic and well-informed wine drinkers.

New York's brewing industry did not return to business as usual after Prohibition's end. Many New York breweries did not reopen. Still, as late as 1962, New York City produced 10 percent of the beer consumed in America, but brewing in the city was a dying industry. The Jacob Ruppert Brewing Company survived until 1965. In 1969, Schlitz closed its Brooklyn plant, and Schaeffer's, the city's last large brewery, closed in 1976. But during the following decade, brewing revived. In 1984, the Manhattan Brewing Company opened in a Soho restaurant. Three years later, the New Amsterdam Brewing Company began producing beer in Manhattan. Although they did not survive for long, they revived New Yorkers' interest in locally made beer. The Manhattan Brewery in Soho opened in 1984. Today Manhattan sports two breweries (Chelsea Brewing Company, at Chelsea Piers, and 508 Greenwich, a restaurant where the proprietor makes his own beer); Brooklyn, three (Brooklyn, Sixpoint, and KelSo); and Queens, one (SingleCut). The Greenpoint Beer Works in Brooklyn's Clinton Hill brews beer at Heartland Brewery, a chain of seven brewpubs in Manhattan launched in 1995. The Brooklyn Brewing Company brewed its first beer in 1996 and today is the city's largest brewery.

Soda continued to be bottled in New York. The Pepsi-Cola Bottling Company in College Point, Queens, continues to bottle soda, and its bottles have "New York" printed on top. Soda fountains closed after World War II, but several have opened recently in all five boroughs.

Not everyone was happy with sugary soda. In 2013, the city forbade the sale of sugary drinks in containers larger than sixteen ounces in restaurants, movie theaters, and other eating places. This has been challenged in court and may not take effect, but it has made New Yorkers aware that sugary sodas contain a large amount of calories. As of this writing, the decision has been appealed and it is still in the courts.

Some New Yorkers developed new, nonalcoholic beverages. In 1972, three entrepreneurs launched a very small company, called the Unadulterated Food Products, Inc., in Brooklyn. They sold fruit juices, sodas,

Heartland Brewery in Union Square, Manhattan, 2013. Courtesy of Kelly Fitzsimmons

and seltzers in wide-mouth bottles. The products were sold in health food stores, promoted with the slogan "Made from the best stuff on Earth." This "new age" marketing approach was highly successful, and the company marketed other beverages, such as lemonade. In 1988, Unadulterated Food Products launched its first flavored tea. In 1993, the company changed its name to the Snapple Beverage Company. Now part of the large multinational Dr. Pepper Snapple Group, it has high international sales—and burgeoning competition.

Still other New Yorkers have opened juice bars. In 1996, Doug Green opened Liquiteria in the East Village. He served raw, cold-press juices, and he promptly became the guru of the juice movement. Others, such as Denise Mari and Doug Evans of Organic Avenue, jumped on the juice wagon. National chains, such as Jamba Juice and Red Mango, have opened outlets in the city. Today, hundreds of establishments offer juice and smoothies to New Yorkers.

CHAPTER SIX

~

Eateries

To a stranger, New-York must seem to be perpetually engaged in eating. Go where you will between the hours of 8 in the morning and 6 in the evening, and you are reminded that man is a cooking animal. Tables are always spread; knives and forks are always rattling against dishes; the odors of the kitchen are always rising. Is the appetite of the Metropolis ever appeased?

This was how the reporter and author Junius Henri Browne introduced his chapter on restaurants in his *Great Metropolis: A Mirror of New York* (1869). The only difference between then and now is that in the city that never sleeps, it also never stops eating. It didn't start out this way.

Taverns and Gardens

The city's first commercial eating establishments were taverns. Drinking, of course, was their primary function—eating was an afterthought. The sale of alcoholic beverages was where taverns made their main profits—just as it is in most New York restaurants today. The City Tavern may have been New Amsterdam's first tavern. Constructed in 1643, it was a two-story building with a basement. It could house several travelers and occasionally prisoners. It was also a place of business where public and private deals were transacted. In addition to selling beer, wine, and brandy, it also sold food, although precisely what kind of food has not survived. Other taverns were soon constructed, one by a Frenchman who named it The White Horse, a name that will be commonly employed by subsequent taverns. Another was opened by a Metje Wessels, whose "eating house" served beer and wine in 1656, and it became the place for dinners and festivities. Precisely what was served was not recorded. The exception was the terrapin, which was noted as one of the most popular dishes. Perhaps the Dutchman Adriaen van der Donck was referring to this when he wrote in 1655, "Some persons prepare delicious dishes from the water terrapin which is luscious food."

Traditionally, American taverns were licensed to sell wine for consumption on the premises; inns were licensed to lodge travelers and to sell beer and ale. Over time, these distinctions broke down—taverns also lodged travelers, and both taverns and inns sold beer, ale, wine, and cider. By the early eighteenth century, rum was the prevailing beverage served in taverns. Higher-class establishments also offered coffee, tea, and chocolate. Taverns also served food. Unlike restaurants, which arrived in America in the early nineteenth century and provided menus (or bills of fare, or whatever they were), taverns served whatever was available, and diners usually had little or no choice as to their victuals.

Dutch taverns survived the English takeover of the city, but English taverns soon outnumbered them. Some, such as those operated by Roger Baker, Michael Howden, and John Parmyter, served the gentry. Elias Chardavoine's victualing house served French food, something that was quite unusual at the time. France, of course, was known for its haute cuisine, which was greatly appreciated by England's wealthy, but most Americans considered it effete and a waste of money.

By the 1730s, the social life of the city revolved around taverns, one of which invited diners to sample "the most Dishes of Meat" in the "best Order," and "drink the richest Wine," according to a newspaper advertisement. In 1775, Edward Bardin's tavern served "Roast Beef, Veal, Mutton, Lamb, Ducks and Chickens, Gammon, Lobsters, Pickled Oysters, Custards, and Tarts of Different Kinds. Chicken Pies ready for Supper every night. Tea and Coffee every afternoon." The number of taverns and other alcohol sellers increased rapidly as the population grew.

The upper classes, particularly those engaged in businesses, frequented coffeehouses. In 1696, Lieutenant John Hutchins opened a coffeehouse called the King's Arms; it became the unofficial headquarters of English émigrés in New York. Many more coffeehouses were opened in New York City during the early eighteenth century, serving good food as well as beverages.

Some taverns sported "gardens," offering summertime entertainment—fireworks, concerts, plays, and outdoor dining. A 1763 advertisement for the "Spring Gardens" offered the "best of green tea &c. Hot French rolls will be provided. N. B. Pies and tarts will be drawn from 7 in the evening till 9, where gentlemen and ladies may depend on good attendance; the best of Madeira, mead, cakes, &c." The most popular tavern garden was Vauxhall, named for the garden in London. It offered "Reception of Ladies, Gentlemen, etc., and will be illuminated every evening in the Week; Coffee, Tea, and Hot Rolls at any hour in the day, neat Wines and other Liquors, with Cakes."

The city's most famous early garden was constructed by William Niblo, an Irish immigrant, who, in 1823, purchased the grounds of a small circus, called "The Stadium," at the corner of Broadway and Prince Street. There he opened Niblo's Garden, featuring a restaurant and concerts. It quickly became one of the most important eating establishments. Particularly popular was its ice cream and its sherry cobblers, which were sipped throughout the gardens. The British aristocrat and philosopher Thomas Hamilton dined at Niblo's in 1833 and described his meal of "oyster soup, shad, venison, partridges, grouse, wild-ducks of different varieties, and several other dishes."

Taverns thrived well into the nineteenth century, but their functions— drinking, eating, and sleeping—were increasingly replaced by hotels, bars, saloons, boardinghouses, and independent restaurants. Taverns survived well into the twentieth century, but by then, they were little different than saloons and bars of the time. Some taverns became quite popular and famous: the White Horse Tavern in Greenwich Village was frequented by writers, actors, poets, counterculture leaders, and political activists in the 1950s and 1960s; and the Stonewall Inn tavern, also in Greenwich Village, is credited with launching the gay rights movement in America in 1969.

Hotel Dining

The nation's first luxury hotel was New York's City Hotel, built in 1794. For almost half a century the four-story, block-long hostelry on lower Broadway was New York's premier inn, the place where wealthy and celebrated visitors stayed when they visited the city. The hotel operated on the American plan, where guests paid both for rooms and all meals (in contrast to the "European plan," which included breakfast only). Manhattan businessmen ate dinner or had tea in the hotel's dining room. Dinners often included choices of twelve to sixteen meat, poultry, or seafood dishes along with vegetables and fruit.

By the mid-1830s many New York hotel dining rooms were serving *la haute cuisine française*. At the Globe Hotel at 66 Broadway, customers enjoyed "excellent French cookery," according to an English visitor. He was even more taken with the food at the palatial Astor House, which employed

Astor House, Broadway and Vesey Streets in New York City, 1907. Courtesy of the Library of Congress. Reproduction Number: LC-DIG-ds-01872

French chefs to run its dining rooms. Menus were incredible as illustrated by the Astor's "Table-d' Hôtel" for Wednesday, March 21,1838:

Vermicelli Soup
Boiled Cod Fish and Oysters
Boiled Corn'd Beef
Boiled Ham
Boiled Tongue
Boiled Turkey and Oysters
Boiled Chickens and Pork
Boiled Leg of Mutton Oyster Pie
Cuisse de Poulet Sauce Tomate
Poitrine de Veau au Blanc
Salade de Volaille
Ballon de Mouton au Tomate
Téte de Veau au Marinade
Casserolle de Fomme de Terre garnie

Compote de Pigeon
Rolleau de Veau à la Jardiniere
Côtelettes de Veau Sauté
Filet de Mounton Piqué aux Ognons
Ronde de Bœuf
Fricandeau de Veau aux Epinards
Côtelettes de Mouton Panée
Macaroni au Parmesan
Roast Beef
Roast Pig
Roast Veal
Roast Leg of Mutton Roast Goose
Roast Turkey
Roast Chickens
Roast Wild Ducks
Roast Wild Goose
Roast Guinea Fowl
Roast Brandt
Queen Pudding
Mince Pie
Cream Puffs
Dessert.

When the Astor House opened, guests paid three dollars per week for room and full board. Its bar was one of the largest in the city, and it offered a prodigious free lunch for all customers who bought drinks. Not surprisingly, the prices escalated rapidly as well-to-do foreign visitors discovered the hotel.

The success of the Astor House encouraged others to build luxury hotels. At the former site of Niblo's Garden on Broadway at Prince Street, Stephen Van Rensselaer built the Metropolitan Hotel in 1852. Its restaurant became one of the most important in the city. The St. Nicholas Hotel was built on Broadway at Broome Street and cost the unheard of price of one million dollars. It had two dining rooms and two taprooms. In the dining rooms, one English visitor in 1856 was amazed at the number and variety of dishes and beverages from which diners could choose:

Two soups, two kinds of fish, ten boiled dishes, nine roast dishes, six relishes, seventeen entries, three cold dishes, five varieties of game, thirteen varieties of vegetables, seven kinds of pastry, and seven fruits, with ice-cream and coffee. The wines numbered eight brands of Madeira, seventeen of sherry, eighteen of champagne, six of port, four of Burgundy, twenty of hock, sixteen of claret, six sauternes, nine varieties of brandy, three liqueurs, and Scotch ale, India pale-ale, and London porter.

The Fifth Avenue Hotel facing Madison Square surpassed all hotels in New York when it was completed in 1859, and its menu at its restaurant was impressive. Its culinary delights, however, were topped with the completion of New York's most famous hotel and restaurants at the Waldorf Astoria Hotel, which started as two separate hotels. William Astor, the grandson of John Jacob Astor, built the Waldorf Hotel in 1893 on Fifth Avenue and Thirty-fourth Street. Four years later, his cousin, John Jacob Astor III, built the Astoria Hotel on a lot adjacent to the Waldorf. A corridor between the two hotels was constructed, and the complex became known as the Waldorf Astoria; it is generally referred to, however, as the Waldorf.

The Waldorf was particularly famous for its dining rooms. One reason was a Swiss immigrant, Oscar Tschirky, who arrived in New York in 1883 and worked as a busboy at Hoffman House and later waited tables at Delmonico's. Before long he became head of the restaurant's catering department, where he became popular with some of New York's most famous people. Tschirky joined the staff at the Waldorf two months before it opened. His management skills helped launch the hotel's restaurants. He was put in charge of its private dining rooms, which were frequented by the city's most famous people, such as the financier J. P. Morgan, the actress Lillian Russell, and the wealthy, overweight businessman and gourmet Diamond Jim Brady. Tschirky made a point of remembering what important guests preferred to eat and drink. His success in the dining rooms elevated him to the position of hotel steward responsible for supplying and preparing all the restaurants with provisions, and he managed all of the restaurant staff, including thirty-five chefs and hundreds of employees. The restaurants served French cuisine, and Oscar, as he was called (because most Americans were unable to pronounce his last name, he asserted in his autobiography), proclaimed that eating at the Waldorf was just as good as eating in a top Parisian restaurant.

Tschirky instituted a number of changes at the hotel that were later adopted by other restaurants. Traditionally, upper-class menus were written in French; the Waldorf's menus were written in English, although a bilingual menu was available on request. It was not the first restaurant in America to do so, but other city restaurants soon followed its lead. Another change was in the number of items listed on the menu. Some haute cuisine restaurant menus had reached gargantuan proportions, weighing in at a thousand items. Tschirky maintained the quality of the French food served at the hotel but

DINNER

MONDAY, OCTOBER 19, 1903

BLUE POINT OYSTERS   LITTLE NECK CLAMS

SOUPS
MUTTON BROTH   HOT OR COLD CONSOMME   PURÉE OF TOMATOES

HORS D'ŒUVRE
STUFFED OLIVES   CROMESQUI OF TERRAPIN À LA BALTIMORE   TOMATOES
RADISHES   CELERY   OLIVES

FISH
BOILED LIVE CODFISH, EGG SAUCE   FRIED SMELTS, TARTAR SAUCE
POTATOES, PARISIENNE   CUCUMBERS

BOILED
TURKEY, SHRIMP SAUCE   BEEF TONGUE, ROBERT SAUCE
HAM AND SPINACH   CORNED BEEF AND CABBAGE

ROAST
RIBS OF BEEF   LOIN OF VEAL, TOMATO SAUCE   SPRING GOSLING
YOUNG CHICKEN   HAM, CHAMPAGNE SAUCE   TURKEY, CRANBERRY SAUCE

ENTREES
FRICASSEE OF CHICKEN, COUNTRY STYLE
HAMBURG STEAK AU JUS   LOIN OF PORK BRAISE À LA ROUENNAISE
APPLE FRITTERS GLACÉ, RUM SAUCE

LEMON SHERBET

GAME
MALLARD DUCK   GROUSE, CURRANT JELLY

COLD
BONED CAPON   PÂTE DE FOIE-GRAS   MEATS   PICKLED LAMBS' TONGUES

SALADS
CHICKEN   LOBSTER   POTATO   LETTUCE

VEGETABLES
BOILED POTATOES   MASHED POTATOES   BOILED SWEET POTATOES
BOILED SPANISH ONIONS   BRUSSELS SPROUTS   BEETS   GREEN CORN ON COB
MARROW SQUASH   CHOPPED SPINACH   MASHED TURNIPS
STEWED TOMATOES   CORN FRITTERS   NEW STRING BEANS
FRIED EGG PLANT   CAULIFLOWER AU GRATIN

RICE   SPAGHETTI A LA NAPOLITAINE

PASTRY
ALBION PUDDING, WINE SAUCE
PLAIN RICE PUDDING   SLICED APPLE PIE
COCOANUT PIE   BLANC-MANGE   WAFER JUMBLES
ASSORTED CAKES

DESSERT
FROZEN MARRON PUDDING   VANILLA AND PISTACHE ICE CREAM
ASSORTED NUTS   RAISINS   PINEAPPLE   ORANGES   BANANAS
PLUMS   APPLES   PEARS   PEACHES AND CREAM
NIAGARA GRAPES   CONCORD GRAPES   DELAWARE GRAPES   TOKAY GRAPES

PHILADELPHIA CREAM, ROQUEFORT, EDAM, BRIE AND MILD CHEESE
COFFEE   TEA

Menu from the Fifth Avenue Hotel, 1903. Courtesy of the Library of Congress.
Digital id: rbpe 1310100a http://hdl.loc.gov/loc.rbc/rbpe.1310100a

Palm Court dining room at the Waldorf Astoria Hotel, circa 1902. Courtesy of the Library of Congress. Reproduction Number: LC-DIG-ds-02798

simplified the menu and decreased the number of courses served. Other city restaurants soon followed his lead with this innovation as well.

In January 1907, the Waldorf Astoria made a bold move—it put up a sign on the hotel's bulletin board announcing that "ladies without escort will be served in the restaurants at any hour." This broke an unwritten rule of ignoring single women who sat down at its restaurants. Upper-class restaurants had "discouraged" unescorted women diners. Waiters ignored them and refused to take their orders. This policy, of course, did not apply to wealthy women known at the restaurants. Women could dine in private meeting rooms at hotels and restaurants. On April 20, 1868, the city's prominent women intentionally met at Delmonico's large meeting room on its second floor and formed the Sorosis Club, the nation's first club for professional women. It sent a shock wave through the city, but the club continued to meet, usually for lunch at meeting rooms of high-end restaurants, such as the Waldorf Astoria.

The Waldorf restaurants were the first upper-class eateries in the city to announce that single women could dine alone, and strong public pressure forced them to reverse this policy shortly after they made it, but it did begin public discussion and some eateries changed. At the time, single women could dine at tea rooms and at the Women's Lunch Club, where exotic salads and "ice cream overpoured with maple syrup and walnuts, and other innovations of endless charm" were served, reported a writer. In 1909, women shoppers were served lunches "with expedition and sometimes with courtesy" on the top floors of department stores. When the Nineteenth Amendment to the Constitution granted women the right to vote in 1920, single women demonstrated their freedom by visiting speakeasies, nightclubs, and restaurants throughout the city, including the Waldorf.

The Waldorf influenced what Americans ate. The hotel restaurants popularized chafing dishes, which they used to prepare two of their iconic dishes: chicken à la king and lobster Newburg. Neither of these dishes originated at the Waldorf, but it did originate the "Waldorf salad," consisting of chopped celery, apples, and mayonnaise, artistically arranged on a bed of lettuce. Walnuts and other items were added later. It quickly became popular throughout the nation, as did "Oscar" sauce, a sauce that the hotel bottled and sold.

Prohibition closed most of New York's haute cuisine restaurants; the Waldorf restaurants did survive, but they did not thrive. Tschirky believed that "Prohibition ruined fine cooking and robbed America of some of its most distinctive native dishes," such as terrapin stew and lobster Newburg, for the well-to-do who could afford these dishes and were not interested in them without accompanying alcohol.

The owners of Waldorf and Astoria agreed in 1929 to move their hotels to make way for the Empire State Building and to relocate to Park Avenue, where the now merged Waldorf Astoria Hotel was even grander than their previous incarnations. It had three dining rooms, one of which was the Palm Court, where Tschirky served as maître d'hôtel until he retired in 1943. His influence survived as other restaurateurs studied and copied his mode of operating.

Oyster Saloons

Oysters were one of New York's most prominent and cherished foods. From the earliest colonial days, vendors sold them on the streets. Small wagons provided New Yorkers with oysters, "biscuits, pepper, and ginger beer; in short, for a few pence, the carter or mechanic has a whet which might satisfy even a gourmand." Others sold oysters flavored by ketchup for a penny apiece from "rude huts, paralytic shanties" along the East River. Those who frequented "these al fresco oyster-houses are longshoremen, truckmen, stevedores, sailors, and others of that ilk, and a very large bowl of oyster soup, not stew, can be obtained for 5 cents." Others sold oysters from "floating-houses," which preserved live oysters for several days by placing them in baskets in the cellar and attic of the oyster boat.

A step up from the floating houses were a large number of "oyster saloons," "oyster and coffee saloons," and "oyster and lager beer saloons." They were mainly constructed in cellars and typically identified themselves with balloons made of "bright red muslin stretched over a globular frame of rattan or wire and was illuminated at night by a candle placed within." Most oysters were served raw, but some were cooked in various ways. Many establishments were on the "canal street plan," which meant that you could eat as many oysters as you liked for twelve cents. By 1835, an estimated five thousand New Yorkers were engaged in retailing oysters.

Rumors abounded that bartenders gave spoiled oysters to those who ate too many.

Charles Dickens, visiting New York in 1842, wrote that he considered such places "pleasant retreats" with "wonderful cookery of oysters, pretty nigh as large as cheese plates." Another British visitor reported that "there is scarcely a square without several oyster-saloons; they are aboveground and underground, in shanties and palaces. They are served in every imaginable style escolloped, steamed, stewed, roasted, 'on the half shell,' eaten raw with pepper and salt, devilled, baked in crumbs, cooked in *pates*, put in delicious sauces on fish and boiled mutton."

According to Scottish poet and journalist Charles Mackay who visited New York in 1859, the oysters were

> cooked in twenty, or, perhaps in forty or a hundred, different ways. Oysters pickled, stewed, baked, roasted, fried, and scolloped; oysters made into soups, patties, and puddings; oysters with condiments and without condiments; oysters for breakfast, dinner, and supper; oysters without stint or limit—fresh as the fresh air, and almost as abundant—are daily offered to the palates of the Manhattanese, and appreciated with all the gratitude which such a bounty of nature ought to inspire.

Oyster cellars catered to the well-to-do as well as the less affluent. Upper-class oyster bars were filled with mirrors, pictures, and other artistic enhancements. Tables could be closed off with curtains, which provided customers with privacy. Less ornate cellars had a counter at one side. Behind it, oyster shuckers, frequently blacks, quickly opened oysters "for their customers, who swallow them with astonishing relish and rapidity." Good shuckers could open 3,500 oysters a day—but the average was about 2,500.

The greatest concentration of oyster houses was found along Canal Street, but again, according to an English visitor in the 1860s, the oyster should be called "the national dish; it is at least the great dish of the Atlantic States." He continued,

> The oyster is the *sine qua non* of all dinner parties and picnics, of all night revels and festive banquets. For tenpence you may have a large dish of them, done in any style you will, and as many as you can consume. The restaurants ostentatious and humble are in the season, crowded with oyster lovers: ladies and gentlemen, workmen and seamstresses, resort to them in multitudes, and for a trifle may have a right royal feast.

Oysters were so plentiful that everyone thought the supply was inexhaustible. But there was a limit. The beds were overharvested, and production rapidly declined in the 1840s. To meet demand, oysters were shipped in from Long Island Sound and then from the Chesapeake Bay. Estimates varied as to how many vessels were engaged in the oyster trade: some said 1,500; others said ten times that. But it was a dying occupation. Pollution and untreated human waste that drained into the harbor destroyed oyster beds. The beds in Harlem River were closed in the 1870s. Health scares associated with them frightened New Yorkers away from the dives and street vendors. Many oyster saloons became seedy, and upper-class New Yorkers migrated to other eateries. When oysters were thought to have caused a typhus outbreak in the 1890s, more beds were closed by health officials. By 1916, most oyster beds in New York Bay were closed or destroyed by pollution. The most iconic oyster restaurant in the city today is the Grand Central Oyster Bar, which opened in 1913. It imports all of its oysters from Long Island and other areas where oysters thrive. Its signature dishes include oyster pan roast and oyster stew.

Boardinghouse Fare

A British actor who immigrated to America in 1797 reported that New York was more a village and a collection of inns than a real city. But he was delighted with the culinary choices at one upscale boardinghouse: "[It

Oyster Bar Restaurant, Grand Central Terminal, Manhattan, 2013. Courtesy of Kelly Fitzsimmons

served] fish, ham, beef, boiled fowls, eggs, pigeons, pumpkin pies, lobsters, vegetables, tea, coffee, cider, sangaree, and cherry-brandy!" A later British visitor to New York also thought well of the fashionable boardinghouse where he stayed:

> In the first-rate boarding-houses of the American commercial capital, there is an entire absence of all vulgarity. The attendance and culinary arrangements are after the models of some of the best English private establishments, and the general tone of the society refined enough for the most fastidious; nor are the expenses so exorbitant as in many a noisy, disagreeable hotel.

Boardinghouses had been common in New York since colonial days. As merchants, clerks, salesmen, seamstresses, mechanics, and immigrants streamed into the city in the early nineteenth century, lower Manhattan became crowded. The island's well-to-do sold their three- and four-story houses and moved uptown. Entrepreneurs purchased the old houses, subdivided the rooms, and converted them into boardinghouses. As landlords made more money selling liquor and other provisions than they did by renting out the rooms, they often converted the parlors or cellars into saloons, or made them into grocery stores that sold liquor. There were not enough old houses to meet the needs of incoming immigrant families, so entrepreneurs began purchasing old nonresidential buildings and converting them into boardinghouses.

Some boardinghouses catered to specific groups, such as Germans, Irish, or Chinese. Others catered to specific professions, such as actors. They were less expensive than hotels, and guests often remained in residence for long periods of time. Guests were typically served three meals a day. In 1842, Walt Whitman, then a twenty-two-year-old New York journalist, proclaimed that the "universal Yankee nation" was a "boarding people." But sixteen years later he grossly exaggerated in proclaiming that three-quarters of the adults in New York City lived in boardinghouses.

Boardinghouse fare depended on the proprietors, and many residents were unhappy with what they were served. Asa Greene, author of the novel *The Perils of Pearl Street* (1834), recorded his impressions of the food served by a boardinghouse landlady he called "Mrs. Conniption." Breakfast consisted of salted shad or mackerel, dried beef steak, and occasionally stale sausages, or heavily salted pork, and bread that was "heavy as a grindstone." Water "drawn from the Manhattan hydrant or the pump" was converted into a hot drink by the addition of "a small quantity of damaged coffee, burnt crust, or roasted rye, well pulverised." Dinner included cheap meat (mutton, beef, or pork), which "was dry as a chip, and totally destitute of any inviting qualities." Vegetables consisted of "watery potatoes, sliced beats, boiled cabbage, and so forth." Sour apple dumplings, rice pudding with molasses, tart apple pies "with the crust as strong as sole-leather," or "shrivelled peaches" were served for dessert. The tea table consisted of dry bread with "extra-salted butter," and weak tea that was made with a "thimbleful of tea . . . put into a quart, a gallon, or some other assignable quantity of water." This was flavored with small amounts of brown sugar and watered-down milk.

In the same spirit, Thomas Butler Gunn, author of *The Physiology of New York Boarding-Houses* (1857), wrote that "meals were uniformly served up 'neither cold, nor hot.'" The soups "might have been improved by a less liberal allowance of grease and unground pepper, of which latter there always remained a deep sediment—as of small shot—in each plate."

Vegetarian Eateries

Other boardinghouses were established by vegetarians and temperance advocates. These were promoted or inspired by Sylvester Graham. In 1833, Asenath Nicholson launched a temperance boardinghouse. She teamed up with Graham to institutionalize his dietary principles in her establishment, and she later published the first "Graham" recipes devised in accordance with his precepts. Other Graham boardinghouses opened, and many survived until late in the nineteenth century. Noted guests at such places included New York newspapermen Horace Greeley and William Lloyd Garrison. The aforementioned Thomas Butler Gunn was surprised and pleased with the offerings at one of the Graham houses:

> We had no meats, no fish, no gravy-soups. Tea and coffee were also rejected, as stimulants. But every variety of vegetable appeared at our table, as also fruit and pastry. (No butter entered into the composition of the latter, that being a tabooed article.) Bananas, melons, peaches, grapes, oranges, cherries, pineapples; all the daintier forms of Vegetarian fare were provided with a liberal hand. The display, indeed, exceeded our expectations.

The New York Vegetarian Society was organized in 1852; it organized dinners. One in 1894 held at the St. Denis Hotel in 1894 offered an impressive menu:

Soup.
Cream of celery.

Relishes.
Olives. Tomatoes. Cucumbers. Salted Almonds. Pickled Walnuts. Haricot beans on bread with curry sauce.

Removes.
Braised lettuce with mushroom sauce and celery croquettes.
Stewed oyster plant with rissole and sweet potatoes Lyonnaise.
Brussels sprouts, cream sauce.
Lemon ice.
French peas, country style.
Baked stuffed tomatoes with spaghetti a la Milannaise.
Fried squash, Creole style, with corn fritters.
Mixed salad with toasted crackers.

Sweets.
Rice and apricots. Croute of mixed fruits. Orange salad. Nesselrode pudding.

Dessert.
Stilton, Roquefort, and Camembert cheese. Fruits of the season. Nuts. Raisins. Cakes. Tea. Coffee. Chocolate.

Vegetarian boardinghouses went out of business by 1900, but vegetarian restaurants, such as The White Rose or The Laurel, were operating in the city. These sold vegetarian steaks, cutlets, filets, and duck. According to one author in 1904, their vegetables were "amazingly" well cooked; he also reported that their mushroom and nut dishes were outstanding, a black cream of mushroom soup was "worthy of a plutocrat" and the coffee made from peanuts was delicious. The publication of Upton Sinclair's *Jungle* (1906) and other exposes about the meatpacking industry encouraged many New Yorkers to become vegetarians. Vegetarian restaurants survived and today thrive as do vegan and raw food restaurants.

Tenements

Boardinghouses were so profitable that entrepreneurs began converting large warehouses and other buildings into "tenant houses," later called tenements. A large brewery erected in 1792 in the Five Points neighborhood, for instance, was in 1837 converted into a dwelling that eventually housed more than seven hundred Irish and African Americans. Unlike boardinghouses, tenements did not provide food for those renting rooms and often did not have kitchens.

As more immigrants flooded into the city, entrepreneurs converted larger old buildings for multiple dwellings. The rooms were tiny—often just big enough for a bed—and most did not have running water, heat, ventilation, or indoor plumbing. Instead, there were outdoor privies with inadequate sewage systems. Water had to be carried in buckets from wells or pumps on the street. New York City and State passed laws to improve conditions in tenements, but the laws often went unenforced. As more immigrants moved into the tenements, they became dangerously overcrowded. According to the *New York Tribune*, garbage was set in boxes on the streets: the waste was "composed of potato-peelings, oyster-shells, night-soil, rancid butter, dead dogs and cats, and ordinary black street mud." The garbage boxes formed "one festering, rotting, loathsome, hellish mass of air poisoning, death-breeding filth, reeking in the fierce sunshine, which gloats yellowly over it like the glare of a devil whom Satan has kicked from his councils in virtuous disgust."

As more immigrants streamed into the city, more tenements were created to house them. In 1900, there were 42,700 tenement buildings in New York, housing almost 1.6 million people. Jacob Riis's exposé *How the Other Half Lives: Studies among the Tenements of New York* (1890) concluded that more than half a million people living in the tenements were either begging for food or subsisting on charity.

One building that was, surprisingly, converted into a tenement was Fraunces Tavern. Originally built as a family home, it was converted into a tavern in 1762. In the early nineteenth century, it was converted back into a house, with street-level shops added later, before it ended up as a tenement for immigrants. In 1904, the building was bought by the New York chapter of the Sons of the American Revolution, who tried to restore the building to its original eighteenth-century condition. Today, it claims to be the oldest surviving building in Manhattan; it functions as a museum and a restaurant serving food and beverages loosely based on colonial fare.

Another tenement building, at 97 Orchard Street on the Lower East Side, was built in 1864. It was designed to have twenty three-room apartments. Each apartment—about 325 square feet—would typically house a family of seven or eight. There was no running water and no toilets, although the apartments did have small kitchens. Residents were able to prepare simple meals. In 1988, this became the Tenement Museum.

Room in The Tenement Museum , 97 Orchard Street. Courtesy of the Library of Congress. Reproduction Number: LC-DIG-highsm-14234

Foreign Food

By the mid-nineteenth century, restaurants, bistros, and cafes thrived in New York, as did more affordable oyster houses and other inexpensive eating establishments. Manhattan alone had an estimated five or six thousand restaurants and eating houses. They ranged from the elegant and expensive Delmonico's to "the subterranean sties where men are fed like swine, and dirt is served gratis in unhomoeopathic doses" with "broken earthen-ware, soiled table-cloths, and coarse dishes," as a New York reporter wrote in 1869.

Many restaurants served "foreign" food, and some were widely frequented. "Gosling's French and American Dining Saloons" on Nassau served a thousand customers a day at lunch. It was good and cheap. In 1843, three customers ate "roast veal farci, with two slices of bread, potatoes, a pickle, and a 'smaller' of beer," and the total cost for all three diners was about thirty cents. By comparison, a meal for three at Delmonico's cost more than fifteen dollars. Henri Mouquin's opened in 1857 on Fulton and Nassau. Their "diner du jour" consisted "of soup, one entree, and cut of roast meat with one vegetable, and cheese with bread at discretion." It cost "25 cents, with a pint of red wine at 12 cents extra," according to a magazine writer in 1866. Mouquin later moved his restaurant uptown to Twenty-eighth Street and Sixth Avenue where he upped the prices and became a "rendezvous for epicures."

Chinese, Italian, and German restaurants thrived in New York by the late nineteenth century. Chop suey joints became common in Five Points (an area later called Chinatown) beginning in the late nineteenth century. By 1898, eleven Chinese restaurants could be found on Mott and Pell Streets. By the 1930s, Chinese restaurants were common even on Times Square. Italian restaurants opened as immigrants from Italy flooded into the city, but in the 1890s, they rapidly increased as New Yorkers fell in love with spaghetti joints where meals were accompanied by a bottle of red wine. Others became very popular, such as the one opened by Stefano Moretti on Fourteenth Street in the 1860s. German restaurants were common in New York by the 1870s. They were located off streetcar lines and sold German foods and wines. Some served the city's well-to-do, such as Lüchow's in Manhattan and the Peter Luger Steak House in Williamsburg.

Chophouses, "adaptations" of English grillrooms, were also common. In the 1860s, they were clustered around Houston and Bleecker Streets. They served a wide range of foods, such as served "stewed tripe, liver and bacon, mutton-chops, porter-house steak, and cuts from 'joints.' The bill of fare is a written one hung up at the bar. The prices are moderate, and the food better cooked than in almost any of the other eating-houses." The De Soto, the leading chop-house in 1866, was run by an English immigrant named William H. Garrard. It was frequented by actors and "dramatic critics" who ate "broiled kidneys and Welch rarebits" and drank ale and cocktails. Forty years later, among the popu-lar chophouses were Farrish's on John Street, Engel's near Herald Square, and Browne's on Broadway near Fortieth Street. These were "much frequented" by "actors and singers and have fascinating collections of old prints and quaint photographs." They were inexpensive. For "a chop, baked potato, a bit of water-cress, plenty of good bread, and English pickles," the cost was forty to eighty cents. They also served "broiled kidneys, porterhouse steaks, imported Bass, porter, or stout, Scotch ale, or half and half (properly pronounced "'arf 'n' 'arf"), served in the pewter and drawn from the wood, are also to be had at their best at these places, and at a reasonable price."

By the time that the Depression hit, foreign food was readily available, as a writer noted in 1931:

> Within a few square miles, you can sample the foods of India, Syria, Japan, and Normandy; you can eat the foods of the French, the German and the Irish; the specialties of the Italians and the Swedes and the Russians and the Danes. You can drink Turkish, European and Florentine coffee; rose-water or Danish beer. You can revel in Smorgasbord, Hors d'oeuvres, or Antipasto; and buy a meal for 50 cents or 50 dollars.

There were also Jewish restaurants. The most famous was the Café Royal, on Second Avenue, then the heart of New York's Yiddish rialto. It opened in 1908 and quickly became the place where socialists, artists, writers, and Yiddish performers mingled. In his book *The Strangest Places* (1939), Russian immigrant Leo Calvin Rosten proclaimed the Café Royal to be "the Delmo-nico's, the Simpson's and the Fouquet's of Second Avenue, all in one." He continued, "Everybody who is anybody in the creative Jewish world turns up at the Café Royal at least one night a week. To be seen there is a social duty, a mark of distinction, and an investment in prestige."

Foreign and ethnic food was and is a defining element in the city's food-scape, and today restaurants offer foods and beverages from hundreds of dif-ferent national, regional, and ethnic groups.

Speed Dining

Until the mid-nineteenth century, New Yorkers engaged in business went home for afternoon dinner. As the city grew and residences were separated from places of employment, lunchrooms emerged. They typically offered fast service and cheap food. Most customers ate quickly and returned to work. An English visitor in 1828 described the "Plate House," one of the city's early quick-service lunch establishments, as a long, narrow, dark room with two rows of boxes "just large enough to hold four persons." Attendants glided "up and down, and across the passage, inclining their heads for an instant first to one box, then to another, and receiving the whispered wishes of the company, which they straightway bawled out in a loud voice, to give notice of what fare was wanted." As customers ordered their food, attendants yelled them out: "Three beef, 8 !" "Half plate beef, 4!" "One potato, 5!" "Two apple pie, one plum pudding, 8!" The numbers at the end identified the table. Other colloquial names for dishes were "a plate of Siamese Twins" (fish balls); "woodcock" (pork and beans); "boned turkey," "corduroy," and "West Broadway" (hash); "Irish goose" (codfish, baked or boiled); and "a plate of Tennessee, and be quick about it" (hot corn bread). Within seconds the food was delivered. Customers ate in silence, ate quickly, and left.

Time was money, whether at a restaurant or in a boardinghouse. Speed of delivery and speed of eating was everything. In the 1830s, an Englishman described breakfast at his boardinghouse:

> Here was no loitering nor lounging; no dipping into newspapers; no apparent lassitude of appetite; no intervals of repose in mastication; but all was hurry, bustle, clamour, and voracity, and the business of repletion went forward, with a rapidity altogether unexampled. The strenuous efforts of the company were, of course, soon rewarded with success. Departures, which had begun even before I took my place at the table, became every instant more numerous, and in a few minutes the apartment had become . . . "a banquet-hall deserted."

Another reported that New Yorkers spent "from five to ten minutes for breakfast, fifteen to twenty for dinner, and ten for supper. . . . Each person, as soon as satisfied leaves the table without regard to his neighbors; no social conversation follows."

Later in the century, a French visitor observed, "In five minutes they manage to gulp down a certain amount of food, pay and go. An intelligent barkeeper attracts customers by the facilities he can offer for rapid feeding. 'Try our quick lunch' is stuck up in the streets."

And there was noise. As an American reporter noted in 1869,

> From 12 o'clock to 3 of the afternoon, the down-town eating-houses are in one continuous roar. The clatter of plates and knives, the slamming of doors, the talking and giving of orders by the customers, the bellowing of waiters, are

mingled in a wild chaos. The sole wonder is how any one gets anything; how the waiters understand anything; how anything is paid for, or expected to be paid for. Everybody talks at once; everybody orders at once; everybody eats at once; and everybody seems anxious to pay at once.

Most lunchrooms were mom-and-pop shops that sold sandwiches, soup, and few other items. By the 1920s, lunchroom chains began to develop in New York. Most chains had only two or three establishments. These shared a name and were advertised as a system. Large chains might also have had central food distribution and preparation. One such chain was W. F. Schrafft's, launched by Frank Shattuck in 1898 as a candy store in Boston. By 1915, Schrafft's had extended its operation to New York City. By 1922, the chain had twenty-two stores.

Faster and more efficient ways of feeding workers continued to emerge in the city. One solution that developed was the Exchange Buffet, which opened in 1885 across the street from the New York Stock Exchange. It catered only to males, who proceeded down a long buffet containing items such as sandwiches, salads, and cakes to eat and tea, coffee, or milk to drink. They picked the foods that they wanted and juggled them in their hands to tall counters where they ate standing up. They bused their own dishes, tallied their own bill, and then told the cashier what he owed. This self-service operation based on the honor system was surprisingly successful, and the company opened thirty-five more establishments in Manhattan and Brooklyn during the next few years.

Other businessmen saw crowds surging about the Exchange Buffet and developed their own model. In 1889, William and Samuel Child opened their first lunchroom on the main floor of the Merchants Hotel. Cleanliness was an important part of the operation, and they dressed waitresses in white aprons and white caps. Unlike the Exchange Buffet, they catered mainly to women. They are also credited with introducing the tray, so that customers didn't have to juggle their dishes. This was so successful that the brothers opened more cafeterias, more than one hundred by 1925.

Cafeterias particularly thrived in large institutions—corporate dining rooms; government offices; museums; military installations, such as Governor's Island; and prisons, such as Riker's Island. New York YMCAs opened their first cafeteria in 1916. New York schools soon opened cafeterias for their students. By 1929, the city had 786 cafeterias.

A restaurant chain that thrived during the Depression was Chock full o'Nuts, which was launched by a Russian immigrant, William Black, who had opened a nut stand in a basement in Times Square in 1926. The chain was successful, and Black opened eighteen additional shops around the city. When the Depression hit, he converted his nut shops into budget luncheonettes, charging a nickel each for coffee and a sandwich consisting of cream cheese, chopped nuts, and lightly toasted date-nut bread. He later added soup and pie to the menu. By the 1950s, he owned twenty-five outlets in Manhattan and two in Brooklyn. In 1953, he came out with his own brand of coffee, also called Chock full o'Nuts. It later expanded to a chain with 125 restaurants. Although the chain did not survive, its brand of coffee did.

Yet another type of self-service operation that thrived in New York was the coin-operated vending machine. They were developed in the United Kingdom in the 1880s. The Thomas Adams Gum Company began selling gum in vending machines on New York's elevated train platforms in 1888. Coin-operated machines offered the means to sell food in many places without the need for a sales force. They took off nationally in 1901, when F. W. and H. S. Mills debuted penny-in-the-slot machines, which became ubiquitous across America shortly thereafter selling gum and candy.

Europeans began selling a wide variety of foods through vending machines, especially in transportation hubs. Philadelphians Joseph Horn and Frank Hardart ordered the coin-operated machines from a German firm and, in 1902, opened America's first Automat. These were self-service operations that dispensed food through coin-operated machines with glass windows. Food, such as sandwiches, pies, coffee cake, cookies, pudding, hot dogs, vegetables, and side dishes, was prepared in advance and placed in glass compartments so that customers could see what they were buying. Heated or refrigerated compartments provided hot and cold food. Empty compartments were filled by workers who prepared food behind the row of machines.

In December 1902, James Harcombe, a New York restaurateur, opened the first Automat in New York. It was fifty feet long and twenty-five feet wide, but it had "an attractive front and a handsome interior," reported the *New York Times*, and it should have, for Harcombe spent seventy-five thousand dollars in lavishly decorating the restaurant. *Scientific American* stated that, when compared with the average café, the Automat was "illuminated with extravagant splendor but is a dismal place compared with it." He advertised it as "Europe's Unique Electric Self-serving Device for Lunches and Beverages. No Waiting. No Tipping. Open Evenings until Midnight." Prices ranged from a nickel to a quarter. To compete with high-end restaurants, the Automat offered a wild assortment of lavish dishes, including "lobster à la Newberg." In addition to food and coffee, it also offered beer, wine, and cocktails. Despite widespread promotion, the restaurant did not thrive, and it closed about 1907.

Horn & Hardart expanded its operation to New York City in 1912, and within a few years, the company operated fifteen Automats in the city. In September 1922, the company opened a combination Automat cafeteria, which they claimed was the largest restaurant in the city with the capacity to feed ten thousand New Yorkers daily. (But one of the most poignant images of the Automat, painted by Edward Hopper in 1927, was a woman alone drinking a cup of coffee in an Automat.) In order to maintain the quality of its operations, the company opened a central commissary that supplied all of its operations in New York. Horn & Hardart did well during the 1920s and thrived during the Depression. In 1933, the company did something unusual—it hired Francis Bourdon, a classically trained chef who had worked at top restaurants in Europe and America, to run its commissary, a position he held for the next thirty-five years. He developed new recipes, gave the chain some prestige, and guaranteed that the quality of food remained the same in every outlet.

After World War II, Horn & Hardart expanded to fifty outlets in the city, and by 1950 most had converted into cafeterias. Then decline set in. It was a combination of issues—New York City began charging tax on food, and it was impossible to put pennies into the nickel slots. The company lost money on its popular high-quality coffee, so it upped the price to a dime. Business declined when they began to water down their coffee and decrease the quality of their food. Finally, fast-food establishments took away even more business. Within four decades, most automats were closed, many having been converted into Burger King outlets. The last Automat in New York closed in April 1991. But this was not the end of the concept. Many businesses and colleges have cafeterias, where workers and students can acquire food items through coin-operated machines, and of course, coin-operated candy, snack, and soda machines are ubiquitous throughout New York.

Cheap food was available from other eating establishments. By the 1880s, cheap hash houses were common. In these, customers acquired bread and butter, potatoes, and pickles for just fifteen cents. Hamburger steak was available for just eight cents. Even cheaper food could be had at the Italian basement eating houses, which served macaroni, toast, and coffee for a nickel. The winter of 1902 was extremely cold, and many New Yorkers were out of work. Bernarr Macfadden opened a cafeteria for the unemployed at City Hall Park. It charged a penny per course, and when it closed in the spring, it actually made a profit. When the Depression hit in 1929, Macfadden duplicated and expanded his concept. Yet another response to the Depression, at least for the customers who had some money, was the "all you can eat" restaurant. These were restaurants with chairs, tables, and waiters. Customers were charged an entrance fee—sixty cents or a dollar—and then they could eat all they wanted on any item on the menus.

High-End Restaurants

The French and Swiss never immigrated in large numbers to New York, but they had a disproportionate influence on New York food, for many were cooks, confectioners, chocolatiers, bakers, restaurateurs, and café owners. After the French Revolution in 1789, many French refugees came to the United States, where they shared the legacy of French cuisine. One of those who arrived on American shores was Captain Joseph Collet, who opened an ice-cream parlor. The French writer Jean Anthelme Brillat-Savarin wrote admiringly that Collet had "earned a great deal of money in New York in 1794 and 1795, by making ices and sherbets for the inhabitants of that commercial town." Collet opened the "Commercial Hotel"—a fancy name for a boardinghouse with a coffeehouse on the lower floor.

François Guerin opened a confectionery and a small lunchroom on lower Broadway opposite the City Hotel in 1815. He sold "imported and domestic confectionery, inviting specimens of pastry and cake, bottles of choice French cordials, fancy boxes filled with Parisian bon-bons interspersed with the fruits then in market." He also served soup and sandwiches and sardines. Louis Curtillet, an immigrant from Provence, sold "meat pies, plum puddings, *confections de crème glacées*, and *punch à la Romaine*." In the 1840s, John Pinteux's Café de Mille Colonnes offered coffee, juleps, and ice cream. It was patronized by the "gayer bloods, who loved glare and glitter and the noise of Broadway."

In December 1827, Swiss immigrants John and Peter Delmonico opened a little café on William Street, near the harbor. It had just six tables; there, patrons could enjoy European-style pastries, ices, bonbons, cakes, and coffee. In March 1830, the café was expanded into a fine dining establishment that was listed in the city directory as "Delmonico & Brother, Restaurant Français." After a fire swept lower Manhattan and their café was destroyed, the Delmonico brothers bought Collet's café and boardinghouse, while they began to construct a new restaurant.

An enlarged Delmonico's on South William Street opened in 1837. It offered salads and other novel French dishes, and the restaurant became very popular. Its eleven-page menu listed a full selection of French dishes (with English translations opposite), such as Potage aux huitres, Salade de chicorée, Blanquette de Veau à la Perigueux, Meringues à la crème, and an impressive French wine list with Bordeaux, vintage 1825. Delmonico's quickly became the city's premier restaurant where the upper classes and visiting dignitaries dined. While some meals could be had for less than fifteen dollars for three, other meals weighed in at more than eighty dollars per person, a very costly meal at the time. But the food was good. Frederick Marryat, an English naval officer, traveler, and novelist, visited Delmonico's and other French restaurants in the 1830s and reported that they served "excellent" French food. A visiting Frenchman, Georges Savuvin, went even further, when he reported in 1893 that the food served at Delmonico's was "better and more sumptuous" than that served "in the best restaurant in Paris."

Newspapers and magazines reported on the lavish dinners for the city's upper crust, as well as visiting dignitaries and royalty. One dinner and ball attended by eight hundred of New York's social elite cost $350,000, an exorbitant amount in 1897. Another dinner for forty guests cost $10,000, or $250 per dinner, again an unheard of amount at the time.

Delmonico's success encouraged the establishment of other French restaurants. By the mid-1830s, many New York hotels served French food in their restaurants. The Astor House employed French chefs to run its dining rooms, and a number of these men became quite famous. The French influence was clearly visible on the menus of these restaurants as well as the way the food was served via *service à la française* (service in the French style), meaning that all food was served at the same time. Carl Schurz, a

Annual Banquet of the Sons of the Revolution in the State of New York, Delmonico's restaurant, February 22, 1906. Courtesy of the Library of Congress. Reproduction Number: LC-USZ62-139580

German visitor to the city in the 1850s, described this experience at the Union Square Hotel restaurant:

> Some fifteen or twenty negroes, clad in white jackets, white aprons, and white cotton gloves, stood ready to conduct the guests to their seats, which they did with broad smiles and curiously elaborate bows and foot scrapings. A portly colored head-waiter in a dress coat and white necktie, whose manners were strikingly grand and patronizing, directed their movements. When the guests were seated, the head-waiter struck a loud bell; then the negroes rapidly filed out and soon reappeared carrying large soup tureens covered with bright silver covers. They planted themselves along the table at certain intervals, standing for a second motionless. At another clang of their commander's bell they lifted their tureens high up and then deposited them upon the table with a bump that made the chandeliers tremble and came near terrifying the ladies. But this was not the end of the ceremony. The negroes held fast with their right hands to the handles of the silver covers until another stroke of the bell resounded. Then they jerked off the covers, swung them high over their heads, and thus marched off as if carrying away their booty in triumph. So the dinner went on, with several repetitions of such proceedings, the negroes getting all the while more and more enthusiastic and bizarre in their performances.

The French themselves shifted to *service à la russe* (service in the Russian style) during the mid-nineteenth century. This meant that food was served in courses—typically appetizers, salad, soup, and entrées followed by desert. American restaurants did not convert to *service à la russe* until later in the nineteenth century.

French cookery in New York reached a peak at the beginning of the twentieth century, when hotel restaurants run by French or French-trained chefs—at the Waldorf Astoria, Essex House, and Ritz-Carlton, among others—were among the nation's premiere eating places. Wealthy Americans also hired French chefs to preside over their household kitchens.

New forms of restaurants emerged during the late nineteenth century. Louis Sherry opened an elegant restaurant at the corner of Fifth Avenue and Thirty-seventh Street. The restaurant's decor and its French chefs soon attracted New York's social elite as well as those who loved good food. To prepare the food, the restaurant had sixteen chefs and two hundred kitchen employees. Sherry's was soon followed by others. Thomas Shanley, an Irish immigrant, opened a small restaurant on Twenty-third Street in 1891. It was in the old theater district. He drew theatrical celebrities from the theaters, and his business grew. The theater district moved to Times Square, and in 1910 Shanley moved his restaurant to Broadway between Forty-second and

Forty-third Streets. He offered "light entertainment" in addition to the food and liquor. It had an opulent interior, and its food was good and costly but of secondary importance to customers who came for the entertainment, for it had a full orchestra, the first restaurant in the city to have one. Shanley is credited with being the first in New York to launch what would later be called a lobster palace. It was an overnight sensation.

Other lobster palaces emerged about the same time. These included those owned by George Rector and Captain James Churchill, and J. B. Martin's Café Martin, Maxim's, John Murray's Roman Gardens, Reisenweber's, Bustanoby's, and many more. Typically, they were built on or near Longacre Square (later renamed Times Square), the city's theater district. Lobster palaces were expensive, elegantly decorated, and sported live entertainment, such as orchestras, dancing, and floor shows. They served a variety of dishes, but lobster was their signature dish. They also possessed liquor licenses permitting them to serve alcohol throughout the night, and in many ways they were the city's first nightclubs. Selling liquor was where they made their profits.

High-end restaurants also made much of their profits from the sale of liquor that preceded, accompanied, and followed a meal. French restaurants, for instance, particularly featured expensive imported wines as part of their dining experience, and the sale of alcoholic beverages played an important role in their profits. When Prohibition went into effect in 1920, restaurants, particularly lobster palaces and haute cuisine establishments, were hit hard. Louis Sherry saw the writing on the balance sheet and closed his restaurant a few months before Prohibition went into effect. Shanley's closed in March 1923. After nearly a century of glorious history, Delmonico's did the same in May 1923.

There were notable exceptions. The Russian Tea Room opened on Fifty-seventh Street in 1927. Initially, it served as a gathering place for those fleeing the Russian Revolution, but it quickly attracted a wide audience by offering Russian and Continental cuisine. Sardi's restaurant, opened in the theater district by Italian immigrant Melchiore Pio Vincenzo Sardi (aka Vincent Sardi) in 1927, served Italian and French fare; its most popular dishes in 1930 were Moules mariniére, the classic Normandy mussel dish, bouillabaisse, and filet of sole. Other popular exceptions included the "21" Club, which sold liquor throughout Prohibition, and The Colony, which was reborn in the midst of Prohibition. Before World War I, The Colony was a somewhat shady bistro with a gambling den upstairs. Gene Cavallero became headwaiter in December 1919, and in 1921 he teamed up with two other waiters to buy the restaurant. They remodeled the premises in ten days and reopened with a menu of fine French cuisine. The Colony was almost immediately discovered by society matron Anne Vanderbilt (Mrs. W. K. Vanderbilt Jr.), who was followed by other members of New York's fashionable set. It was a very expensive restaurant, and its specialties were chafing dishes, game, and its hors d'oeuvres. By late 1920s, The Colony was so much the favored haunt of New York's wealthy that the restaurant closed during the summer, its clientele having decamped for Europe.

Haute Cuisine Revival

Prohibition ended in December 1933, but by this time, the country was in the depths of the Depression and few restaurants served haute cuisine. This changed after New York hosted the 1939 World's Fair. Located in Flushing Meadow in Queens, the fair had an optimistic theme, "Dawn of a New Day," where visitors could glimpse "the World of Tomorrow." The Food Zone included 150 cows sponsored by Borden and a wheat field—the city's first in sixty-eight years—sponsored by Continental Baking, makers of Wonder Bread. The Beach Nut exhibit illustrated how coffee was grown, harvested, and roasted. Standard Brands exhibited Fleischman's Yeast, Royal Desserts, and Chase & Sanborn Coffee.

More than eighty restaurants were located around the fairgrounds. The Japanese restaurant served sukiyaki; the Italian, spaghetti; the Swedish, a smorgasbord; and the Mexican, chili con carne. Two restaurants emerged from the fair to become New York culinary landmarks. One was opened by Dario Toffenetti, an Italian immigrant and Chicago restaurateur. He acquired the concession for a restaurant at the fair and decided to open a restaurant in New York. At Forty-third Street and Broadway, he built a large modern restaurant complete with an escalator and massive chandeliers. It could seat a thousand people, and the day it opened in August 1940, it served 8,500 customers. It offered simple, low-cost food, such as "Spaghetti a la Toffenetti with Fresh Meat Sauce," supposedly derived from an obscure manuscript that Mrs. Toffenetti had located in Bologna. Toffenetti's restaurant was open twenty-four hours a day, and for almost thirty years it was one of New York's most popular restaurants, serving thousands of customers daily.

A very different type of restaurant was launched by Henri Soulé, the maître d'hôtel at the restaurant at the French Pavillon. The restaurant, which the *New York Times* called "an epicure's delight," served classical French food. Wealthy New Yorkers were familiar with the French cuisine; during Prohibition and the Depression, they had traveled to France, where they dined at the world's finest restaurants. The French restaurant at the

World's Fair, however, attracted a wide audience. Most fairgoers had never before sampled French food; they did so at the Pavillon, and they liked what they tasted.

Henri Soulé remained in New York when the fair ended and opened a restaurant on New York's fashionable Upper East Side in 1941. Hoping to trade on the restaurant's popularity at the fair, he named the establishment Le Pavillon. Soulé was joined by many of his former colleagues, such as Pierre Franey, who had been the *poisson commis* (assistant fish cook). Soulé attracted the rich and famous to dine. Le Pavillon was a solid success from the beginning as New York's social and economic elites—Astors, Cabots, Kennedys, Rockefellers, and Vanderbilts—dined regularly at the restaurant. It survived World War II and thrived during the 1950s. Soulé made a virtue of snobbery. Presumably to protect the sensibilities of his refined customers, he refused entrance to those who did not meet his standards. Soulé is also said to have coined the term "Siberia," referring to the tables closest to the kitchen (considered the worst in any restaurant).

When Henri Soulé died in 1966, the *New York Times* restaurant critic Craig Claiborne eulogized him as the "Michelangelo, the Mozart and Leonardo of the French restaurant in America." Soulé's greatest achievement, according to Claiborne, was his nurturing of restaurateurs and other influential individuals on America's food scene. Pierre Belin and Paul Arepejou, who started at Le Pavillon, opened La Poinière in 1954. Roger Fessaguet, who had moved from Le Pavillon to La Caravelle, made La Caravelle the "incubator for some of New York's better-known chefs." Michael Romano worked with Fessaguet until restaurateur Danny Meyer tapped him to become the chef at the Union Square Café. David Ruggerio went from La Caravelle to Le Chantilly, and Cyril Renaud became the chef and owner of Fleur de Sel.

Le Pavillon survived only a few years after Soulé's death, but French cuisine continued to thrive in New York. A host of restaurants serving a variety of regional French cuisines as well as Escoffier's classics appeared in New York. Lutèce opened in 1961, with Chef André Soltner at the helm. For more than three decades, Lutèce was considered one of the finest restaurants in America. Le Périgord, opened by Georges Briguet in 1964, still upholds the tradition of fine French cuisine in New York. Sirio Maccioni, who came to work at The Colony in 1956, opened Le Cirque with Jean Vergnes in 1974. It has moved premises and transformed itself over the years, but Le Cirque continues to employ notable chefs, and alumni of its kitchens include Alain Sailhac, Jacques Torres, Daniel Boulud, David Bouley, and Michael Lomonaco.

Among New York City's longest-tenured French restaurants are La Gre-
nouille and La Mangeoire, serving classic and country cuisines, respectively;
of more recent vintage but highly regarded are Restaurant Daniel, Jean
Georges, and Le Bernardin.

Management Groups

Joe Baum, a graduate of the Cornell's hotel management school, was hired by
Rikers Restaurant Associates (later renamed Restaurant Associates) in 1953.
It operated twenty-four restaurants in the New York City area. They had just
acquired the Newarker, a restaurant at Newark Airport, then a small regional
airfield. Baum was placed in charge of developing the Newarker.

Baum hired Albert Stockli, a classically trained Swiss chef, to run the
kitchen. Together, they devised an unusual menu with showy, attention-
grabbing features—large portions, sparklers in birthday cakes, and lots of
dishes that were flambéed tableside. The restaurant lost twenty-five thousand dollars in that first year, but it soon became a "destination" eating
place. Despite its location in the airport, the Newarker served a thousand
customers a day—most of them *not* airline passengers—and grossed twenty-
five million dollars a year.

Baum was placed in charge of the Restaurant Associates' specialty restaurants in 1955. He hired big-name consultants, such as James Beard, Julia
Child, Jacques Pépin, Barbara Kafka, and Rozanne Gold, to help him think
through restaurant concepts and menus. Then he recruited top talent to
design and run the restaurants. He is credited with popularizing themed
restaurants, such as the Aurora (French), the Hawaiian Room at the Lexington Hotel (Polynesian, complete with hula dancers), La Fonda Del Sol
(South American), Zum-Zum (German sausage), Quo Vadis (French and
Italian), the Forum of the Twelve Caesars at Rockefeller Center (Roman),
and many others, such as the Brasserie, Hudson River Club, Café Greco,
Tavern on the Green in Central Park, and The Four Seasons. The expenses
were enormous, and Restaurant Associates began to lose money. Baum was
let go in 1970.

A few weeks after leaving the Restaurant Associates, Baum was hired by
the New York Transit Authority to design a world-class restaurant at the top
of the brand-new World Trade Center and to consult on other eateries in the
buildings. He developed the Market Bar and Dining Rooms on the ground-
floor concourse, Windows on the World at the top of the North Tower, and
twenty other eating places for the massive new office complex. Windows on

the World opened in April 1976, quickly becoming a landmark and a destination restaurant for tourists and New Yorkers alike. From then on, Baum continued to design restaurants. He took over and redesigned the Rainbow Room in Rockefeller Center, which reopened in 1988. When Joe Baum died, in 1998, he and Restaurant Associates had created 167 restaurants.

With some notable exceptions, such as The Four Seasons, most of Baum's restaurants have not survived, but his approach has influenced many who came after him: the chefs and restaurateurs Drew Nieporent, Daniel Boulud, Danny Meyer, Jean-Georges Vongerichten, Stephen Hanson, and David Chang have followed in Baum's footsteps, designing new restaurant concepts in New York and around the world. Drew Nieporent, a Cornell hotel management graduate, worked at Tavern on The Green, before he formed the Myriad Restaurant Group, which operates Tribeca Grill, Nobu New York City, The Daily Burger at Madison Square Garden, and thirty-two other restaurants. Danny Meyer created the Union Square Hospitality Group, including the Union Square Café, Gramercy Tavern, Shake Shack, The Modern, Café 2, Terrace 5 and others. Korean American David Chang opened his first restaurant, Momofuku Noodle Bar, in the East Village in 2004. He then opened other restaurants in New York and other cities and created the Momofuku restaurant group to manage them.

Restaurant Workers

The first modern fast-food chain to hit New York was White Castle, which arrived during the Depression. Initially, it sold nickel square hamburgers, soda, coffee, and pie. Hamburgers were prepared on an assembly-line format to fulfill orders as quickly as possible. Outlets stayed open late at night and were often located near businesses, such as newspaper plants, that operated twenty-four hours a day. It served as a model for other fast-food chains that moved into the city after World War II. These included McDonald's, Burger King, Wendy's, Taco Bell, Au Bon Pain, Chipotle, Starbucks, Jamba Juice, and many more.

Today, fast-food chains employ fifty thousand workers in the city. Most are paid minimum wage (currently $7.25 an hour), and most work only part time. Few receive medical insurance, paid sick days, or vacation days. In November 2012 and again in April 2013, workers at McDonald's, Burger King, Wendy's, Taco Bell, and other fast-food chains went on one-day strikes asking for a living wage.

Immigrants form the main workforce behind the food service industry and their suppliers, such as meatpackers, and farm laborers, such as those who pick tomatoes. According to the Restaurant Opportunities Center of New York, 47.5 percent of the restaurant workers in the city were foreign born in 1980; by 2000, this had reached 64.5 percent; today the number is much higher. More than 125,000 immigrants—many undocumented—are employed in the city's restaurants. Most are paid minimum wage—and some even less. The number of undocumented workers in restaurants is likely to increase in future years. As a Manhattan chef and restaurateur explained in 2011, "We always, always hire the undocumented workers. . . . It's not just me, it's everybody in the industry. First, they are willing to do the work. Second, they are willing to learn. Third, they are not paid as well. It's an economic decision. It's less expensive to hire an undocumented person."

In 2011, 69 percent of all small restaurant and other food service business owners in New York City were foreign born. In other culinary sectors, immigrants make up an even larger percentage: 84 percent of small grocery store owners were foreign born, as are most of those employed in other restaurants and grocery stores. A 2007 report, "Unregulated Work in the Global City," conducted by the Brennan Center for Justice, stated that in the food retail industry, "the workforce is almost exclusively immigrant, from Mexico, Central America, Korea, Africa, the Caribbean, and South Asia. Delivery workers are mostly African immigrants."

CHAPTER SEVEN

~

Historic Cookbooks, Dishes, and Recipes

During the last two hundred years, the majority of America's important cookbooks have been brought into being by New York City publishers. Although both Boston and Philadelphia were (and are) home to some major publishing houses, including Little, Brown & Co., Houghton Mifflin, and J. W. Lippincott, New York was and is the capital of the American publishing industry. Many cookbook authors and editors live in the city, and New York's intense restaurant culture gives rise to an entire genre of cookbooks.

Before American authors began churning out culinary works, British authors were dominant. English colonists brought cookery manuscripts and cookbooks with them. British cookery books, such as Martha Bradley's *British Housewife*, E. Smith's *Compleat Housewife*, and Penelope Bradshaw's *Family Jewel*, among others, were sold by 1761 at the Bible and Crown, Hugh Gaine's bookshop on Hanover Square. Beginning in 1790, New York publishers issued reprints of British cookery books. A popular title was Susannah Carter's *Frugal Housewife*, originally published in London in 1772, which was first printed in New York in 1792. The 1803 edition included "an appendix containing several new receipts adapted to the American mode of cooking." It is unknown who wrote the twenty-nine recipes, but eighteen clearly reflect American traditions, such as recipes for making Indian pudding (corn pudding), pumpkin pie, cranberry tarts, and several recipes that are sweetened with maple syrup.

British cookbooks naturally influenced the earliest American cookery writers. Amelia Simmons's *American Cookery* (1796), the first cookbook written by an American, was not unlike the British works that preceded it. *American Cookery*, however, did call for many New World ingredients such as corn and cranberries. It was the first book to offer distinctively American recipes, such as "Indian Slapjack" made from cornmeal. Originally published in Hartford, Connecticut, and reprinted many times, *American Cookery* was not printed in New York until 1822.

The first "New York" cookbook, *The Universal Receipt Book or Complete Family Directory by a Society of Gentlemen in New York* (1814), is attributed to Richard Alsop, a wealthy poet and satirist, who, in fact, resided in Hartford, Connecticut. The Society of Gentlemen had existed off and on since 1749. It consisted mainly of physicians, but by 1814 it had expanded to include a range of well-to-do "gentlemen." For at least a decade, Alsop collected recipes from his friends and acquaintances. Alsop's brother-in-law published it. The culinary recipes were generally reflective of the American diet at the time: some notable exceptions featured ketchup and tomatoes, and there is even a recipe for pineapple ice cream.

As New York became America's financial capital, publishers flocked to the city. Many published cookbooks, although most of their authors were not New Yorkers; they lived elsewhere in the country, or overseas, notably in the United Kingdom and France. Among the more interesting works published in New York include two homemakers encyclopedias. Writer Elizabeth Ellet, who was born upstate but lived much of her life in New York City, wrote a "Domestic Encyclopedia" titled *The Practical Housekeeper* (1857). Her tome, which weighed in at 599 pages, was intended to be a "complete system of Domestic Economy." It was broken down into three sections: "housekeeping, cooking, and drugstore-type concerns (soaps, perfumes, medical guide)." It was revised and reprinted throughout the nineteenth century. A similar work, *The Housekeeper's Encyclopedia* (1861) was written by a "Mrs. E. F. Haskell," and it too went through several printings during the nineteenth century and has recently been reprinted in facsimile. Similar works continued to be published well into the twentieth century. Isabel Ely Lord's *Everybody's Cook Book* (1924), developed at the Pratt Institute in Brooklyn, contained more than 3,400 recipes. *America's Cook Book* (1937), compiled by the Home Institute of the *New York Herald Tribune*, included more than three thousand recipes.

Immigrant and International Cookbooks

Cookbooks by and for immigrants began to appear in the late 1850s. Anna May wrote *Die kleine New Yorker köchin* (The little New York cook). Its recipes were mainly written in German, and the book's intended audience was the new German immigrant population who wished to find work as domestics. First published in 1859, it was reprinted several times. A more influential cookbook was written by a French immigrant, Pierre Blot, who came to the United States around 1855. He founded the New York Cooking Academy, America's first French cooking school, which didn't last long. With financial assistance from the daughter of Commodore Cornelius Vanderbilt, Blot subsequently opened the New York Cooking School, which mainly catered to the wealthy women and their cooks who were interested in studying a simplified version of the classic techniques of French cookery. He wrote articles and two cookbooks, *What to Eat, and How to Cook It* (1863) and *Hand-Book of Practical Cookery* (1867), which went through several printings.

Immigrants and members of ethnic and religious groups have continued to publish cookbooks in New York. Gesine Lemcke, a German immigrant who launched a cooking school in Union Square, published *Desserts and Salads* (1901) and *European and American Cuisine* (1902). In 1918, Mrs. Maria Matilda Ericsson Hammond, who ran a cooking school on East Forty-sixth Street, self-published *The Swedish, French, American Cook Book*; she brought out a Swedish-language edition, *Mrs. Ericsson Hammonds Svensk-Amerikanska Kokbok*, in 1926. Florence Greenbaum, an instructor in cooking and domestic science at the Young Women's Hebrew Association, wrote *The International Jewish Cook Book: A Modern "Kosher" Cook Book* (1918). The book went through four editions; later editions included "1600 recipes according to the Jewish dietary laws with the rules for kashering: the favorite recipes of America, Austria, Germany, Russia, France, Poland, Roumania."

Immigrants who arrived in the United States after World War II have also become part of the New York cookbook landscape. Italian American cookbook authors are legion, and most of them settled in New York. Pino and Fedora Bontempi were pioneers in television cooking history and started a long-running program, "Cooking with the Bontempis," in 1949. They published *The Bontempi Cookbook* in 1965, and it became a standard work. Marcella Hazan, who came to New York from Emilia-Romagna in 1955, opened the School of Classic Italian Cooking in 1969. Her first book, *The Classic Italian Cook Book: The Art of Italian Cooking and the Italian Art of Eating*, was published in 1973; this book and its sequel, *More Classic Italian Cooking*, have become mainstays of the American cookbook shelf. A native of Abruzzo who first came to New York in 1959, Anna Teresa Callen also became a cooking teacher and published several books, including *Food and Memories of Abruzzo* (1998). Lidia Bastianich arrived in New York from

Trieste as a young refugee in 1958. In 1971, she and her husband, Felice, opened a restaurant in Forest Hills, Queens. Their Manhattan restaurant, Felidia, opened in 1981 to great acclaim. Lidia Bastianich's first cookbook, *La Cucina Di Lidia: Distinctive Regional Cuisine from the North of Italy*, was published in 1990. She has since written twelve more books and has been a star of the PBS cooking-show roster since 1998.

Cookbooks for the Working Class

A different direction was set by Juliet Corson who opened the New York Cooking School in 1876. She targeted her teaching at not only middle-class women and their children but also poor and working-class women. Based on her lectures, Corson penned the *Cooking School Text Book and Housekeepers' Guide*, which simplified cooking and promised that anyone who could follow simple directions could become a cook in "twelve easy lessons." At this time, economic woes gripped the country; unemployment was at 14 percent. Wages were cut, leading railroad workers to strike in 1877 and paralyzing the nation. Corson saw that struggling families needed help in selecting and preparing cheap, nutritious meals. At her own expense, she printed fifty thousand copies of a pamphlet, *Fifteen Cent Dinners for Workingmen's Families* (1877). The pamphlet received widespread acclaim, and the recipes were republished in newspapers and magazines across the country. She subsequently published *Twenty-five Cent Dinners for Families of Six* (1878), *Meals for the Million* (1882), and *Family Living on $500 a Year* (1888)—all of which were widely distributed—and the simple and inexpensive recipes reflected what many working-class New Yorkers ate.

Haute Cuisine Cookbooks

Cookery at the other end of the economic spectrum was reflected in the cookbooks authored by New York City restaurant chefs. During the second half of the nineteenth century, the Metropolitan Hotel's restaurant on Broadway was among the city's more fashionable eateries. In 1864, a small softcover book, *250 Rare Receipts, including the Celebrated 100 Metropolitan Hotel Recipes, and over 150 other Valuable Receipts*, was published. Although no author was identified, it was reprinted several times, setting the stage for hundreds of future cookbooks written by chefs who gained fame at New York City's hotels, restaurants, and clubs.

Soon French chefs who worked in New York City restaurants began to write cookbooks. In 1884, Felix Déliée, successively chef at the New York

Club, the Union Club, and Manhattan Club, published a 620-page tome *The Franco-American Cookery Book*, and it was regularly reprinted until 1910. Alessandro Filippini was a Swiss émigré who started out as a cook at Delmonico's in 1848, rose to the post of chef de cuisine, and finally became manager of one of the Delmonico's restaurants. In 1888, when he retired, Filippini began writing cookbooks. The first of these, *The Table* (1889), presented simplified versions of recipes he prepared at the restaurant. One of his later works was *The International Cook Book* (1906). Other Delmonico chefs followed in his footsteps: Charles Ranhofer, a French-born chef who replaced Filippini when he retired, produced his masterwork *The Epicurean* (1894). It was the most comprehensive French cookbook published in the United States up to that time. Unlike Filippini's simplified version of Delmonico's cookery, Ranhofer's imposing tome was extremely detailed and featured menus for every imaginable event and occasion. His work included many of the recipes that made Delmonico's famous, including lobster à la Newberg and baked Alaska. When *The Epicurean* was published, Leopold Rimmer, then in charge of one of Delmonico's dining rooms, bitterly complained that Ranhofer had given "away all the secrets of the house."

Oscar Tschirky, maître d'hôtel at the Waldorf, collected recipes from the chefs at the hotel's restaurants and in 1896 published *The Cook Book by "Oscar" of the Waldorf*. It includes many recipes that the Waldorf was known for, such as the Waldorf salad. Three years later, Annie Clarke published *The New Waldorf Cook Book*, containing more than a thousand recipes for cooking and household management. After World War II, French cookbooks were regularly released by New York publishers. Dione Lucas, a British immigrant, opened a restaurant and cooking school in New York; in 1947, she published her recipe collection *The Cordon Bleu Cook Book*. Until the advent of Julia Child, it was considered the standard work on the subject. Joseph Donon, a chef to New York's wealthy, wrote *The Classic French Cuisine*, published in 1959.

Magazines and Cookbooks

World War I, followed by Prohibition and then by World War II, put a damper on restaurants and cookbooks published by their chefs. But after World War II, haute cuisine restaurants reemerged, and chefs began to publish cookbooks. Chef Louis P. De Gouy, who had studied with Escoffier, worked in many European and American restaurant kitchens, including the Waldorf's. In 1931, De Gouy opened the Institute of Modern and Practical Cooking in New York City. His *Gold Cookbook* (1947) was published the year he died, and his wife and daughter compiled and published several additional cookbooks posthumously. Before his death, he was identified as the "Gourmet chef" for *Gourmet*, a magazine launched in New York by Earle MacAusland in 1941.

MacAusland sought out the best food writers of the day to contribute to his magazine. He was foresighted enough to hire James Beard, who had just published his first cookbook, *Hors D'oeuvre and Canapés, with a Key to the Cocktail Party*; M. F. K. Fisher, whose first book, *Serve It Forth*, had appeared in 1937; Pearl V. Metzelthin, author of the *World Wide Cook Book* (1939); and chef Louis Diat, whose book *Cooking à la Ritz* (1941) included the first published recipe for vichyssoise. Other contributors to *Gourmet* were popular writers such as Joseph Wechsberg, who later wrote *Dining at the Pavillon* (1962), among other culinary books, and the British cookbook writers Jane Grigson and Elizabeth David. Recipes from *Gourmet* were collected and published in cookbooks beginning in 1951.

Other national food magazines got their start in New York. *Food and Wine* was first published in 1978. The brainchild of Michael Batterberry, his wife, Ariane, and three others, Michael Batterberry, who served as the magazine's editor in chief, described the magazine as taking "food seriously but not pompously." The Batterberrys coauthored *On the Town in New York, from 1776 to the Present* (1973), the first "food biography" of New York. In 1988, they launched a trade publication, *Food Arts* magazine.

Saveur was launched in New York in 1994 "to satisfy the hunger for genuine information about food in all its contexts . . . heritage and tradition, home cooking and real food, evoking flavors from around the world (including forgotten pockets of culinary excellence in the United States)." *Saveur* has also published many cookbooks based on recipes that first appeared in the magazine.

Newspapers and Cookbooks

New York newspapers got in on the act as well as they hired food columnists. Ida C. Bailey Allen, author of *Mrs. Allen's Cook Book* (1917), was hired as the food editor of the *New York American* in 1924. She continued to write cookbooks, including *Mrs. Allen on Cooking, Menus, Service* (1924)—reissued eight years later as *Ida Bailey Allen's Modern Cook Book*. Allen hosted a variety of radio cookery programs and eventually wrote more than fifty cookbooks and cook booklets, including *When You Entertain—What to Do, and How* (1932), which promoted Coca-Cola; 375,000 copies were distributed.

Clementine Paddleford served as a food columnist for several New York publications, including the *New York Herald Tribune*, the *New York Sun*, and the *New York Telegram*. Paddleford's weekly readership topped twelve million during the 1950s and 1960s. In 1953, *Time* magazine named her America's "best-known food editor." Her cookbooks included *Recipes from Antoine's Kitchen* (1948), *How America Eats* (1960), *Clementine Paddleford's Cook Young Cookbook* (1966), and her posthumously published *Best in American Cooking: Recipes Collected by Clementine Paddleford* (1970).

Paddleford was soon eclipsed by Craig Claiborne, a Southerner, who was hired by the *New York Times* in 1959 as its first food columnist. He authored *The New York Times Cookbook* in 1961 and revised it in 1980. It sold more than three million copies. Claiborne invited some of America's top French chefs and cookbook writers, including future cookbook writers Pierre Franey, René Verdon, Jean Vergnes, and Jacques Pépin, to cook in his home kitchen. Claiborne noted down their recipes and comments as they prepared a meal and presented the recipes in his newspaper columns. He was later hailed as the man who "demystified haute cuisine, and even made it look like fun." Pierre Franey and Craig Claiborne became friends, and they collaborated on five cookbooks, including *Classic French Cookery* (1970). Claiborne went on to author or coauthor twenty cookbooks, including *The New York Times International Cookbook* (1971), four volumes of *Craig Claiborne's Favorites from the New York Times* (1975–1978), *Craig Claiborne's the New York Times Food Encyclopedia* (1985), and *The Best of Craig Claiborne: 1,000 Recipes from His New York Times Food Columns and Four of His Classic Cookbooks* (1999).

After Claiborne left the *New York Times*, some of his successors also became cookbook authors, such as Molly O'Neill and Amanda Hesser. Other *New York Times* writers who have published cookbooks include Kim Severson and Florence Fabricant, who has written or edited ten cookbooks, including her latest, *The New York Restaurant Cookbook: Recipes from the City's Best Chefs* (2009). Ruth Reichl, who served as the restaurant critic for the *Times* before becoming the last editor of *Gourmet*, published several cookbooks, including *The Gourmet Cookbook: More than 1000 Recipes* (2006); *Gourmet Today: More than 1000 All-New Recipes for the Contemporary Kitchen* (2009), and memoirs, which include recipes.

Celebrity Chefs' Cookbooks

Jacques Pépin immigrated to the United States in 1959 and began working at New York's famous French restaurant Le Pavillon. He left the restaurant after eight months and went to work for the Howard Johnson's restaurant chain. Pépin left Howard Johnson's in 1969 to open La Potagerie, a soup restaurant in New York. A publisher approached him about writing a soup cookbook, which Pépin declined to do, but this discussion launched his career as an author. Among his books are *A French Chef Cooks at Home* (1975); *La Technique* (1976), which stayed in print for the next twenty-two years; its companion volume, *La Methode* (1979; both of these are virtual bibles to many chefs), and *Jacques Pepin's The Art of Cooking* (1987–1988).

In 1949, Edna Lewis, the granddaughter of Virginia sharecroppers, came to cook at Café Nicholson, a restaurant on New York's well-to-do Upper East Side. Her first book, *The Edna Lewis Cookbook* (1972), focused on her experiences at Café Nicholson and her subsequent catering business. After Lewis met Knopf editor Judith Jones, who specialized in cookbooks, she wrote a second book, *The Taste of Country Cooking* (1976), which focused on the culinary experiences of her youth. Lewis continues to work in restaurants, most notably the venerable Gage and Tollner in Brooklyn. She also wrote *In Pursuit of Flavor* (1988) and coauthored, with Scott Peacock, *The Gift of Southern Cooking* (2003).

New York celebrities, chefs, and restaurateurs have continued to publish a wide range of cookbooks. New York theatrical producer Crosby Gaige procured recipes from home economists in each state and compiled them in *New York World's Fair Cook Book: The American Kitchen* (1939). He went on to publish *The Standard Cocktail Guide: A Manual of Mixed Drinks Written for the American Host* (1944).

Frank Case's *Feeding the Lions: An Algonquin Cookbook* (1942) built on the popularity of the Algonquin "Round Table," where New York City's literary and journalistic lights gathered for meals and witty conversation. It included comments from the famous—Dorothy Parker, Robert Benchley, and the like—on their favorite dishes. Some of the other eateries that spearheaded the trend in publishing cookbooks or restaurant "biographies" were The Colony (1945), El Borracho (1950), Lüchow's (1952), The House of Chan (1952), Sardi's (1953), Longchamps (1954), The Lobster (1958), Romeo Salta (1962), and Leone's (1967).

Italian immigrant and restaurateur Sirio Maccioni opened Le Cirque in 1974. He hired some of New York's top chefs, including Alain Sailhac and Daniel Boulud. Along with coauthor Pamela Fiori and Alain Ducasse, he published *A Table at Le Cirque: Stories and Recipes from New York's Most Legendary Restaurant* (2012). French restaurateur Daniel Boulud moved to New York in 1982 and opened the Polo Lounge at the Westbury Hotel. In 1986, he became the executive chef at Le Cirque. He opened his own restaurant,

Daniel, in 1993. He published his first cookbook, *Cooking with Daniel Boulud*, the same year. His latest cookbook is *Cocktails and Amuse-Bouches* (2011), coauthored with mixologist Xavier Herit.

Alsatian André Soltner became chef-owner of Manhattan's Lutèce in 1961, a career that lasted thirty-four years. His *Lutèce Cookbook* (1995) published many of the recipes that made the restaurant a success. Danny Meyer, owner of the Union Square Café, cowrote with Chef Michael Romano *The Union Square Café Cookbook: 160 Favorite Recipes from New York's Acclaimed Restaurant* (1994). A sequel, *Second Helpings from Union Square Café*, was published in 2001.

Smaller but still iconic New York restaurants, many of them ethnic and specialty eateries, also published cookbooks. These include *The Little Italian Cookbook* by Christiana Lindsay and Alfred Lepore (1968), from Caffé Ferrara in Little Italy; *Princess Pamela's Soul Food Cookbook* (1969); *Cooking Creatively with Natural Foods* (1972), by Edith and Sam Brown of Brownie's, a beloved mostly vegetarian restaurant; *Ratner's Meatless Cookbook* (1975) by Judith Gethers and Elizabeth Lefft, from a Jewish dairy restaurant on Delancey Street; Pat Miller's *Serendipity Cookbook* (1999) from the fanciful Upper East Side dessert shop/celebrity clubhouse (Andy Warhol, Marilyn Monroe, and Truman Capote were regulars); and three books published in 1999: Sharon Lebewohl's *Second Avenue Deli Cookbook*, from her family's archetypal Jewish deli; Sylvia

Cheesecakes at Junior's Restaurant, Brooklyn, 2013. Courtesy of Kelly Fitzsimmons

Woods and Melissa Clark's *Sylvia's Family Soul Food Cookbook*, from the re-
nowned Harlem restaurant; and *Welcome to Junior's*, by Marvin and Walter
Rosen, whose father founded the Brooklyn cheesecake mecca.

New York Dishes

New York City cooks, chefs, bartenders, and homemakers have created
untold numbers of original dishes and drinks. Many groundbreaking recipes
were first published in New York. Dishes, recipes, and beverages with the
words "Manhattan," "New York," "Coney Island," or "Waldorf" in their
names, however, did not necessarily originate in the city, although many
have been popularized by New York restaurateurs, cookbook authors, newspaper columnists, pushcart vendors, deli owners, and bartenders. Here are a
few that are often associated with New York over the years.

Manhattan Clam Chowder

The first recipe for a clam chowder containing tomatoes—what is today
typically called "Manhattan clam chowder"—appeared in Jessup Whitehead's *Cooking for Profit* (1893). Whitehead described it as popular in restaurants as a lunch dish, and he subtitled the recipe "Coney Island Style."
Coney Island (now, thanks to landfill, no longer an island) was a Brooklyn
beach resort where a popular amusement park was established in the 1840s.
Joseph Vachon's *Book of Economical Soups and Entrées* (1903) used the
name "Coney Island clam chowder" for a soup made with tomato ketchup
rather than milk. A recipe for "Fulton Market clam chowder" appeared in
The Grand Union Cook Book (1902) by Margaret Compton. The 1931 *Picto-
rial Review Standard Cook Book* called the soup "New York clam chowder,"
and three years later, Virginia Elliot and Robert Jones renamed it "Manhattan clam chowder" for their book *Soups and Sauces* (1934). The name
caught on, but the idea of replacing milk with tomatoes in clam chowder
remains a point of contention between New Yorkers, New Englanders,
and their respective partisans. Chef Louis P. De Gouy, author of *The Soup
Book* (1949), concluded that it was one of those subjects, like politics
and religion, that could never be discussed lightly. In his book, he offered
ninety-eight chowder recipes, including two for "Manhattan-manner" clam
chowder. Leaving the subject more blurred than clarified, De Gouy claimed
that these actually originated in New England.

Regardless of its real origin or ingredients, Manhattan clam chowder
never became as popular as the creamy New England version in the city.

Culinary impresario James Beard described it as a horrendous soup "which resembles a vegetable soup that accidentally had some clams dumped into it." Despite such disparagement, Manhattan clam chowder recipes still appear in cookbooks, and the soup is still found on city restaurant menus.

Lobster à la Newberg

Chefs at fashionable restaurants often flattered the egos of their wealthy patrons by naming dishes after them. As the story goes, in 1876 Ben Wenberg, a wealthy shipowner and a frequent customer at Delmonico's, showed Charles Delmonico an extremely luxurious way of preparing lobster in a chafing dish. Delmonico put the dish on the menu as "Lobster à la Wenberg." For unclear reasons—possibly a falling out between the two men—the name was later changed to lobster à la Newberg. Alessandro Filippini and Charles Ranhofer, both Delmonico's chefs, as well as other nineteenth-century cookbook writers, included recipes for it in their books.

Lobster à la Newberg: Split two good-sized, fine, freshly boiled lobsters. Pick all the meat out from the shells, then cut it into one-inch-length equal pieces. Place it in a saucepan on the hot range with one ounce of very good, fresh butter. Season with one pinch of salt and half a saltspoonful of red pepper, adding two medium-sized, sound truffles cut into small dice-shaped pieces. Cook for five minutes; then add a wine-glassful of good Madeira wine. Reduce to one-half, which will take three minutes. Have three egg yolks in a bowl with half a pint of sweet cream, beat well together, and add it to the lobster. Gently shuffle for two minutes longer, or until it thickens well. Pour it into a hot tureen, and serve hot. *Source:* Alessandro Filippini, *One Hundred Ways of Cooking Fish* (New York: Charles L. Webster, 1892), 66.

Lobster à la Newberg or **Delmonico**: Cook six lobsters each weighing about two pounds in boiling salted water for twenty-five minutes. Twelve pounds of live lobster when cooked yields from two to two and a half pounds of meat with three to four ounces of coral. When cold detach the bodies from the tails and cut the latter into slices, put them into a sautoir, each piece lying flat, and add hot clarified butter; season with salt and fry lightly on both sides without coloring; moisten to their height with good raw cream; reduce quickly to half; and then add two or three spoonfuls of Madeira wine; boil the liquid once more only, then remove and thicken with a thickening of egg-yolks and raw cream. Cook without boiling, incorporating a little cayenne and butter; warm it up again without boiling, tossing the lobster lightly, then arrange the pieces in a vegetable dish and pour the sauce over. *Source:* Charles Ranhofer, *The Epicurean* (New York: R. Ranhofer, 1894), 411.

Baked Alaska

The United States purchased Alaska from Russia in 1867, and there was a flurry of interest about the new territory. Delmonico's began serving a dish called "Alaska Florida." It was described by English writer George Sala, in December 1879 as

> an *entremet* called an "Alaska." The "Alaska" is a *baked ice*. A *beau mentir qui vient de loin*; but this is no traveller's tale. The nucleus or core of the *entremet* is an ice cream. This is surrounded by an envelope of carefully whipped cream, which, just before the dainty dish is served, is popped into the oven, or is brought under the scorching influence of a red hot salamander; so that its surface is covered with a light brown crust. So you go on discussing the warm cream *soufflé* till you come, with somewhat painful suddenness, on the row of ice.

Sala was mistaken about one crucial point: the topping is not whipped cream but meringue, which is a poor conductor of heat. This keeps the ice cream from melting while the meringue browns under the salamander (a heated iron).

Similar recipes soon appeared in other cookbooks and cookery magazines under various names. They were usually simplified versions of Ranhofer's extravaganza, and the name that stuck was "baked Alaska."

Cocktails

Some of America's most celebrated cocktails likely originated in New York or were named after boroughs. The Manhattan—typically made with whiskey, sweet vermouth, and bitters—may have been invented at New York's Manhattan Club during the 1870s. It first appeared in a bartender's guide in 1884. The second edition of Jerry Thomas's *Bar-Tenders Guide* (1887) includes a formula consisting of vermouth, rye whiskey, bitters, two dashes of Curaçao or maraschino, and ice. Today a Manhattan is frequently stirred with ice and then strained into a cocktail glass. (A bartender at the Manhattan Club may also have created the first tomato "cocktail," a mixture of oyster juice, tomato juice, Tabasco sauce, chili pepper sauce, ketchup, and lemon juice.)

New York City's best-known borough was not the only one to have cocktails named for it. The Brooklyn cocktail is credited to one Maurice Hegeman, who moved to Brooklyn from Cincinnati and worked in Schmidt's Café. Schmidt's was the first saloon one encountered after crossing the Brooklyn Bridge from Manhattan. In 1910, Hegeman gave the borough's name to a combination of hard cider, absinthe, and ginger ale. Over the years, the ingredients changed (or perhaps the name was appropriated), and today's Brooklyn cocktail is typically made with whiskey, dry vermouth, and maraschino liqueur. Some credit the Bronx cocktail to Joseph S. Sormani, a Bronx restaurateur who began serving the drink in 1905: it was a blend of gin, orange juice, and vermouth. According to legend, Sormani acquired the recipe in Philadelphia. Others credit the Bronx cocktail to Johnnie Solon, a bartender at the Waldorf Astoria Hotel. The somewhat obscure Queens cocktail consists of gin, pineapple juice, and both dry and sweet vermouth. There's a Staten Island martini—obviously a recent invention—made with coffee vodka, dry vermouth, and lime juice; a cocktail called the Staten Island Ferry is a blend of rum and pineapple juice.

There's no definitive origin story for the martini. Recipes for a drink called the "Martinez" appeared beginning in 1884. The second edition of Jerry Thomas's *Bar-Tenders Guide* (1887) includes one made with gin, vermouth, bitters, two dashes of maraschino liquor, and ice. The following year, Harry Johnson's *New and Improved Illustrated Bartenders' Manual* offered a martini cocktail recipe (gin, vermouth, bitters, Curaçao, gum syrup, and ice) and also illustrations of two different "Martine" glasses. Who precisely invented the martini—and how to concoct a perfect one—have been topics of discussion ever since.

The martini was served in New York from the late nineteenth century onward. A 1930 recipe published during Prohibition included an orange peel, olive, pecan, or walnut in addition to Gordon's gin and vermouth. It was shaken, not stirred. The martini became specifically associated with New York in the 1960s, when businessmen famously gathered for the "three-martini lunch." It became infamous in 1977, when President Jimmy Carter complained bitterly about the "three-martini lunch," which he believed was an inappropriate business expense that was tax deductible. He called for the Internal Revenue Service to remove this and other loopholes. One participant fondly remembered them in a *New York Times* letter to the editor in 1989. They consisted of six-ounce martinis made up of six ounces of gin, a drop of vermouth, and a thin strip of lemon peel floating on the top, surrounded by a handful of silvery slivers of ice. "Straight up" was the way most people drank in the 1960s; ordering "on the rocks" was seen as a sign of weakness, as was the substitution of vodka. Olives displaced too much gin, and the only people who drank Gibsons were the effete heads of publishing companies. The three-martini lunch has disappeared, but the martini continues to thrive in New York.

Waldorf Salad

Waldorf salad is a combination of chopped tart apples, celery, and mayonnaise. The recipe was first published in *The Cook Book by "Oscar" of the*

Waldorf (1896). Author Oscar Tschirky was in charge of the dining rooms at the Waldorf Hotel. According to Tschirky, Waldorf salad was served as a side dish, not as a salad course or main course. The Waldorf salad became an American favorite, and variations emerged. Beginning in 1898, it was usually served on a bed of lettuce. Chopped walnuts were added during the first decade of the twentieth century, and they have become part of the standard recipe. Grapes and raisins are other common additions. At some point the Waldorf salad came to be served as an entrée; a popular variation includes cubes of roast chicken to make it a more substantial dish.

> **Waldorf Salad**: Peel two raw apples and cut them into small pieces, say about half an inch square, also cut some celery the same way, and mix it with the apple. Be very careful not to let any seeds of the apples be mixed with it. The salad must be dressed with a good mayonnaise. *Source:* Oscar Tschirky, *The Cook Book by "Oscar" of the Waldorf* (Chicago: Werner, 1896).

Steaks, Potatoes, and Eggs

Confusion surrounds the term "New York steak." It likely did not originate in New York, but the term has been adopted in many local restaurants. A New York steak is variously defined as a porterhouse steak with the filet removed; a boneless top sirloin; or a strip steak. To make matters more confusing, it can also be called New York strip, New York cut, shell steak, New York sirloin, or sirloin strip. Outside of New York, the term may be used to refer to a completely different cut. (One steak that may have originated in New York is the porterhouse.)

Today the term "Delmonico steak," or "New York steak," refers to two rounds of boneless rib eye tied together with butcher's twine. Charles Ranhofer includes three steak recipes in *The Epicurean* that are named for the restaurant. Here's one:

> **Delmonico Sirloin Steak of Twenty Ounces, Plain** (*Bifteck de Contrefilet Delmonico de Vingt Onces, Nature*): Cut from a sirloin slices two inches in thickness; beat them to flatten them to an inch and a half thick, trim nicely; they should now weigh twenty ounces each; salt them on both sides, baste them over with oil or melted butter, and broil them on a moderate fire for fourteen minutes if desired very rare; eighteen to be done properly, and twenty-two to be well done. Set them on a hot dish with a little clear gravy . . . or maître d'hôtel butter. *Source:* Charles Ranhofer, *The Epicurean* (New York: R. Ranhofer, 1894), 487.

Delmonico's steak is often served with Delmonico potatoes, which are rich mashed potatoes served gratinée—with a browned topping of grated cheese (and sometimes breadcrumbs). Recipes for them were published beginning in 1889. Alessandro Filippini, a former Delmonico's chef, published his own in 1906.

> **Delmonico Potatoes**: Place four good-sized boiled and finely hashed potatoes in a frying pan with one and a half gills cold milk, half gill cream, two saltspoons salt, one saltspoon white pepper and a saltspoon grated nutmeg; mix well and cook on the range for ten minutes, lightly mixing occasionally. Then add one tablespoon grated Parmesan cheese, lightly mix again. Transfer the potatoes into a gratin dish, sprinkle another light tablespoon grated Parmesan cheese over and set in the oven to bake for six minutes, or until they have obtained a good golden colour; remove and serve. *Source:* Alessandro Filippini, *The International Cook Book* (New York: Doubleday, Page, 1906), 204.

Many stories surround the origins of eggs Benedict, but they all agree that the dish was invented in the 1890s in a New York restaurant (usually identified as Delmonico's or one of the restaurants in the Waldorf Astoria hotels). The recipe evolved over the years before being codified as a slice of ham and a poached egg atop an English muffin, lavished with Hollandaise sauce. A "Talk of the Town" item published in the *New Yorker* in 1942 gives credit to Lemuel Benedict, a retired stockbroker who was a veteran of New York's glamorous Gilded Age restaurant scene: he had dined with Diamond Jim Brady at Delmonico's, and Caruso had been a dinner guest in his home. Benedict claimed that forty-eight years earlier (which would have been 1894), in the throes of a hangover, he had ordered breakfast at the Waldorf —"some buttered toast, crisp bacon, two poached eggs, and a hooker of hollandaise sauce"—with which, continues the writer, "he then and there proceeded to put together the dish that has, ever since, borne his name." Oscar Tschirky, author of *The Cook Book by "Oscar" of the Waldorf* (1896), includes a similar recipe, substituting muffins for the toast and sliced chicken for the bacon, but he calls the dish "Philadelphia eggs." Did Lemuel Benedict have a faulty memory or an inflated ego? Or was Oscar Tschirky loath to credit a customer with the creation of such a successful dish? Regardless of its actual origin, eggs Benedict is still a popular brunch choice in the city's restaurants.

> **Philadelphia Eggs**: Split some fresh muffins in two, toast them to a fine color and lay them on a dish. Cut cooked chicken white meat the same size as the half muffin, lay them on top, then a poached egg over, and cover with Hollandaise sauce, made as follows: Melt a quarter of a pound of fresh butter and when quite hot add two raw egg yolks and the juice of half a lemon; whip well till it becomes creamy and consistent, then use. *Source:* Oscar Tschirky, *The Cook Book by "Oscar" of the Waldorf* (Chicago: Werner, 1896), 588.

Coney Island Hot Dogs

New Yorker Charles Feltman has often been credited with selling America's first hot dog—a sausage served in a bun. In 1871, Feltman, an immigrant from Hanover, Germany, is reported to have operated a pushcart near the Coney Island amusement park in Brooklyn, selling sausages on rolls with sauerkraut. In Germany, such sausages are called, among other names, Frankfurters (i.e., from Frankfurt) or Wieners (i.e., from Wien, [Vienna]). By the 1890s, Feltman's ten-cent specialty had come to be called a "hot dog," and his business had grown from a pushcart into a large restaurant with table service that sold a variety of foods including sausages from individual serving stands.

The genius behind the most famous hot dog stand in New York—and America—is Nathan Handwerker, a Polish immigrant who worked at Feltman's restaurant. Handwerker stayed at Feltman's for a year and then took three hundred he had saved from his wages and opened a hot dog stand a few blocks away. Handwerker cooked his hot dogs on a twelve-foot grill and sold them for a nickel apiece, thus undercutting his former boss. To keep the customers coming, Handwerker installed signs with horns that sounded like fire-engine sirens. When the subway arrived at Coney Island in 1920, people from all over the city could visit Coney Island for a nickel, and a hot dog from "Nathan's Famous Frankfurters" (or simply "Nathan's Famous") was a

The Original Nathan's Hot Dog stand on Coney Island, 2013. Courtesy of Kelly Fitzsimmons

must for beachgoers. Nathan's began marketing retail packages of its beef frankfurters, based on Ida Handwerker's original recipe, in grocery stores, and they are now sold nationwide. There are also hundreds of Nathan's franchises around the country. Every summer, on the Fourth of July, Nathan's sponsors a highly publicized hot dog–eating contest on the boardwalk at Coney Island. Contestants down as many hot dogs (and buns) as they can in ten minutes. The current records are sixty-five for a male contestant and forty for a woman.

Hamburgers

Hamburgers—a cooked ground beef patty in a bun—had been sold in New York since the late nineteenth century. Their main advantage was that they were cheap and easy to make. Street vendors with a grill could sell them as could diners, cafés, stands, and restaurants. During the Depression, so many hamburger places opened up in Times Square that it became known as "Hamburger Row." Another type of hamburger operation entered the city in 1933—White Castle, a chain launched more than a decade before in Wichita, Kansas. Within a few years, fifteen White Castle outlets were established in the city offering cheap hamburgers, coffee, soda, and apple pie.

Hamburgers remained one of New York's favorite foods. It was served in virtually every coffee shop, restaurant, and café. The Hamburger Heaven, a chain launched during the Depression, thrived after the Second World War. It served relatively expensive burgers, cakes, and coffee. Another chain, Burger Heaven, which today has three outlets, opened in the 1940s. Other restaurateurs made their own burgers and gave them exotic names—the Prima Burger, the Plush Burger, and Phoebe's Whamburger. The P. J. Clarke chain was famous for its bacon cheeseburger, which was proclaimed "the Cadillac of burgers" by Nat King Cole. Beginning in the 1970s, national hamburger chains McDonald's and Burger King emerged. There were also local chains, such as the Shake Shack, which was launched in Madison Square Park in 2004.

The hamburger was also a menu item on upper-class restaurants. In 1975, New York's famous "21" Club introduced the "21 Burger," priced at $21. It was served "nude"—without a bun. Burger connoisseurs pronounced it "the best burger in the world," and it was undoubtedly the most expensive in the world at that time. In New York City in 2001, four-star chef Daniel Boulud opened db Bistro Moderne, a more casual cousin to his elegant Restaurant Daniel. On the menu was the "db Hamburger," a ground sirloin patty stuffed with the rich, tender meat of beef short ribs as well as foie gras and truffles. At twenty-nine dollars, it quickly became a smash hit, and the burger was featured in the *New York Times* and culinary magazines. It was as if the gaunt-let had been thrown down, and other restaurateurs began to vie for the title of "best burger"—and highest price.

Marc Sherry, owner of New York's venerable Old Homestead Steakhouse, offered a forty-one-dollar hamburger, with Kobe beef, lobster, mushrooms, and microgreens on a Parmesan twist roll. Daniel Boulud retaliated with the "db Hamburger Royale" with double truffles for nine-nine dollars. This culinary creation, served only during truffle season, won the *Guinness Book of Records*' certificate for the most expensive commercial hamburger in the world at the time.

Many New York restaurants have their special hamburgers.

Bagels, Cream Cheese, and Lox
The point of origin for the bagel, a small doughnut-shaped bread, has been disputed, although it seems to have Eastern European roots. Bagels are un-usual in that they are boiled before being baked, giving them a glossy finish. Jewish bakers in New York were making bagels, and street vendors were selling them, as early as the 1880s. During the early twentieth century, bagel factories opened, and bagels were sold in delicatessens. These small, plain, ring-shaped breads were little known outside Jewish neighborhoods until Polish-born Harry Lender brought the bagel to a wider American audience: by 1955, his baking plant was packaging bagels, six to a plastic bag, and these became a standard item in supermarkets nationwide. As bagels became popu-lar, they lost their original characteristics to become bigger, softer, puffier, and sweeter. Embellished and flavored bagels became the norm, where once the only choices were "plain" and "egg." American bagels were topped with poppy seeds, sesame seeds, onions, garlic, or coarse salt, or swirled with cinnamon and raisins. A wide variety of frozen and fresh bagels are sold in supermarkets and are served in coffee shops, diners, and fast-food chains.

The combination of bagels and cream cheese likely originated in New York. Though the Jewish immigrants from Eastern Europe were familiar with soft, unripened cheeses, such as cottage cheese, milk was relatively scarce in their rural villages. Only the very rich would have had the luxury of add-ing cream to the pressed, soft curds, which is how cream cheese is made. Rather, the immigrants first encountered cream cheese upon their arrival in the United States. It had been made as early as 1841; an upstate New York farmer, William Lawrence, began mass producing it in 1877 under the name "Philadelphia Cream Cheese." By the early 1880s, there were several cream cheese brands to be found in New York City markets. Cream cheese, however, was an expensive "fancy cheese," still beyond the budgets of the newly arrived immigrant families. By the early 1920s, however, the children of these immigrants had climbed the rungs of social mobility and were able to afford such luxuries. In addition, the mass production of cream cheese by corporations such as Phenix, beginning in 1903, had lowered the price of the cheese. Finally, the taste of cream cheese underwent a transformation with the introduction of a new high-fat cream cheese by Breakstone Brothers Dairy in 1923.

In the early 1940s, newspapers reported that the combination of bagels and lox was sold by New York delis as a Sunday morning treat. Historically, lox was salmon cured in a salt brine; today, it usually refers to smoked salmon. After World War II, virtually everyone, even Bob Hope, was eating bagels, cream cheese, and lox. In 1951, a show called *Bagels and Yox*, billed as the "Yiddish American Revue," played on Broadway. The following year, the *New York Times* identified the combination of bagels, cream cheese, and lox as "an old New York Sunday morning tradition," and reported that "together they're magnificent; apart they're only wonderful, according to fanciers." For many New Yorkers, bagels and cream cheese are typical breakfast or brunch treats.

Bialys—chewy, flat rolls—have also become an iconic New York food. They are similar to bagels but are not boiled before baking; rather than having a glossy, hard exterior, they are flour dusted and yielding to the bite. Instead of a hole, the bialy has a depression in the middle which is filled with onions, garlic, or other seasoning. Unlike the bagel, which is now commonly sold throughout America, the bialy remains very much of New York—especially when eaten fresh from the oven at Kossar's bakery on the Lower East Side.

Corned Beef, Pastrami, and Reuben Sandwiches

In the late nineteenth century, New York delicatessens sold a variety of cured, smoked, salted, and brined meats, including corned beef and pastrami. Developed long before artificial refrigeration, "corning" is a way of preserving meat by coating it heavily with salt. Corned beef is simply salted beef, which was part of British and Irish culinary traditions that came to America in colonial times. It is usually made from a brisket, a fatty, flavorful cut. Recipes for preparing and cooking corned beef appear in many nineteenth-century American cookbooks. Corned beef is one of the few traditional Irish foods to be recognized as such in the United States; the combination of corned beef and cabbage is a must for St. Patrick's Day celebrations in New York. Here's one recipe from New York cookbook teacher and author Juliet Corson:

Corned Beef Brisket: Choose about seven pounds of the navel end of the brisket of corned beef; wash it well in plenty of cold water; put it over the fire in a large pot containing sufficient cold water to cover the beef, and let it slowly approach the boiling point, removing all scum as it rises. The beef can either be left flat, or the bones be taken out and a compact roll be made of it, secured by a string. Boil the beef steadily and gently for four hours after it begins to boil; it may then be served hot, or may be pressed until cold before it is used.

Cabbage is usually served with corned beef; cooked according to directions given among the vegetable recipes, it is excellent; or it may be boiled with the beef, only it should not be boiled longer than just time enough to make it tender, which is less than half an hour usually. *Source:* Juliet Corson, *Miss Corson's Practical American Cookery* (New York: Dodd, Mead, 1886), 338.

By the late nineteenth century, corned beef became a staple item in New York delicatessens. Today corned beef sandwiches are still a top-of-the-menu item at the city's kosher and Jewish-style delis.

The making of pastrami is a complicated process involving brining, drying, spicing, smoking, and then steaming a piece of meat. The seasonings may include salt, peppercorns, garlic, paprika, ginger, and other spices. The method probably evolved in Asia Minor, possibly in Turkey, and eventually took hold in Romania (once ruled by the Turks), where goose breast was a favorite meat for making pastrami.

The technique of pastrami making was brought to New York by Romanian Jews in the late nineteenth century. There are two conflicting (and undocumented) stories about the first New York deli to serve pastrami. One claim is made for Sussman Volk, a Lithuanian immigrant who opened a butcher shop on Delancey Street in New York in 1888. In a 1953 article in *Collier's* magazine, Jacob Altman, president of the Manhattan Provision Company, claimed that Volk had acquired the recipe for making pastrami from a Romanian immigrant. Once Volk began offering pastrami in his butcher shop around 1903, according to Altman, there was such a demand for it that he turned the shop into a restaurant specializing in pastrami sandwiches. Others credit Willy Katz, an immigrant, who, in 1903, entered into a partnership in the Icelandic Brothers Delicatessen on Ludlow Street on the Lower East Side. Katz's Deli now stands at the corner of Houston and Ludlow, a mecca for pastrami lovers and a rare survivor of the immigrant era in a neighborhood that has become hip, upscale, and polyglot.

The Reuben sandwich—layers of corned beef, Swiss cheese, sauerkraut, and Russian or Thousand Island dressing on rye or pumpernickel—was invented in New York by Arnold Reuben, a German immigrant who opened a small deli on the Upper West Side about 1908. He later moved to Fifty-eighth Street and expanded his business into a restaurant that specialized in sandwiches. The first located print reference to a "Reuben sandwich" is in

Reuben sandwich at Katz's Deli, Manhattan, 2013. Courtesy of Kelly Fitzsimmons

a 1927 newspaper article that described special sandwiches Reuben devised for celebrities who frequented his restaurant late at night, after the theater. Around 1914, he came up with the "Annette Seelos Special" for one of Charlie Chaplin's leading ladies. It consisted of "ham, cheese, turkey, cole slaw and dressing." While not quite today's Reuben, the Annette Seelos Special was its clear antecedent.

Reuben's restaurant attracted celebrities even during the Depression, when Arnold Reuben spent one hundred thousand dollars "flossing up his two sandwich shops," which had grown, according to a 1933 newspaper article, "to a national institution." British dignitaries visiting the city in 1937 visited one of these restaurants to dine with celebrities and enjoy "a Reuben Sandwich," which was a generic term for the fifty or so different sandwiches that Arnold Reuben served. One called the Col. Jay Flippen's sandwich consisted of "corned beef on toasted rye bread with a thin slice of Swiss cheese melted over the top, mustard and cole slaw," which was very close to today's Reuben.

Joseph Oliver Dahl, a New York restaurant expert and prolific author, changed the name for this combination in his *Menu Making for Professionals in Quantity Cookery* (1939). His "Ruben" sandwich consisted of "Rye Bread, Switzerland Cheese, Sliced Corn Beef, Sauerkraut, Dressing." The book was intended for use in "Hotels, Restaurants, Clubs, Schools, Fountains,

Tearooms, Resorts, Camps, Cafeterias, Hospitals and Institutions." This book was widely distributed, and it went through several reprintings through 1950. It standardized the formula, although when it hit menus, the spelling was changed to "Reuben." It became a staple in New York in many of the city's "Jewish-style" delis even though the combination of corned beef and Swiss isn't kosher (meat and cheese may not be eaten together). Many other sandwiches, such as pastrami and corned beef on rye, were also popularized by New York's delis and restaurants.

New York Cakes
One of the most iconic New York foods that emerged into the mainstream is Jewish-style cheesecake. New Yorkers consumed cheesecake since colonial times, and it was not much different from that of the cheesecakes that other Americans (and Europeans) consumed. These were made from ricotta cheese, cottage cheese, curd cheese, sour cream, or farmer's cheese, and the crust was typically made of pastry. During the early twentieth century, a very different type of cheesecake, made from cream cheese, emerged in New York delis and restaurants. It was smoother than other cheesecakes. Arnold Reuben claimed to have originated this recipe in 1928. During the following decade, his cheesecake became popular in New York, and he began to ship it to other places. An article in the *Los Angeles Times* in 1939 reported that he shipped it "anywhere from New Orleans, to London to Paris." The shipping charges were often four times more than the cost of the cheesecake, but people were willing to pay for it. He later complained that his recipe was stolen by others, specifically Leo Lindermann.

Lindermann was a German-Jewish immigrant who opened Lindy's, a restaurant near Times Square in 1921. By 1948, he was selling a velvety cream-cheese-based cheesecake, plain or with sweet fruit toppings. It had a cookie-like crust, and the cake was flavored with citrus zest. Another cheesecake seller was Junior's in Brooklyn. It had been established in 1950 by Harry Rosen, who was born on the Lower East Side, sits on a thin layer of sponge cake, and is flavored only with vanilla. Sylvia Balser Hirsch, a Texan transplanted to New York City, provided New York's upscale restaurants and gourmet shops with a distinctive vanilla cheesecake (and a range of other desserts) in the 1970s and 1980s under the name "Miss Grimble." Her preference was for cookie-crumb crusts.

Other New York cakes were also popular—at least for a time. Ebinger's Baking Company was a small family-owned chain in Brooklyn that began on Flatbush Avenue in 1898. It was known for its classic lemon cupcakes, "crumb buns," and its Brooklyn Blackout Cake, a very dark devil's food layer cake with custardy chocolate filling and frosting; the whole cake was coated with a layer of chocolate cake crumbs. The chain folded in 1972, but memories of its Blackout Cake remain alive for those lucky enough to have sampled the original. Many bakers and cookbook writers have tried to replicate the original recipe, which has not survived.

Yet another iconic New York dessert cake is the Charlotte Russe. In the classic French recipe for this dessert (a "Russian" charlotte), a mold is lined with ladyfingers or slices of cake and then filled with whipped cream or custard and chilled so that it can be sliced. The New York City version is made as an individual serving: a disk of yellow sponge cake is placed in the bottom of a cylindrical paper case, and whipped cream is piped in until it mounds on top. The confection is topped with a maraschino cherry (and sometimes with chocolate sprinkles). Sometimes the paper case was made in two parts, so that the bottom can be pushed up as the cream was consumed. As the Charlotte Russe was mostly whipped cream, it was a cool-weather specialty, sold only in the autumn and winter. These iconic treats were typically sold in bakeries and candy stores from the 1930s to the 1960s; there is hardly any place in the city that still makes them.

Egg Creams

Nonalcoholic drinks made with raw eggs, cream, and fizzy water were popular soda-fountain fare in the late nineteenth century; chocolate and vanilla syrups were the most common flavorings. To make a more affordable treat, the egg and cream were sometimes eliminated, and the simplified "egg cream" was a mixture of milk and chocolate syrup, frothed with carbonated water (usually seltzer, dispensed from a blue- or green-glass bottle topped with a silvery syphon). Several Brooklynites have been credited with its invention, including Louis Auster. Typically made with Fox's U-Bet Chocolate Syrup (invented by Brooklynites Herman and Ida Fox in 1895), egg creams were standard fare in soda fountains and "candy stores" (corner grocery/paper/ sweet shops) throughout New York by the 1920s. Vanilla egg creams arrived in the 1950s, as did coffee-flavored ones. The egg cream largely disappeared in the late twentieth century, although it can still be found in some quintessential New York City restaurants, such as Junior's in Brooklyn, and in surviving "candy stores," mostly in the outer boroughs.

Cookies

Several cookies originated in New York City; the best known is the Oreo, a round cookie with vanilla cream sandwiched between two dark chocolate wafers. The National Biscuit Company (later Nabisco), which was based in the city until the 1950s, introduced Oreos in 1912 to compete with Sunshine Bakeries' Hydrox Biscuit Bonbons, which had come on the market two years earlier. Oreos were produced in the National Biscuit Company bakeries, on Ninth Avenue between Fifteen and Sixteenth Streets—a block where the street sign now reads "Oreo Way." Oreos are arguably the most famous commercial cookies in American history.

A New York favorite, but less successful elsewhere in the country, is the Mallomar, a round biscuit that tastes something like a Graham cracker, topped with a dome of marshmallow and coated in dark chocolate. These were first made by Nabisco in 1913, at the same bakeries where Oreos were produced. Because the chocolate coating melts in warm temperatures, Mallomars are made and sold only in the autumn and winter; 70 percent of the total production is snapped up by New Yorkers.

Even more iconic to New York is the black-and-white cookie, which is typically sold in bakeries and delis. It is a large, somewhat soft, chewy cookie frosted half and half with chocolate and vanilla icing.

Pretzels

Pretzels, which were made in similar ways to bagels, were sold in New York by the 1860s. Street vendors carried them on long poles, a custom that would survive for decades. Today, big, somewhat soft pretzels are sold from the same carts that offer hot dogs and, in the winter, roasted chestnuts. Even in the early days they were usually made by professional bakers, but some old recipes for home-baked pretzels have survived.

> **Pretzels:** Sift together two cupfuls of flour, one teaspoonful of salt and a pinch of ginger; add one egg beaten, one-third of a cupful of butter, one-half of a yeast cake dissolved, and stir in enough sweet milk to make a very stiff dough; beat with biscuit roller until smooth, and let rise; cut off small pieces and roll them between the hands into strips, form small rings, pinch the ends of the dough together, and let rise; put them a few at a time in salted boiling water, let cook until they begin to come to the top of the water, take out quickly, sprinkle with salt, put in a greased pan, and bake a light brown. *Source:* Miss Sigel, "Pretzels," *Table Talk* 27 (February 1912): 102.

The New York City food scene has come a long way since, where the city now stands, Lenape Indians hunted game; gathered nuts, berries, and oysters; caught shad and sturgeon; and grew maize, squash, and beans using slash and burn agricultural methods. Almost four hundred years ago European colonists introduced Old World foods and beverages into the area, and over the succeeding centuries, immigrants—first from Western Europe and later from the rest of the world—streamed into the city, bringing their own food culture. These contributions are all ingredients in the simmering, ever-changing culinary stew that is New York City food.

To meet the culinary needs of the city's 8.3 million residents and its fifty-two million annual visitors, New York has developed one of the most complex food systems in the world: there are more than fifty thousand restaurants; some five thousand street food vendors and food truck operators; tens of thousands of supermarkets, corner stores, bodegas, delis, greenmarkets, meat markets, wine shops, and bakeries; and hundreds of soup kitchens and food pantries. If past is prologue, New York City's unique, quixotic culinary life will continue to sustain, surprise, confuse, and amuse anyone lucky enough to eat there.

~

Bibliography

New York Histories

Allen, Irving L. *City in Slang: New York Life and Popular Speech*. New York: Oxford University Press, 1993.

Anbinder, Tyler. *Five Points: The 19th Century New York City Neighborhood That Invented Tap Dance, Stole Elections, and Became the World's Most Notorious Slum*. New York: Free Press, 2001.

[Beard, Frank]. *The Night Side of New York: A Picture of the Great Metropolis after Nightfall*. New York: J. C. Haney, 1866.

Bernard, John. *Retrospections of America, 1797–1811*. Edited by Laurence Hutton and Brander Matthews. New York: Harper & Brothers, 1887.

Booth, Mary L. *The History of New York City*. New York: W. R. C. Clark, 1860.

Browne, Junius Henri. *The Great Metropolis: A Mirror of New York*. Hartford, CT: American Publishing, 1869.

Burrows, Edwin G., and Mike Wallace. *Gotham: A History of New York City to 1898*. New York: Oxford University Press, 1999.

Campbell, Helen. *Darkness and Daylight: Lights and Shadows of New York Life*. Hartford, CT: A. D. Worthington, 1891.

Cantwell, Anne-Marie E., and Diana diZerega Wall. *Unearthing Gotham: The Archaeology of New York City*. New Haven, CT: Yale University Press, 2001.

Carmer, Carl. *The Hudson*. New York: Farrar & Rinehart, 1939.

Chambers, Julius. *The Book of New York: Forty Years' Recollections of the American Metropolis*. New York City: Book of New York, 1912.

Danckaerts, Jasper, and Peter Sluyter. *Journal of a Voyage to New York*. Brooklyn: [The Society], 1867.

Dayton, Abram C. *Last Days of Knickerbocker Life in New York*. New York: G. W. Harlan, 1882.

Diehl, Lorraine B. *Over Here! New York City during World War II*. New York: Smithsonian Books/HarperCollins, 2010.

Erenberg, Lewis A. *Steppin' Out: New York Nightlife and the Transformation of American Culture*. Chicago: University of Chicago Press, 1981.

Ferguson, William. *America by River and Rail*. London: J. Nisbet, 1856.

Goodfriend, Joyce D. *Before the Melting Pot: Society and Culture in Colonial New York City, 1664–1730*. Princeton, NJ: Princeton University Press, 1992.

Haenni, Sabine. *The Immigrant Scene: Ethnic Amusements in New York, 1880–1920*. Minneapolis: University of Minnesota Press, 2008.

Harlow, Alvin F. *Old Bowery Days: The Chronicles of a Famous Street*. New York: D. Appleton, 1931.

Harris, Charles Townsend. *Memories of Manhattan in the Sixties and Seventies*. New York: Derrydale Press, 1928.

Hasswell, Charles H. *Reminiscences of an Octogenarian of the City of New York*. New York: Harper & Brothers, 1897.

Hughes, Rupert. *The Real New York*. New York: Smart Set, 1904.

Jacobs, Jaap. *The Colony of New Netherland: A Dutch Settlement in Seventeenth-Century America*. Ithaca, NY: Cornell University Press, 2009.

———. "'It Has Pleased the Lord That We Must Learn English': Dutch New York after 1664." In *Dutch New York between East and West: The World of Margrieta van Varick*, edited by Deborah L. Krohn and Peter Miller, 55–65. New Haven, CT: Yale University Press, 2009.

Jameson, J. Franklin, ed. *Narratives of New Netherland, 1609–1664*. New York: Charles Scribner's Sons, 1909.

Janowitz, Meta F., and Diane Dallal, eds. *Tales of Gotham, Historical Archaeology, Ethnohistory and Microhistory of New York City*. New York: Springer, 2013.

Kernan, Frank J. *Reminiscences of the Old Fire Laddies and Volunteer Fire Departments of New York and Brooklyn*. New York: M. Crane, 1885.

Krohn, Deborah L., and Peter Miller, eds. *Dutch New York between East and West: The World of Margrieta van Varick*. New Haven, CT: Yale University Press, 2009.

Levinton, Jeffrey S., and John R. Waldman, eds. *The Hudson River Estuary*. Cambridge: Cambridge University Press, 2006.

Mackeever, Samuel Anderson. *Glimpses of Gotham, and City Characters*. New York: National Police Gazette Office, [1881].

Mayer, Grace M. *Once upon a City: New York from 1890 to 1910*. New York: Macmillan, 1958.

McKay, Ernest A. *The Civil War and New York City*. Syracuse, NY: Syracuse University Press, 1990.

Mensch, Barbara. *South Street*. New York: Columbia University Press, 2007.

Morris, Lloyd R. *Incredible New York*. New York: Random House, 1951.

Peterson, Arthur Everett, and George William Edwards. *New York as an Eighteenth Century Municipality*. New York: Columbia University Press, 1917.

Reitano, Joanne R. *The Restless City: A Short History of New York from Colonial Times to the Present*. New York: Routledge, 2006.

———. *The Restless City Reader: A New York City Sourcebook*. New York: Routledge, 2010.

Riis, Jacob August. *How the Other Half Lives: Studies among the Tenements of New York*. New York: Charles Scribner's Sons, 1890.

Sandler, Corey. *Henry Hudson: Dreams and Obsession*. New York: Citadel Press, 2007.

Shepp, James W., and Daniel B. Shepp. *Shepp's New York City Illustrated: Scene and Story in the Metropolis of the Western World*. Chicago: Globe Bible, 1894.

Shorto, Russell. *The Island at the Center of the World: The Epic Story of Dutch Manhattan and the Forgotten Colony That Shaped America*. Prince Frederick, MD: Recorded Books, 2004.

Singleton, Esther. *Social New York under the Georges, 1714–1776*. New York: D. Appleton, 1902.

Smith, Matthew Hale. *Sunshine and Shadow in New York*. Hartford, CT: J. B. Burr, 1868.

Spann, Edward K. *Gotham at War: New York City, 1860–1865*. Wilmington, DE: Scholarly Resources, 2002.

Still, Bayrd. *Mirror for Gotham: New York as Seen by Contemporaries from Dutch Days to the Present*. New York: New York University Press, 1956.

Vanderbilt, Gertrude Lefferts. *The Social History of Flatbush, and Manners and Customs of the Dutch Settlers of Kings County*. New York: D. Appleton, 1881.

van der Donck, Adriaen. *A Description of the New Netherlands*. Edited by Thomas F. O'Donnell. Syracuse, NY: Syracuse University Press, 1968.

Van Dyke, John C. *The New New York*. New York: Macmillan, 1909.

Wilson, James Grant, ed. *The Memorial History of the City of New York, from the First Settlement to the Year 1892*. 4 vols. [New York]: New-York History, 1892–1893.

City Food Histories

Batterberry, Michael, and Ariane Batterberry. *On the Town in New York: The Landmark History of Eating, Drinking, and Entertainments from the American Revolution to the Food Revolution*. New York: Routledge, 1999.

Grimes, William. *Appetite City: A Culinary History of New York*. New York: North Point Press, 2009. *Appetite City* television series: http://a002-vod.nyc.gov/html/appetite_city.php?id=1221.

Lawson, Annie H., and Jon Deutsch, eds. *Gastropolis: Food and New York City*. New York: Columbia University Press, 2008.

Schwartz, Arthur. *Arthur Schwartz's New York City Food: An Opinionated History and More Than 100 Legendary Recipes*. New York: Stewart, Tabori & Chang, 2004.

Shulman, Robin. *Eat the City: A Tale of the Fishers, Trappers, Hunters, Foragers, Slaughterers, Butchers, Farmers, Poultry Minders, Sugar Refiners, Cane Cutters, Bee-keepers, Winemakers, and Brewers Who Built New York.* New York: Crown, 2012.

Chapter 1. The Material Resources: Land, Water, and Air

Grumet, Robert S. *First Manhattans: A History of the Indians of Greater New York.* Norman: University of Oklahoma Press, 2011.

Homberger, Eric. *The Historical Atlas of New York City: A Visual Celebration of 400 Years of New York City's History.* New York: Henry Holt, 1994.

Koeppel, Gerard T. *Water for Gotham: A History.* Princeton, NJ: Princeton University Press, 2000.

Lewis, Tom. *The Hudson: A History.* New Haven, CT: Yale University Press, 2005.

Otto, Paul. "Intercultural Relations between Native Americans and Europeans in New Netherland and New York." In *Four Centuries of Dutch-American Relations,* edited by Hans Krabbendam, Cornelis A. van Minnen, and Giles Scott-Smith, 178–91. Albany: State University of New York Press, 2009.

Pritchard, Evan T. *Native New Yorkers: The Legacy of the Algonquin People of New York.* San Francisco: Council Oak Books, 2002.

Sanderson, Eric W. *Mannahatta: A Natural History of New York City.* New York: Abrams, 2009.

Chapter 2. From Colonization to the Present

Bluestone, Daniel. "'The Pushcart Evil.'" In *Landscape of Modernity,* edited by David Ward and Oliver Zunz, 287–312. New York: Russell Sage Foundation, 1992.

Bradley, Elizabeth L. *Knickerbocker: The Myth behind New York.* New Brunswick, NJ: Rivergate Books, 2009.

Cahn, William. *Out of the Cracker Barrel: The Nabisco Story, from Animal Crackers to Zuzus.* New York: Simon & Schuster, 1969.

Federal Writers Project. *The Italians of New York.* New York: Random House, 1938.

French, Earl R. *Push Cart Markets in New York City.* Washington, DC: Agricultural Economic Bureau, USDA, 1925. http://naldc.nal.usda.gov/download/CAT10675911/PDF.

Kellar, Jane Carpenter, comp. and ed. *On the Score of Hospitality: Selected Receipts of a Van Rensselaer Family, Albany, New York, 1785–1835; A Historic Cherry Hill Recipe Collection.* Albany, NY: Historic Cherry Hill, 1986.

Loukaitou-Sideris, Anastasia, and Renia Ehrenfeucht. *Sidewalks: Conflict and Negotiation over Public Space.* Cambridge, MA: MIT Press, 2009.

Ray, Krishnendu. "Exotic Restaurants and Expatriate Home Cooking: Indian Food in Manhattan." In *The Globalization of Food,* edited by David Inglis and Debra Gimlin, 213–26. Oxford: Berg, 2009.

Restad, Penne L. *Christmas in America: A History.* New York: Oxford University Press, 1995.
Serventi, Silvano, and Françoise Sabban. *Pasta: The Story of a Universal Food.* Translated by Antony Shugaar. New York: Columbia University Press, 2002.
Sijs, Nicoline van der. *Cookies, Coleslaw, and Stoops: The Influence of Dutch on the North American Languages.* [Amsterdam]: Amsterdam University Press, 2009.
Taylor, Dennis S., et al. "Street Foods in America: A True Melting Pot." *World Review of Nutrition and Dietetics* 86 (2000): 25–44.

Chapter 3. A Culinary Stew: Immigrants and Their Food

Balinska, Maria. *The Bagel: The Surprising History of a Modest Bread.* New Haven: Yale University Press, 2008.
Bayor, Ronald H., and Timothy Meagher, eds. *The New York Irish.* Baltimore: Johns Hopkins University Press, 1996.
Bercovici, Konrad. *Around the World in New York.* New York: Century Co., [1924].
———. "The Greatest Jewish City in the World." *Nation,* September 12, 1923, 259–61.
Binder, Frederick M., and David M. Reimers. *All the Nations under Heaven: An Ethnic and Racial History of New York City.* New York: Columbia University Press, 1995.
Burgess, Thomas. *Greeks in America.* Boston: Sherman, French, 1913.
Diner, Hasia R. *Hungering for America: Italian, Irish, and Jewish Foodways in the Age of Migration.* Cambridge, MA: Harvard University Press, 2001.
Ernst, Robert. *Immigrant Life in New York City, 1825–1865.* New York: Kings Crown Press, 1949.
Foner, Nancy, ed. *New Immigrants in New York.* New York: Columbia University Press, 2001.
Gabaccia, Donna R. *We Are What We Eat: Ethnic Food and the Making of Americans.* Cambridge, MA: Harvard University Press, 1998.
Golden, Harry. *The Greatest Jewish City in the World.* New York: Doubleday, 1972.
Hendricks, Glenn L. *The Dominican Diaspora: From the Dominican Republic to New York City; Villagers in Transition.* New York: Teachers College Press, Columbia University, [1974].
Khandelwal, Madhulika Shankar. *Becoming American, Being Indian: An Immigrant Community in New York City.* Ithaca, NY: Cornell University Press, 2002.
Korrol, Virginia Sánchez. *From Colonia to Community: The History of Puerto Ricans in New York City.* Berkeley: University of California Press, 1994.
Laguerre, Michel S. *American Odyssey: Haitians in New York City.* Ithaca, NY: Cornell University Press, 1984.
Marx, Jeff. "The Days Had Come of Curds and Cream: The Origins and Development of Cream Cheese in America, 1870–1880." *Food, Culture and Society* 15 (2012): 177–95.

Min, Pyong Gap. *Caught in the Middle: Korean Communities in New York and Los Angeles.* Berkeley: University of California Press, 1996.

Pozzetta, George E. "The Italians of New York City, 1890–1914." PhD diss., University of North Carolina at Chapel Hill, 1971.

Rischin, Moses. *The Promised City: New York's Jews, 1870–1914.* Cambridge, MA: Harvard University Press, 1962.

Sánchez Korrol, Virginia. *From Colonia to Community: The History of Puerto Ricans in New York City.* Berkeley: University of California Press, 1994.

Wang, Xinyang. *Surviving the City: The Chinese Immigrant Experience in New York City, 1890–1970.* Lanham, MD: Rowman & Littlefield, 2001.

Ziegelman, Jane. *97 Orchard: An Edible History of Five Immigrant Families in One New York Tenement.* New York: Smithsonian Books/HarperCollins, 2010.

Chapter 4. From Garden to Grocery: A Tour of Markets, Vendors, and Other Food Sellers

Benepe, Barry, and John L. Hess. *Greenmarket: The Rebirth of Farmers Markets in New York City.* New York City: Council on the Environment of New York City, [1978].

Caldwell, Alison. "Will Tweet for Food: The Impact of Twitter and New York City Food Trucks, Online, Offline, and Inline." *Appetite* 56, no. 2 (April 2011): 522.

The Cries of New-York. New-York: Printed and sold by S. Wood, Juvenile Book-store, 1808.

DeVoe, Thomas F. *The Market Assistant.* New York: Hurd and Houghton, 1867.

———. *The Market Book Containing a Historical Account of the Public Markets.* Vol. 1. New York: Printed for the author, 1862.

Great Atlantic & Pacific Tea Company. *Colonel Goodbody's Red Setter Menus.* Montvale, NJ: Author, n.d.

———. *Grocery Catalogue 1912.* Glen Cove, NY: Author, 1912.

Hutcheson, John C. "The Markets of New York." *Harper's,* July 1867, 229–36.

Levinson, Marc. *The Great A&P and the Struggle for Small Business in America.* New York: Hill and Wang, 2011.

Mendelson, Anne. "To Market, to Market: A Profile of Thomas F. De Voe." *NY-Foodstory* 1 (Fall 2012): 3, 14–16, 18.

Seiger, Karen E. *Markets of New York City: A Guide to the Best Artisan, Farmer, Food, and Flea Markets.* New York: Little Bookroom, 2010.

Slantez, Priscilla Jennings. "A History of the Fulton Fish Market." *Log of the Mystic Seaport* 36 (Spring 1986): 14–25.

Tangires, Helen. *Public Markets.* New York: W. W. Norton, Library of Congress, 2008.

———. *Public Markets and Civic Culture in Nineteenth-Century America.* Baltimore: Johns Hopkins University Press, 2003.

Walsh, William I. *The Rise and Decline of the Great Atlantic & Pacific Tea Company.* Secaucus, NJ: Lyle Stuart, 1986.

Wasserman, Suzanne. "Hawkers and Gawkers: Peddling and Markets in New York City." In *Gastropolis: Food and New York City*, 153–73. New York: Columbia University Press, 2009.

White, Charles Henry. "The Fulton Street Market." *Harper's*, September 1905, 616–23.

Chapter 5: Drinking in the City

Anderson, Will. *The Breweries of Brooklyn: An Informal History of a Great Industry in a Great City*. Croton Falls, NY: Anderson, 1976.

Bryson, Lew. *New York Breweries*. Mechanicsburg, PA: Stackpole Books, 2003.

Byles, W. Harrison. *Old Taverns of New York*. New York: Frank Allaben Genealogical Company, 1915.

DeGennaro, Jeremiah J. "From Civic to Social: New York's Taverns, Inside and Outside the Political Life of the United States after the Revolution." Master's thesis, University of North Carolina at Greensboro, 2008.

Mitchell, Joseph. *McSorley's Wonderful Saloon*. New York: Pantheon, 1992.

"Old New York Coffee-Houses." *Harper's*, March 1882, 481–99.

Smith, Andrew F. *Drinking History: Fifteen Turning Points in the Making of American Drink*. New York: Columbia University Press, 2012.

Chapter 6: Eateries

Beriss, David, and David Sutton, eds. *The Restaurants Book: Ethnographies of Where We Eat*. Oxford: Berg, 2007.

Berry, Rynn, and Chris Abreu-Suzuki, with Barry Litsky. *The Vegan Guide to New York City*. 17th ed. New York: Ethical Living, 2010.

Bradley, Jimmy, Andrew Friedman, and David Sawyer. *The Red Cat Cookbook: 125 Recipes from New York City's Favorite Neighborhood Restaurant*. New York: Clarkson Potter, 2006.

Brody, Iles. *The Colony*. New York: Greenberg, 1945.

Bromell, Nicolas. "The Automat: Preparing the Way for Fast Food." *New York History* 81, no. 3 (July 2000): 300–312.

Chappell, George Shepard. *The Restaurants of New York*. New York: Greenberg, 1925.

Dearing, Albin Pasteur. *The Elegant Inn: The Waldorf-Astoria Hotel, 1893–1929*. Secaucus, NJ: Lyle Stuart, 1986.

Diehl, Lorraine B., and Marrianne Hardart. *Automat: The History, Recipes, and Allure of Horn & Hardart's Masterpiece*. New York: Clarkson Potter, 2002.

Erenberg, Lewis A. *Steppin' Out: New York Nightlife and the Transformation of American Culture, 1890–1930*. Westport, CT: Greenwood, 1981.

Evans, Meryle R. "Knickerbocker Hotels and Restaurants 1800–1850." *New-York Historical Society Quarterly* 36 (1952): 377–410.

Fairchild, Henry Pratt. *Greek Immigration to the United States*. New Haven, CT: Yale University Press, 1911.

Federman, Mark Russ. *Russ & Daughters: Reflections and Recipes from the House That Herring Built*. New York: Schocken, 2013.

Freeland, David. *Automats, Taxi Dances, and Vaudeville: Excavating Manhattan's Lost Places of Leisure*. New York: New York University Press, 2009.

Gamber, Wendy. *The Boardinghouse in Nineteenth-Century America*. Baltimore: Johns Hopkins University Press, 2007.

Garrett, Thomas Myers. "A History of Pleasure Gardens in New York City, 1700–1865." PhD diss., New York University, 1978.

Haley, Andrew P. *Turning the Tables: Restaurants and the Rise of the American Middle Class, 1880–1920*. Chapel Hill: University of North Carolina Press, 2011.

James, Rian. *Dining in New York*. New York: John Day, 1930.

Lebewohl, Sharon. *The Second Avenue Deli Cookbook: Recipes and Memories from Abe Lebewohl's Legendary Kitchen*. New York: Villard, 1999.

Maccioni, Sirio, and Peter Elliot. *Sirio: The Story of My Life and Le Cirque*. Hoboken, NJ: Wiley, 2004.

Manzo, Joseph T. "From Pushcart to Modular Restaurant." *Journal of American Culture* 13, no. 3 (Fall 1990): 13–21.

Mariani, John, with Alex Von Bidder. *The Four Seasons: A History of America's Premier Restaurant*. New York: Crown, 1994.

Meyer, Danny, and Michael Romano. *The Union Square Café Cookbook: 160 Favorite Recipes from New York's Acclaimed Restaurant*. New York: HarperCollins, 1994.

Rimmer, Leopold. *A History of Old New York Life and the House of the Delmonicos*. New York, 1898.

Sardi, Vincent, and Richard Gehman. *Sardi's: The Story of a Famous Restaurant*. New York: Henry Holt, [1953].

Schriftgiesser, Karl. *Oscar of the Waldorf*. New York: E. P. Dutton, 1943.

Segrave, Kerry. *Vending Machines: An American Social History*. Jefferson, NC: McFarland, 2002.

Shuldiner, Alec Tristin. "Trapped behind the Automat: Technological Systems and the American Restaurant, 1902–1991." PhD diss., Cornell University, 2001.

Slomanson, Joan Kanel. *When Everybody Ate at Schrafft's: Memories, Pictures, and Recipes from a Very Special Restaurant Empire*. Fort Lee, NJ: Barricade Books, 2006.

Thomas, Lately [pseudonym for Robert V. P. Steele?]. *Delmonico's: A Century of Splendor*. Boston: Houghton Mifflin, 1967.

Wechsberg, Joseph. *Dining at the Pavillon*. Boston: Little, Brown, 1962.

Where and How to Dine in New York: The Principal Hotels, Restaurants and Cafés of Various Kinds and Nationalities Which Have Added to the Gastronomic Fame of New York and Its Suburbs. New York: Lewis, Scribner, 1903.

Williams, Ellen, and Steve Radlauer. *The Historic Shops and Restaurants of New York*. New York: Little Bookroom, 2002.

Zagat Survey. *New York City Restaurants 2009*. New York: Author, 2008.

Chapter 7: Historic Cookbooks, Dishes, and Recipes

[Alsop, Richard.] *The Universal Receipt Book or Complete Family Directory by a Society of Gentlemen in New York*. New York: I. Riley, 1814.

Appel, Jennifer, and Allysa Torey. *The Magnolia Bakery Cookbook: Old-fashioned Recipes from New York's Sweetest Bakery*. New York: Simon & Schuster, 1999.

Astor, Mrs. Jane. *The New York Cook-Book*. New York: G. W. Carleton, 1880.

Bastianich, Lidia. *Lidia's Italian Table*. New York: William Morrow, 1998.

Blot, Pierre. *What to Eat, and How to Cook It*. New York: D. Appleton, 1863.

Bradley, Jimmy, Andrew Friedman, and David Sawyer. *The Red Cat Cookbook: 125 Recipes from New York City's Favorite Neighborhood Restaurant*. New York: Clarkson Potter, 2006.

[Centaur]. *New York Receipt Book*. New York: Centaur, 1881.

Claiborne, Craig. *The New York Times Cook Book*. New York: Harper & Row, 1961.

Clark, Annie. *The New Waldorf Cook Book*. New York: F. Tennyson Neely, 1899.

Corson, Juliet. *Miss Corson's Practical American Cookery*. New York: Dodd, Mead, 1886.

Filippini, Alessandro. *One Hundred Ways of Cooking Eggs*. New York: Charles L. Webster, 1892.

———. *One Hundred Ways of Cooking Fish*. New York: Charles L. Webster, 1892.

———. *The International Cook Book*. New York: Doubleday, Page, 1906.

———. *The Table: How to Buy Food, How to Cook it, and How to Serve It*. New York: Charles L. Webster, 1889.

Greenbaum, Florence Kreisler. *The International Jewish Cook Book: A Modern "Kosher" Cook Book*. New York: Bloch, 1918.

Hesser, Amanda. *The Essential New York Times Cook Book: Classic Recipes for a New Century*. New York: W. W. Norton, 2010.

Lahman, DeDe, Neil Kleinberg, and Michael Harlan Turkell. *Clinton St. Baking Company Cookbook: Breakfast, Brunch and Beyond from New York's Favorite Neighborhood Restaurant*. New York: Little, Brown, 2010.

Lewis, Edna. *The Taste of Country Cooking*. New York: Alfred A. Knopf, 1976.

Lewis, Edna, and Evangeline Peterson. *The Edna Lewis Cookbook*. Indianapolis: Bobbs-Merrill, 1972.

May, Anna. *Die kleine New Yorker köchin* [The little New York cook). New York: Verlag von Steiger, 1859.

Mayor Mitchel's Food Supply Committee. *Hints to Housewives*. New York: Author, 1917.

O'Neill, Molly. *New York Cookbook*. New York: Workman, 1992.

Pépin, Jacques. *The Apprentice: My Life in the Kitchen*. Boston: Houghton Mifflin, 2003.

Ranhofer, Charles. *The Epicurean*. New York: R. Ranhofer, 1894.

Rose, Peter G., trans. and ed. *The Sensible Cook: Dutch Foodways in the Old and the New World*. Syracuse, NY: Syracuse University Press, 1989.

[Sauer Company]. *Fifty Recipes on Flavoring by a Famous New York Chef*. Richmond, VA: C. F. Sauer, [1920s].

Schwartz, Arthur. *Arthur Schwartz's New York City Food: An Opinionated History and More than 100 Legendary Recipes*. New York: Stewart, Tabori & Chang, 2004.

Sigel, Miss. "Pretzels." *Table Talk* 27 (February 1912): 102.

Tschirky, Oscar. *The Cook Book by "Oscar" of the Waldorf*. Chicago: Werner, 1896.

~

Index

~

About the Author

Andrew F. Smith has taught culinary history at the New School in New York since 1995. He is the author or editor of twenty-five books, including *American Tuna: The Rise and Fall of an Improbable Food* (2012), *Drinking History: 15 Turning Points in the Making of American Beverages* (2012), and *Food and Drink in American History: A "Full Course" Encyclopedia* (2013). He serves as the editor in chief of the *Oxford Encyclopedia on Food and Drink in America* (2013) and series editor for the Edible series. He has written more than three hundred articles in academic journals, popular magazines, and newspapers, and has served as historical consultant to several television series. For more about him, visit his website: www.andrewfsmith.com/.